HARRYING

HARRYING

Skills of Offense in Shakespeare's Henriad

Harry Berger, Jr.

Fordham University Press

New York 2015

Visit us online at www.fordhampress.com.

Library of Congress Cataloging-in-Publication Data

Berger, Harry, Jr., 1924– author.
Harrying : skills of offense in Shakespeare's Henriad / Harry Berger, Jr.—First edition.
pages cm
Includes bibliographical references.
ISBN 978-0-8232-5662-4 (cloth : alk. paper)—
ISBN 978-0-8232-5663-1 (pbk. : alk. paper)
1. Shakespeare, William, 1564–1616—Histories. 2. Shakespeare, William, 1564–1616—Language. I. Title.

PR2982.H36 2015
822.3'3—dc23
2015008871

Printed in the United States of America

17 16 15 5 4 3 2 1
First edition

to Peter Erickson

With deep gratitude for many years of friendship

and for his generosity

and for his remarkable critical insight

Contents

Preface

Harrying continues the interpretive project I began many decades ago when I began to practice what I've called reconstructed old New Criticism. This consists in revising the kind of close reading first developed during the 1940s by the so-called New Critics—revising it in terms of a particular hypothesis: The language Shakespeare's characters speak always says more than they mean to say. They try to say one thing. Their language says other things that often question the speakers' motives or intentions. *Harrying* explores the effects of this linguistic mischief on the representation of all the Henriad's major figures. But it centers on the portrayal of Falstaff and on the bad faith that darkens the language and performance of Harry, the Prince of Wales who becomes King Henry V.

In *Imaginary Audition* and *Making Trifles of Terrors* I treated *Richard II* as a drama of self-deposition in which the king seems to manage his own undoing and even to select his own heir and maneuver him into usurping the crown. I argued that Richard II and Richard III "share a mordancy of language" which is "sharpened by the bemused, delicious, blank-eyed perception that they can be the knaves they are and get away with so much." What distinguishes them is that whereas in Richard III's world everyone deserves what he does to them, Richard II is more selective in his choice of victims: "He acts as if he deserves everything he can do or get done to himself." *Harrying* begins with three chapters that resume and develop, and in some instances modify, this argument.

This project wouldn't have gotten off the ground without the support and contributions of many friends and colleagues. First and foremost, Nina Levine and Peter Erickson. It gives me the greatest pleasure to thank them for sharing their profound understanding of this book in rich and perceptive reports that led me to make many changes in the version they encountered. Once again, as so often in the past, Peter's understanding of what I was trying to do was clearer and deeper than mine, and he guided me along interpretive paths I wouldn't otherwise have taken or even found.

I've been both lucky and blessed to have spent so many years working with—or, more accurately, under the guidance of—two remarkable editors and human beings at Fordham University Press: Helen Tartar and Tom Lay. This was much more than a working relationship: We were a family. The family also includes my wife and best interlocutor, Beth Pittenger, whose love and critical insight have sustained me and improved my thinking and writing for thirty years.

Finally, I'm deeply indebted to Lea Puljcan Juric, Helen Hill, and Teresa Jesionowski. To Lea for her excellent work checking, completing, and revising the citations in *Harrying.* To Helen for turning the mountains of messy pages I made her climb into a green meadow of legible prose. To Teresa for her superb copy editing of the manuscript.

My daughters, Cynthia and Caroline Berger, and Cynthia's son, Ezra Berger, didn't have much to do with the actual writing of this book. But along with Beth, they have everything to do with the love that's warmed my life like California sunlight ever since the middle of the last century.

1. *Misanthropology in* Richard III

Shakespeare's *Richard III* is a play about a "real" historical person, a dead tyrant whose wickedness is guaranteed by textual authority. Throughout the play he moves downstage and "addresses" an audience that he assumes is familiar with him and his story. He performs frequently enough "before" that audience to make him seem aware of their scrutiny even when he's bustling about upstage in the midst of his plots and perversions. It's obviously important to him to maintain contact with, and also to maintain rhetorical control over, an audience to whom his present doings are (as we say nowadays) history. But what kind of history are they, and what's his particular problem with that history?

During the first thirty-one lines of Richard's opening soliloquy his references are vague enough to suggest that his audience possesses general if not detailed familiarity with the sources in Thomas More, Edward Hall, and Raphael Holinshed, as well as with the history covered by the three *Henry VI* plays that precede *Richard III.* The most specific references, "this sun of York" and "Grim-visaged war" (1.1.2, 9), still presume familiarity with the story.[1] At the end of the soliloquy, the sudden drop into the details of his "plots" and "inductions" against "Clarence and the King" produces the same effect, although the details will be explained as soon as the soliloquy is over and the action begins. Finally, his "descant on mine own deformity" (1.1.27) is a strong allusion to the sources I mentioned.

So it is that from the opening lines of the play, Shakespeare presents us with a protagonist who seems aware of an audience that knows who he is and where he comes from. Furthermore, he seems eager to explore and test and possibly challenge a prefabricated image of himself floating around in the public domain. Richard's performance may be straightforward in that he wears his villainy on his sleeve, but it is complicated by two possibilities. First, the play represents him as a camp version of the Tudor scapegoat. Second, the play represents him presenting himself as a camp version of the Tudor scapegoat.

This view of Richard is not my invention. It has been advanced and explored with variations in a large body of critical work during the past five decades or so. My own sense of the play responds to a particular version of the view, one that can be traced back to A. P. Rossiter (1961) and Nicholas Brooke (1968), and then forward to more recent studies by Patricia Parker and Linda Charnes.

Rossiter argues that since Richard is "in effect God's agent," an "angel with horns," the play reveals justice to be the work of a divine will "as pitiless as the Devil's." As a result, "the naive, optimistic, 'Christian' principle of history, consoling and comfortable, modulates into its opposite." Nevertheless, the play is more than "a 'debunking' of Tudor myth." Rather it interrogates the "absolutes" and "certainties" that myth offers, and it "leaves us with relatives, ambiguities, irony."[2]

Brooke concedes that since the play celebrates the Tudor victory over the tyrant, it ratifies the working of the "gigantic machine" of "Christian order behind the seeming chaos of human affairs." But he argues persuasively that this Christian-Tudor theme gets challenged by the play's attention to Richard's merry melodrama of misanthropy, by its delight in his self-delight, and by its focus on his high-spirited villainy—theater effects produced primarily through the medium of soliloquy. The cost of the oppressive and deterministic Christian plot that underwrites "the whole Tudor theory of history" is thus measured in theatrical terms. In other words, the necessities of the killjoy plot curtail our pleasure in Richard's histrionic and irrational exuberance.[3]

Brooke's accomplishment is to have shown how Shakespeare uses the villain's role to parody Tudor ideology and its appropriation of the gigantic Christian machine. This theme was subsequently developed by Parker and Charnes. Parker argues that the play depicts its protagonist as the product of the bad faith with which Tudor historiography demonized Richard and sanctified Henry VII: Richard's "unnatural" deformity and fiendishness are the creation of the official Tudor histories. Shakespeare's character is presented as the scapegoat that "a particular official construction of history might retroactively require."[4]

This construction is what Charnes calls *notorious identity*. She carries Parker's idea a little further by suggesting that Shakespeare's character *presents himself as* the Tudor scapegoat. Her argument is that the Richard who performs the villain's discourse tries but ultimately fails to dissociate himself from the notorious identity the Tudors saddled him with. As she and others point out, when he says, "I am determinéd to prove a villain," he probably means that he is resolved, committed, to proving himself a villain in a way that will put his sources to shame. But the phrase also means that he is preordained to be a villain and can't do anything about it, can only replay the role imposed on him by Tudor ideology. Charnes argues that by the end of the play Richard realizes that "he has determined nothing for himself."[5] But I think a slightly different view of the matter opens up if we follow Brooke's lead and focus on Richard's theatrical high jinks.

What makes him a vital and compelling villain is that he fully actualizes a vital and compelling duplicity built into the rhetorical structure of the villain's discourse: The speaker tells himself one thing and tells everyone else onstage another, and among the things he tells himself is that he tells himself one thing and tells everyone else another. He all but flaunts his villainy in his victims' faces as if daring them to find him out. He would clearly like to invert the victim's slogan, which, in the form King Lear gives it, is "I am more sinned against than sinning." But the inversion is troubled by an ambiguity.

The obverse of Lear's complaint is "I am more sinning than sinned against." This is the formula for the villain's discourse. It also happens to be the confessional theme of the sinner's discourse. Until very late in the play, Richard labors successfully to keep the villain's boast from being contaminated by its formulaic double and moral opposite. From the start he looks for chances to sharpen up his villain talk. This is why he soliloquizes so much. It's also why Lady Anne offers him a world-class target. At the end of the first scene, the murderer of Anne's husband and father-in-law struts his nasty plan to make amends by marrying "the wench." The trouble is that in the ensuing scene her complicity challenges his claim to autonomous malfeasance.

During their stimulating discussion of *Richard III*, Jean Howard and Phyllis Rackin claim that the women in the play "are deprived of theatrical power and agency"—deprived, that is, by Shakespeare. Borrowing an idea from Susan Jeffords, they argue that Richard monopolizes the stage with his "performative masculinity."[6] But I'm not sure that this claim holds for Anne, who seems to know something about performative femininity and who enthusiastically competes with Richard in histrionic flummery. I prefer an argument that was advanced in different forms by Marguerite Waller and John Jowett: Anne deprives *herself* of agency and does so through her enjoyment of theatrical power. "Susceptible to the . . . erotic charm of theater," she revels in her declamatory performance of the victim's discourse.[7]

It is she, Waller notes, who "sets the terms for scene 2" by defining herself as "poor Anne" and flaunting her new independence as a mourning widow:[8]

> Set down, set down your honorable load,
> If honor may be shrouded in a hearse,
> Whiles I a while obsequiously lament
> Th'untimely fall of virtuous Lancaster. (1.2.1–4)

She works the pathos of repetition and then pauses archly for a categorial check on her choice of adjectives. But the real damage is done by the indefinite quantifier, "a while." It warns us to settle down, settle down, because we know she aims the "lamentations of poor Anne" at an audience more substantial than the lowly attendants in her cortège. She's waiting for Richard.

Though she titles her little act "Th'untimely fall of virtuous Lancaster," her passion is more vengeful than elegiac. It quickly veers toward vilification of the villain. Then, as if that swerve profanes the ground beneath the dead king, she tells her servants to pick up the hearse and move on, but immediately orders them to put it down again so she may properly "lament King Henry's corpse." She still waits for Richard.

At this moment the object of her fury appears on cue and offers a helping hand. He repeats her order, bullies the servants, and, in the guise of shoring up her authority, he begins to reduce it. Thus it isn't only Shakespeare who deprives Anne of agency. Richard joins in. But it isn't only Richard. Anne joins in. As Waller and Jowett convincingly show, the seduction scene that follows is partly driven by her exercise of the power of self-disempowerment. She *gets* herself seduced.

After his gratuitous offer of help spurs her to take her execration to its climax, Richard blithely catches Anne's curses and bounces them back as literary hyperboles. She calls him a devil, and he calls her a saint, "adopting" and adapting "her constellation of terms."[9] She chooses to accept his adaptation, to join his Petrarchan dance, to follow his lead. He in turn offers her—and she assumes—the illusory autonomy of the Cruel Fair whose expiring victims implore her to murder them, but only by metaphor.

It takes two to play that game. Jowett notes that when she calls Richard "dissembler," her "chiding is that of the resentful though forgiving lover," empowered to "exercise mercy."[10] Finally she accepts his ring, and, with the very phrase intended to deny she's surrendering, she surrenders herself: "To take is not to give." "Poor [widow] Anne" the victim has discovered a new role. Enough of grieving and cursing. She'll become a tease. Her words herald the onset of excitement and lawlessness, the throb of an impulse that joins the sinner to the villain in the discordant harmony of "more sinning than sinned against."

"Was ever woman in this humor wooed? / Was ever woman in this humor won?" These lines introduce a soliloquy characterized by Waller as a "self-serving, long-winded, but unfounded assessment" of what just happened. Richard describes it admiringly as a conquest "carried out in the face of every improbability."[11] But he has to persuade his audience as well as himself that he took what the audience just saw Anne give. He needs someone, some disinterested connoisseur of good villainy, with whom he can share the secrets he can't divulge to his potential victims without jeopardizing his ability to victimize. He seems (perhaps unbeknown to himself) to have found such a connoisseur in Anne.

The effect of sandwiching the seduction between soliloquies is to increase our sense that Richard performs the entire seduction scene with one eye on the audience those soliloquies evoke. He aims his performances downstage toward an audience whose voyeuristic relation to the onstage community of victims reinforces his, an audience of superior wit and judgment capable of rewarding him with the appreciation, the applause, the respect, and the loathing he deserves.

This is an audience presumably aware of the fact that the first tetralogy blandly dishes out such "staples of early Tudor propaganda" as "the pious role-playing" of Henry VII along with his campaign to get Richard demonized and Henry VI sanctified.[12] In the play's most hilarious episode, act 3, scene 7, Shakespeare has Richard perform a wicked parody not only of Henry VI but also of the religious myth of legitimacy that was instituted at Richard's expense by his Tudor successor.

The objective of that scene is to get the Mayor and citizens of London to support his claim to the throne. He and his hatchet man, the Duke of Buckingham, cook up a plan in which, with the commons present, Richard appears aloft in all his sanctity—standing between two bishops, clutching his prayer book, full of Christian blather. He can't imagine why his devotions are being disturbed by such worldly fluff as kingship. He spends a long time proclaiming his unfitness to rule and keeping his future subjects on the hook.

This little charade makes fun of the saintly king, Henry VI, who, in the preceding play, had been equally reluctant to rule and who was captured with prayer book in hand before Richard killed him. In addition, Richard's prominent display of a devotional text as a dramatic prop caricatures the more general—and Machiavellian—use of such texts in the theater of propaganda. As he camps up his villain's role, Shakespeare's audience is entitled to wonder whether Shakespeare's Richard is getting his revenge on the Tudors for their slander of his prototype—whether he isn't belatedly mocking the chronicle myth that empowers Richard, and that lets him get away with murder just long enough to establish the new order on the cornerstone of his deformed body.

Act 3, scene 7 is high comedy, but Richard's performance becomes puzzling as soon as we ask at whom it's aimed and what it seems intended to accomplish. Is it protracted because his onstage auditors are hard to convince? Anne Righter Barton calls it "a little comedy, drawn out at some length," and notes that here, as elsewhere, "ingenuous souls are deceived" by "the brilliance of Richard's performance."[13] Barton finds it odd that Shakespeare's concentration on its brilliance leads him to diverge on this point from the source of the scene in Thomas More's life of Richard. The citizens in More's "account . . . are all perfectly well aware of the deception involved," whereas Shakespeare "gives no indication whatsoever that the Mayor's cry, 'God bless your Grace' . . . , or the citizens' 'Amen' is insincere."[14] But this isn't quite right, because at the beginning of the scene there *are* indications that qualify the onstage spectators' show of sincerity.

Act 3, scene 7 begins with Richard asking Buckingham how the citizens reacted when he enumerated the reasons why Richard should be king. Buckingham delivers the following report: They responded with speechless fear and diffidence, and when he asked what "this wilful silence" meant, the Mayor explained that the people were not accustomed to being addressed by anyone but a civic official called the Recorder. On being urged to repeat the message, the Mayor nervously attributed it to Buckingham: "Thus saith the Duke, thus hath the Duke inferred, / But nothing spoke in warrant from himself" (3.7.27–28).

At this point, Buckingham continues, some of his goons planted in the citizen audience shouted, "God save King Richard!" and he, taking "vantage of those few," thanked the citizens for the "love to Richard" evinced by "this general applause and cheerful shout" (3.7.31–35). Having thus been royally conned, the Mayor and his deputation appear before Richard.

During the long stretch of pious palaver that follows, the Mayor manages to interject four one-line comments, three of which are smarmy endorsements, and the last of which is followed by Buckingham's "Long live King Richard" and the ratifying choric "Amen," the only sound uttered by the Mayor's taciturn townspeople.

This meager evidence can't be used to determine whether Richard's civic auditors are taken in by his performance—whether the auditors are ingenuous and deceived or simply cowed by fear into compliance. But several other passages in the play throw light on this question and even contextualize the citizen response within the boundaries of a well-defined pattern. The strange goings-on in act 3, scene 7 are sharply illuminated by three episodes that precede it. All the speakers in them except one, the Duke of Clarence, are minor characters.

1. In act 1, scene 4, we find Clarence in prison, thanks to Richard, who will shortly have him killed. After Clarence describes a terrible dream he had to the keeper of the Tower, Sir Robert Brakenbury, he falls asleep, and Brakenbury muses on the hard life of princes who "have but their titles for their glories, / An outward honor for an inward toil" (1.4.72–73). At that point the murderers arrive and show him the commission from Richard that orders him to deliver Clarence into their hands. Reading the commission, Brakenbury says, "I will not reason what is meant thereby, / Because I will be guiltless from the meaning" (1.4.85–86). He thus dissociates himself from Clarence's murder in the very speech act that makes the murder possible: "There lies the Duke asleep," he continues, "and there the keys," and he then leaves the room.

2. The second episode occurs in the same scene. Richard had lied to Clarence, telling him it wasn't he but their brother, King Edward, who threw him in jail. Clarence's nightmare drives him to confess to Brakenbury that he was in effect Edward's hit man: "I have done those things / Which now bear evidence against my soul / For Edward's sake" (1.4.64–66). This leads one critic to claim that the nightmare "illustrates the terrible powers of conscience" and that Clarence responds with "deeply moving contrition."[15]

I don't see that at all, since, when the murderers confront him a few minutes later, Clarence gets over his attack of conscience as if it were an attack of hives. He proclaims himself innocent in a speech that disingenuously confuses the moral or spiritual with the legal senses of that term (1.4.187–94). In the lengthy debate with the murderers that follows, he shifts the blame to his brother and pleads extenuating circumstances.

Clarence's words give no evidence that he's doing more than trying to make the murderers feel guilty enough to spare his life and, in the process, trying to displace and mitigate the guilt he himself had previously acknowledged. By "no evidence" I mean that there are no traces in his language of the kind of self-dividedness we see at work in the language of Edgar or Cordelia in *King Lear,* or of King Henry IV; therefore, there is no way of telling whether Clarence is trying to persuade or deceive himself as well as the murderers.

On the other side, the two murderers are preoccupied with the theme of conscience before they approach Clarence. It takes them some fifty lines of manly banter to domesticate their fear of the "blushing shamefaced spirit" that "makes a man a coward" (1.4.119, 122). In their subsequent debate with Clarence they seem intent on keeping conscience at bay with rationalizations that he is just as eager to pick apart. He half succeeds, since one of the murderers contracts a bad case of the scruples. But half-success is no success at all: When the second murderer repents and thinks on Pontius Pilate, it is only after his accomplice has done Clarence in. So in the case of all four figures—Brakenbury, Clarence, and the two murderers—an overview of this scene reveals a strongly marked pattern in which attacks of conscience are either preemptively warded off or wrestled down.

The clarity of the pattern varies along class lines. The knight Brakenbury efficiently and briskly dissociates himself from Clarence's murder, demonstrating the mastery of moral choreography essential to minor officers who serve wicked princes. Following this, the murderers, who entered the scene talking salty colloquial prose and leave it speaking verse, seem humorously garrulous and clumsy by contrast.[16] Their anxiety, their desire to justify their act to themselves, their fear of damnation, and their effort to deal with it, are transparent and explicit. They work through the dialogue of conscience in a manner repeated by nobody else until Richard's soliloquy in act 5, scene 4. In doing this, they alert us to the conspicuous absence of this moral process from the rest of the play.

Their performance of the dialogue highlights Clarence's backpedaling from his confession of guilt into what appears (again by contrast) to be an elaborate and painstaking process of evasion. The debate between Clarence and the murderers is in verse, and it features the competing rationalizations by which each party uses religious arguments to justify its position. The shift into verse contributes to the effect of rationalization because, as George T. Wright brilliantly observes, in Shakespeare's time what "is cast into verse is not the official word-hoard of the culture but is material that is being mythologized in our presence, material whose importance is not inherent but is asserted by the act of treating it in verse."[17]

3. My third episode is act 3, scene 6, which consists of a single soliloquy by a Scrivener. It concludes Richard's management of the murder of Lord Chamberlain Hastings. In act 3, scene 1, at line 190, Richard has a quick answer to Buckingham's question about how to deal with the intransigent Hastings: "Chop off his head, man." He follows through in act 3, scene 4, at line 81 ("Off with his head"), and Catesby, his counsellor, displays the fruits of decapitation in act 3, scene 5, at line 20. In the next scene, the Scrivener enters "with a paper in his hand" and tells us he has just "engrossed" the document that will be used to rationalize or justify the beheading:

> This is the indictment of the good Lord Hastings,
> Which in a set hand fairly is engrossed,
> That it may be this day read o'er in Paul's.
> And mark how well the sequel hangs together.
> Eleven hours I spent to write it over,
> For yesternight by Catesby was it brought me;
> The precedent was full as long a-doing.
> And yet within these five hours lived Lord Hastings,
> Untainted, unexamined, free, at liberty. (3.6.1–9)

This is new information: Six hours before Hastings lost his head, the Scrivener began copying the indictment from a "precedent" that must have been commissioned several hours earlier—some time soon after (if not before) Richard's breezy "Chop off his head, man" (3.1).[18]

After proudly admiring his handiwork, the Scrivener goes on to reflect on the state of the world:

> Here's a good world the while! Why, who's so gross
> That cannot see this palpable device?
> Yet who's so bold but says he sees it not?
> Bad is the world, and all will come to naught
> When such ill dealing must be seen in thought. (3.6.10–14)

He exclaims against the timorousness of those who look the other way—while he timorously looks the other way. The word "gross" recalls the engrossing—the legal script—he just admired, and the demonstrative force of the phrase "this palpable device" glances back toward his contribution to the badness he deplores. Together, these details combine the sense of moral obtuseness with the blinders of the draftsman's delight in his skill.

In some ways, the most telling statement in the play is the Scrivener's "all will come to naught / When such ill dealing must be seen in thought." "In thought" is usually glossed as "silently" (you have to keep what you see to yourself in order to stay out of trouble), but two other senses of the couplet clamor for attention: The world is in a sorry state (1) when everyone is aware of, and nobody bothers to hide, the wicked thoughts behind ill dealing, and (2) when you can't avoid awareness of the ill dealing in your own thought—just such ill dealing as the Scrivener's knowing complicity in implementing "this palpable device." His speech act both acknowledges and evades, both accuses and excuses, his complicity.

According to Robert Weimann, Brakenbury's lament and the Scrivener's soliloquy qualify their speakers for inclusion among those Shakespearean figures who move downstage and share with the audience "generalized truth in a choric mode." Such minor figures, Weimann argues, "help to embody . . . a naive and joyous, or bitter, sense of freedom from the burden of the ruling ideologies and concepts of honor, love, ambition, and revenge."[19] But Brakenbury and the Scrivener articulate only a sense of the burden. Unlike their betters in the play, they—along with Clarence's murderers—are represented as having scruples they have to overcome. By their little exercises in evasion and casuistry they make themselves the instruments—passive or active, willing or unwilling—of the aristocratic thugs who perpetrate their treacheries in the name of honor, love, ambition, revenge, and Christian justice.

In each of these three episodes a feathery nuance of bad conscience or self-dislike is betrayed in the midst of the practice of moral evasion. Conscience has been described as one of the play's "leading themes, woven through it as through a piece of music."[20] But among the major players, the princes and magnates, the music of conscience is limited to a series of arias all of which are motivated by portents or the certain expectation of death. For these figures it's restricted to the "music at the close," as in King Edward's cadenzas (2.1) or in the more perfunctory laments of Hastings and Buckingham, who don't express guilt or contrition so much as remorse at having blindly brought on themselves the poetic justice of the Christian plot: "Wrong hath but wrong, and blame the due of blame" (5.1.29).

Those of the lower orders who do Richard's dirty work provide a different model. The murderers of Edward's sons were filled "with conscience and remorse" by their deed (4.3.20). Like the second murderer in the encounter with Clarence, they feel remorse for what they do to others. Hastings and Buckingham are aggrieved by what they foolishly allow others to do to them. In the first and most complicated performance of the theme Clarence moves from contrition to rationalization.

These episodes show that in a community dominated by Christian discourse, conscience is a force to be reckoned with. But they also show it to be a force the Christians *can* reckon with. They have at hand a set of arguments or moves enabling them both to fend off attacks of conscience in themselves and to provoke them in others. The voice of conscience is both conspicuous and conspicuously ineffective. It's kept under control by the strategies we saw at work in the language of Brakenbury and the Scrivener, strategies for disarming or overcoming scruple and for redistributing complicities from oneself to others. The behavior of the citizens and mayor in act 3, scene 7 may best be understood in this context.

"Who is so gross / That cannot see this palpable device? / Yet who's so bold but says he sees it not?" These lines introduce the problem of the next scene (3.7), and suggest an answer to the question I asked about it: For whose benefit is Richard's sanctimonious charade performed, and what is it intended to accomplish? The Scrivener's rhetorical questions register the disingenuous response of the ordinary citizen, and this is precisely the response Thomas More depicts in his account of the event represented in this scene (3.7).

More tells us that when the citizens were assailed by the histrionic skullduggery of Buckingham and Richard, they "wel wist there was no man so dul that heard them, but he perceiued wel inough, that all the matter was made [up] betwene them"—they knew the whole performance was humbug. Nevertheless, More continues, in a phrase that has a wicked bite to it: "Menne must sommetime for the manner sake not bee a knowen what they knowe." Citizens who knowingly blind themselves to the realpolitik of "Kynges games" have recourse to a kind of ritual complicity: "Somme excused that agayne, and sayde all must be done in good order."[21]

If we assume not only that the citizens aren't deceived but also that Richard doesn't expect to deceive them, why does it go on so long? Its duration, its gratuitous protraction, renders it more hilarious, at least to Richard's offstage audience and readership. The pleasure of showing up a faint-hearted citizenry has to be shared with a more discriminating audience than the Mayor and the citizens.

Consider the touching moment when, after Buckingham feigns impatience and leads the citizens offstage, Richard altruistically agrees to overcome his sense of unfitness and yield to his countrymen's importunate entreaties. Catesby implores him to call Buckingham back and "accept their suit," and Richard reluctantly confesses himself moved by their plea:

> Would you enforce me to a world of care?
> Well, call them again. I am not made of stones,
> But penetrable to your kind entreats,
> Albeit against my conscience and my soul. (3.7.201, 203–5)

Since the two speakers are alone, this exchange may have the force of a stage whisper intended to be overheard by the contingent that just moved offstage. Yet it lends itself equally well to another scenario. It may be gratuitous histrionics: The two thespians are in their element, they've gotten up a head of steam, and they don't want to stop even though nobody is present to appreciate their art. But somebody is: They perform for their own delectation. In effect, they continue to mock the citizens and giggle at what Richard can get away with.

They aren't doing this because the citizens are fools. On the contrary, he can get away with murder precisely because they aren't fools, because they don't swallow the outrageous fiction but, like More's citizens, pretend "not bee a knowen what they knowe" lest (as More puts it a few sentences later) some royal thug "might hap to breake" their heads.[22] The excessive length of his performance betrays a perverse moralism on Richard's part: It justifies the farce by showing how much everyone lets him get away with, and so it mocks the citizens' desire for the ritual cover that helps them excuse their complicity in usurpation on the grounds that it was "done in good order."

It may be true that Richard prevails over victims who "acquiesce in evil" and "deserve their fate" because they are "all guilty."[23] But guilty conscience differs from objective culpability. Remember how Brakenbury, the murderers, and the Scrivener acquiesce in the victimization of others. The villain is empowered by their disingenuous acts of rationalization. Much of the work performed by the sinner's discourse in *Othello* and *King Lear* is relegated in *Richard III* to the gigantic Christian machine that operates, so to speak, not behind the guilty victims' eyes, but behind their backs. With the exceptions noted, the weakness of conscience is directly proportional to the power of the machine. Very little in *Richard III* resembles what happens in the language of the soliloquies of Edgar and Harry, or even in the language of Richard II. *Their* language throws the shadow of an unknown fear over the seeming knowledge of the self-justifying arguments they ensconce themselves in, the stories they tell themselves and others. It is the fear that they are more sinning than sinned against not only *while* but also *because* they claim to be more sinned against than sinning.

The rhetorical pressure of self-justification betrays the lurking suspicion that the projects they defend may be reprehensible and the defense in bad faith. Both Edgar and Richard II are the sites of a language animated by recurrent flashes of anger which, when self-directed, signify the speaker's desire to put himself in danger—to get hurt, punished, judged, as (he suspects) he deserves. Thus the drama of self-representation played out at the level of discourse gives "conscience" a meaning radically different from the one it receives in *Richard III*. In the terms of moral pathology the former denotes a chronic condition induced discursively, the latter an acute condition induced situationally.

This distinction is most obvious in the play's major example of an attack of conscience, the soliloquy in act 5, scene 3 that responds to the parade of Richard's ghostly victims urging him to "despair, and die." The soliloquy divides the speaker in two. He argues with himself, judges himself, defends himself, threatens himself, feels sorry for himself, confesses and denies his villainy, and finally acknowledges himself a sinner who will die unloved and unpitied. But above all, he's putting on a show for his offstage fans in the audience, as the phrase "There's none else by" coyly reminds us. It's as if Shakespeare's Richard is talking to and commenting on the Tudor Richard, maybe trying to solicit support for a psychologically and morally more ambiguous figure than the one delivered by the history books.

Yet for all its rhetorical fireworks, its rodomontade of rhetorical shifters, the soliloquy is psychologically simple to the point of caricature. In the brief space of twenty-five lines Richard races through a selection of the self-reflexive sentiments that get more intricately worked out in the soliloquies of such speakers as Hamlet, Edgar, Lear, Macbeth, and the three kings of the Henriad. In Richard's performance, the sentiments go off like a string of Chinese firecrackers:

> O coward conscience, how thou dost afflict me!
> ....
> What do I fear? Myself? There's none else by.
> Richard loves Richard: that is, I am I.
> Is there a murderer here? No. Yes, I am.

Then fly. What, from myself? Great reason why:
Lest I revenge. What, myself upon myself?
Alack, I love myself. Wherefore? For any good
That I myself have done unto myself?
O no, alas, I rather hate myself
For hateful deeds committed by myself.
I am a villain—yet I lie: I am not.
Fool, of thyself speak well. Fool, do not flatter.
My conscience hath a thousand several tongues,
And every tongue brings in a several tale,
And every tale condemns me for a villain.
Perjury, perjury, in the high'st degree,
Murder, stern murder, in the direst degree.
All several sins, all used in each degree,
Throng to the bar, crying all, "Guilty, guilty!"
I shall despair. There is no creature loves me,
And if I die, no soul will pity me.
And wherefore should they, since that I myself
Find in myself no pity to myself?
Methought the souls of all that I had murder'd
Came to my tent, and every one did threat
Tomorrow's vengeance on the head of Richard. (5.3.178, 181–205)

He seems to throw himself, if not on the audience's mercy, then on its pity: Unloved, unwept, even he can't feel pity for the villain he was determined to be.

But look again at the last three lines, because they modulate his tone and change its emphasis:

Methought the souls of all that I had murder'd
Came to my tent, and every one did threat
Tomorrow's vengeance on the head of Richard. (5.3.203–5)

The supple cadencing of these lines produces a calmer speaker, someone more worried about "tomorrow's vengeance" in battle than about eternal judgment. Still, the last five lines are an indirect appeal for pity and sympathy. To me, they convey his sense of the futility of his effort of persuasion, his sense that such a plea will and should be dismissed by any audience familiar with the life and death of the Richard concocted by the Tudors. This is, after all, the audience he has to persuade. But the tone of his appeal, dangerously close to a whine, constructs it as an audience he can't persuade. And so in the final lines he begins to prepare the audience for his next and last role: the role of the defiant heroic underdog he'll assume in his dash toward death.

Of course, if the soliloquist really had an audience, it would be likely to think his bravado pathetic. Had he been able to play himself in theater, those who might have found his glee and gusto attractive could be imagined to resign themselves more easily to his career as villain than to the shameless way in which he spends his last moments hogging the stage, especially since Richmond virtually ignores him after killing him.

His fifth-act histrionics go flat because they so conspicuously lack the "mocking, blasphemous, slangy" effervescence of the early soliloquies in which he "rendered ridiculous" the "pieties and proprieties . . . of the divine scheme of things."[24] But to miss this effect at the end of the play is to remind oneself that it was there earlier. It's to acknowledge the irruption and loss of what Hibbard calls Richard's "authentic voice," a loss sharpened by the bland recuperation of those pieties and proprieties in Richmond's language.[25]

I noted that Richard's irruption of bad conscience is externally induced by the ghosts in the Christian machine. The ghosts are now the spectral patrons of the new regime, instruments of poetic justice and Tudor justification. In good Christian fashion, the dead awaken and get a second chance to save the realm and to be saved from the devil who deprived them of their first life. But there's something rotten in England. For when you recall the careers of most of these figures, you realize that their conversion from Richard to Richmond is little more than another turn in the endless pirouette of turncoats who have been discredited by their behavior during the Wars of the Roses. In his ghostly exit performance, Clarence continues where he left off in act 1, scene 4: He represents himself only as a poor victim seeking justified revenge, whereas Buckingham's little speech glides quickly past his guilt to dwell on Richard's.

Considering the behavior in life of most of those ghosts, we're entitled to be skeptical about the Christian conscience they mediate. Such skepticism produces an odd if momentary effect: Despite all we know, Richard appears in this episode to be the target of a conspiracy of bad faith. And since Richmond concludes the play with a resounding and resoundingly predictable speech of conciliation and hope, the conspiracy is guaranteed to continue into the new regime.

Richmond's voice and victory appear to be the medium through which God manifests his plan for reconciliation and for the supersession of Plantagenets by Tudors. But the situation is more complicated than that, and one source of the added complication is the figure of Queen Margaret. Henry VI's widow has often been described as the play's voice of history, its voice of prophecy, the voice that best articulates the workings of the gigantic machine. When she begins act 4, scene 4 with a soliloquy that recalls Richard's in act 1, scene 1, she joins hands with him in bitter gratitude for his contributions to her revenge. That juncture is short-lived.

Act 4, scene 4 is notable for its parade of Senecan speech conventions. Its chief effect is to reassert through Margaret the ferocious spirit of an archaic blood feud and of the Lancastrian desire for revenge. She embodies the force that isolates Richard and guarantees Richmond's victory. Richmond replaces Richard as Margaret's avenger. If you look at these events through her eyes, if you imagine that in addition to being providential history they are scenes in a "frantic play" of revenge, then Richmond's triumph becomes her triumph. Incidentally, he arrives onstage only after Margaret's final exit. It is as if he replaces her, an idea that makes it hard for me to resist a bizarre casting fantasy in which Margaret and Richmond are played by the same actor.

Margaret's soliloquy, her theatrical asides, and her reference to herself as the spectator of "a frantic [revenge] play" position her as a Lancastrian outside observer. She speaks as if to her fans offstage who have missed her and wonder where she has been since her last appearance (in 1.3): "Here in these confines slyly have I lurk'd / To watch the waning of mine adversaries" (4.4.3–4). But in act 4, scene 4 she stops lurking and comes out swinging. She is responsible both for the rapprochement with her Yorkist rivals and for the shape it takes. She turns her fellow victims from groaners to cursers and thus mobilizes their active support for Richard's enemies:

> Think that thy babes were fairer than they were
> And he that slew them fouler than he is.
> Bett'ring thy loss makes the bad causer worse.
> Revolving this will teach thee how to curse. (4.4.114–17)

Teaching how to curse: One could say that the upshot of Margaret's instruction is the legend, the notorious identity, of Richard III, and that the "sweetness" of Richmond—"what a stick he is," complains Dover Wilson[26]—is informed by a variant of her advice: "Bett'ring thy *gain* makes the bad causer worse."

Richmond, the relatively mealymouthed hero who kills the monster and becomes Henry VII, the first Tudor king, was the grandson of Henry V's widow and the son of Henry VI's half-brother. He was therefore a member of the House of Lancaster. His seizure of the throne from the bloody dog of York can be described as the work of divine providence.

But Margaret's intervention sharpens the point of a different idea. She offers an interpretation of this "play" that casts a long shadow over the benign providential story in which the Tudor God sends his image, the "upright, just, and true-disposing" Richmond, to save England. In her view, the story of Richard III becomes the dramatization by Tudor apologists of a Lancastrian curse on York. The apologists have something to apologize for: The Wars of the Roses were concluded, and the Tudor dynasty inaugurated, by another Lancaster's de facto usurpation and regicide eighty-five years after the violent accession of the first Lancastrian king.

In discussing act 3, scene 7, I noted that Richard's lengthy charade mocked the citizens' desire for the ritual cover that would excuse their complicity in usurpation. They pretend "not bee a knowen what they knowe" lest they spoil the play and get clobbered. I now add that the same rationale may be extended to the play's account of Richmond. Like a scared citizen, the play seems to excuse, to legitimize, and indeed to idealize, what Sigurd Burckhardt has more realistically depicted: Richmond's triumph is only another in the long "series of successions by combat in which kings who are lacking in potency are supplanted (and usually killed) by others who prove their right to the title by their ability to seize it."[27]

Richard III doesn't fully disown knowledge of its complicity with the Tudor cause. Even as it differentiates Richard's sentiments and speech patterns from Richmond's, it links them together by an insistent echoic doubling. This effect has been discussed with deep insight by several critics and editors, most notably Barbara Hodgdon and John Jowett. I conclude with a pastiche of quotations from the former's classic essay in *The End Crowns All.*

Richmond's "promises to restore the cultural order" Richard "disrupted . . . raise eerie echoes of Richard's earlier claims to protect Elizabeth's children and England's future." Such echoes suggest to Hodgdon that "replacing a false tyrant with a true king simply exchanges one fiction for another, each marked by the same rhetorical mask." Even Richmond's "flamboyantly coherent [final] appeal" to "the idea of union, legitimacy, authority, peace, and prosperity . . . recirculates traces of doubt and strain."

He mentions traitors and treason three times in his closing speech, and his anxious exhortations not only critique the lack of "religious and communal values" in the world the play has imagined. Reaching forward in time, they also "critique the lack of those values in the world of its audience."[28] But these are the values Richard has consistently invoked and continuously mocked. And his mockery prevails because, as Hodgdon shows, the end does crown all. She brilliantly picks out the final theatrical insult the staged play levels at Richmond.

When the actor playing Richard shakes off his character's death and "rises to take a curtain call," it's inevitably to the applause of spectators who were delighted by his nasty exploits and who don't regret having cheered him on. Their "applause acknowledges their complicity with his playing, if not with his ability to manipulate both rhetoric and history to his own advantage."[29] The referent of "his" in this statement, the object of applause, is as much Richard as the actor. Linda Charnes argues that by the end of the play Richard realizes "he has determined nothing for himself."[30] But Hodgdon's perception gets him out of his blind alley. He has determined the actor to be a villain and to bring "hell's black intelligencer" back to life. Thanks to his mock resurrection, "Richard yet lives," a darkling entertainer.

This villainous parousia is merely theatrical, but to respond to it is to be reminded at the end that *Richard III* is very much a Christian play. As such, it is a portrayal of failed Christianity, not, however, of religion per se but of the Tudor production of a Christianizing historiography. The religious dimension is important. Because the sinner's discourse articulates attitudes toward guilt and bears the imprint of confessional practices, its Christian provenance is obvious, and this prompts the following genealogical fantasy: The ironic conception of redistributed complicities developed in Shakespeare's subsequent plays were precipitated out of a critique of the unrealized possibilities of *Richard III* as an experiment in Christian melodrama.

In the several isolated episodes that glance at the mechanisms for overcoming scruple, *Richard III* shows how the villain is empowered by those disingenuous acts of rationalization. It shows, for example, how Brakenbury, the murderers, Cardinal Bourchier (in 3.1), and the Scrivener acquiesce in the victimization of others. But with the exception of Anne in act 1, scene 2, there are no discursive signs that characters acquiesce in their own victimization—that they collaborate with their victimizer in the way Gloucester and Edgar collaborate with Edmund, Cordelia with Lear, Othello with Iago (and Desdemona with Othello), Falstaff with Harry,

Richard II with Bolingbroke, Don Pedro and Claudio with Don John, and Prospero with his usurpers. Stanley Cavell argues that Othello has "a *use for* Iago that reciprocates Iago's *use of* him."[31] The difference that energizes this symbiosis is registered in the distinction between the more passive "have a use for" and the more active "make use of." Both the relative passivity of the former and the active if covered desire it implies are marked in the discursive performances of featured victims in the plays after *Richard III*.

Many of these figures (victims as well as victimizers) tell themselves and others self-justifying stories that betray the pressure of a particular fear: the fear that what they do to others may be worse than what others do to them. In the discursive activity of Richard II, Falstaff, Othello, Gloucester, Lear, and Prospero the pressure is manifested by their complicity in bringing about their own victimization, suffering, or downfall. Where villains are involved, the imprint of that complicity is variously registered, but what is common to the situations of Don John, Edmund, and Iago is that something more than mere obtuseness in their victims allows the villains to get away with as much as they do.

The villain's proud claim to be more sinning than sinned against is ironically framed within a network of discourses that reveals how much he is obligated to his victims. It is they whose use for him empowers him, which is to say it disempowers him since it places his power at least partly in their gift. If they don't give him all, they give him more than he wants, for whatever he is given he can't take, and the ability to take is the soul of manly villainy. Othello's "I am bound to thee for ever" (3.3.217) resonates with a dramatic irony no less deadly than the discursive irony of Iago's answering pledge, "I am your own for ever" (3.3.479).[32] Such a mutually castrating marriage, freely entered into by both parties, is not a possibility that troubles the language of Richard III and his victims. Nevertheless, the structure of that lethal symbiosis is discernible in Richard's interaction with the Christian plot.

2. *"Here, Cousin, Seize the Crown"*

The Triumphant Fall of Richard, the Self-Harrier

Two groups of English history plays by Shakespeare appeared between 1590 and 1600, near the end of the long reign of Elizabeth (1558–1603). She was the last member of a Tudor dynasty that had ruled uninterruptedly since 1485, when Henry VII displaced Richard III from the throne. The historical range covered by the two tetralogies extends from the last days of Richard II in 1399 to the death of Richard III in 1485.

The most important of the sources from which Shakespeare drew his material were the chronicles of Edward Hall (1548) and Raphael Holinshed, the latter in the revised version prepared by several hands and published in 1587.[1] Hall's chronicle was slanted toward glorification of the Tudors, correlated with an emphasis on divine providence and justice. The 1587 version of Holinshed has been called a political "counterstatement" to Hall, but it contains frequent assertions of the same moral and ideological commitments.[2]

Hall's history details the Wars of the Roses, the chaotic struggles for control of the throne waged throughout most of the fifteenth century by factions clustered about the rival houses of Lancaster and York. He locates the cause of this disorder primarily in the murder of Richard II by Bolingbroke and secondarily in Richard's deposition. Bolingbroke consequently endured an "Unquiete Time" as Henry IV, the first Lancastrian ruler. The crown was appropriated from his grandson, Henry VI, to a series of Yorkist kings during a period of mayhem that culminated in the murderous regime of the tyrant Richard III.

In Hall's account, England is not redeemed from this hell until the Lancaster-connected Henry Richmond defeats Richard III, becomes the first Tudor monarch (Henry VII), and unites the warring houses by marrying the daughter of Richard's brother and predecessor, Edward IV. Those responsible for the 1587 Holinshed return at critical moments to the moral and providential themes that dominate Hall's master narrative.[3] So, for example, Holinshed follows Hall in affirming that it was because Bolingbroke "had with wrong usurped the crowne and not onelie violentlie deposed king Richard but also cruellie procured his death; for the which undoubtedlie, both he and his posteritie tasted such troubles, as put them still in danger of their states till their direct succeeding line was quite rooted out by the contrarie [Yorkist] faction."[4]

The order in which Shakespeare's two tetralogies appeared reverses the historical sequence. The later regimes of Henry VI, Edward IV, Edward V, and Richard III are treated in the first tetralogy, which begins with the death of Henry V. The second tetralogy goes back in time to the deposition and death of Richard II, and concludes with Henry V's conquest of France. Thus not only Elizabethan readers but also playgoers familiar with the material covered by the first tetralogy could watch the events in any part of the second tetralogy unfold with full knowledge of what they would lead to. This combination of hindsight and foresight was exploited by Shakespeare in staging the central dilemma of Richard II: Richard is a bad king, and his opponents initially seem justified in their efforts to curb his abuses of power, but usurpation and regicide are crimes against the divine order.

Modern commentators fully appreciate the ambivalent and dynamic characterization this dilemma makes possible. Their appreciation often leads them to praise Shakespeare for the innovative manner in which he dramatized the moral message he found in Holinshed and Hall. For example, in one of the most compelling accounts of the way the orthodox teaching has been conveyed by the play's manipulation of its audience, Phyllis Rackin argues that Shakespeare initially alienates the audience from Richard and aligns it with Bolingbroke, but that later, as political power moves from Richard to Bolingbroke, the sympathies of the audience are transferred from Bolingbroke to Richard.[5]

Rackin brilliantly shows how the comic and unresolved series of challenges that open act 4, scene 1 diminish Bolingbroke's stature and foreshadow the disorder that will mar his regime in the Henry IV plays. In the deposition scene "Bolingbroke has all the political power, but Richard has all the theatrical power" ("Role of the Audience," 272, 269). When Richard prophetically "attributes the Wars of the Roses to divine vengeance for the sin of deposing him, the audience is prepared to believe him" because they know the prophecy is true (271). If the audience is initially maneuvered into cheering Bolingbroke on, by the end of the play Richard's valiant death and Bolingbroke's guilty remorse encourage it to "withdraw from complicity in the dangerous act of rebellion" and thus to endorse "the familiar judgment of the Tudor historians" (271, 281).

Other commentators have found in Shakespeare's histories a skeptical treatment of the Tudor insistence on the divine right of kings and the divine institution of kingship. Before glancing at an example of this interpretation, it will be helpful to have before us the four specific aspects of the idea of kingship mentioned by various speakers at various points in the play.

1. Succession to the throne is hereditary and governed by the law of primogeniture (the firstborn son is heir), and is part of a larger system in which laws of property and genealogy govern the transmission of rights, privilege, and power.[6] Richard inherited the throne from his grandfather, Edward III, because Edward outlived his oldest son, Richard's father.

2. Though kings and aristocrats may inherit "rights and royalties" by the same set of rules—"if that my cousin king be king in England, / It must be granted I am Duke of Lancaster" (2.3.122–23)—kingship is set apart and further reinforced by the idea that it was divinely instituted: The kingship is created by God; its occupants are appointed by God and serve only at His pleasure; the properly invested ruler is God's deputy and earthly representative.[7]

3. "Tudor political theorists and propagandists were always ready to quote St. Paul to the effect that all power is from God, whence it followed that the subject owed obedience, as a matter of religious duty, to the de facto ruler."[8] This principle of nonresistance, to which John of Gaunt appeals in excusing his inaction (1.2.1–7, 37–41), must be obeyed even if rulers "be wicked and wrong doers."[9]

4. The problematic relation of a bad ruler to the office was dealt with by either invoking or resisting the distinction enshrined in the doctrine of the king's two bodies. This is "a legal fiction developed in the Middle Ages" in order to stabilize "an artificial separation of the king's physical body from his spiritual or legal existence as a ruler."[10] The actual relations developed by Elizabethan jurists between the King's "Body natural and . . . Body politic" were much more complex than that between person and office, especially when the "Body natural" belonged to a Queen, and they needn't concern us here.[11]

This divided political structure reappears in the theatrical division between actor and role. Anne Righter (Barton) observes that in Shakespeare's portrayals of flawed "Player Kings," the "contrast between the individual and the part he assumed at the moment of coronation is so obvious that it evokes the image of the actor."[12] Richard II's histrionic flamboyance has made the actor/king relation the subject of a large body of criticism, most of it adverse. Of more particular importance for Richard is that since Tudor lawyers were hardly the only ones who continued to hedge the royal office in the aura or rhetoric of religion, two questions specifically raised in this play would not be lost on its audiences. Can the ruler appropriate the divine charisma of the office as his own personal quality, or power, or protection? Can the personal wickedness of a bad ruler like Richard contaminate the office?[13]

These questions have been explored by modern interpreters who focus—not surprisingly—on the relation between Richard's view of the king's divine right and his own problematic behavior. Proponents of the view that the play treats Tudor doctrine skeptically often identify the force of its critique with the unflattering characterization of Richard. It is easy to concur with the claim that if Richard is an advocate of divine right he is unconvincing. But is he an advocate? What if it can be shown that the play represents him not as an advocate but as a critic, not as one who means simply to assert the ideology but as one who mocks and undermines it? To go back a step, what would it take to show this? What shift of interpretive perspective would be required to refocus Richard as not only the *object* but also the chief *source* of the play's mockery?

To begin with the most obvious distinction between narrative and theater, Holinshed's medium and Shakespeare's, the dramatist represents characters only through the words they speak to and about each other. That could be a severe restraint, a challenge to overcome. Unlike the chronicler, the playwright can't represent himself describing actions, commenting on character, and sympathizing or criticizing in his own voice. Characters can only be represented in and performed by their speech. But by the same token the playwright can represent characters representing themselves in a more sustained and consistent manner than in poetry or prose mediated by a narrator.

The powers of description, representation, and interpretation can best survive the passage from narrative to theater if they are transferred to and wholly vested in dramatic speakers. One of the ways the author of Shakespeare's plays met this challenge was to develop the art of representing self-representation. His speakers seem aware that in their words and actions they represent themselves to others. In their efforts to control the effects of their self-representation they use their language the way actors do. They try to impose on their auditors a particular interpretation of the persons they pretend to be.

How would a reading of *Richard II* that picks out this emphasis on self-representation be affected by it? What would happen if we focus on the self-interpretation that Richard performs for the benefit of his auditors? And performs for his own benefit as well, since a performer can't represent himself to others without at the same time representing himself to himself? My answer is that it would make it more difficult to accept the common view of Richard as a politically incompetent knave undone by his own folly. On the contrary, this shift of perspective would confirm that throughout the play Richard plays the Bad Richard with wry "in your face" gusto as if he is asking for trouble.[14]

Holinshed's view of Richard is interestingly ambivalent. He represents Richard as the victim of his own folly but shuttles back and forth between sympathizing with or apologizing for him and lambasting his "insolent misgovernance" and loose living. The chronicle keeps its reader in touch with a prelapsarian Richard, the anointed king who "knew his title just, true, and infallible; and his conscience cleane, pure, and without spot of envie or malice," and who was "a right noble and woorthie prince" before succumbing to "the frailtie of wanton youth" and the influence of evil counselors.[15]

As I see it, Shakespeare took up Holinshed's unthematized ambivalence, sharpened its focus, and transferred it to Richard as the attitudes, or set of attitudes, his language shows him to perform not only before others but also before himself. This hypothesis allows us to treat reactions to Richard by his auditors as mirrors or echoes of his reaction to himself. So, for example, Phyllis Rackin's fine account of the way the play's opening scenes work "to make Richard contemptible in the eyes of the audience" becomes a clue to the way Richard works to make himself appear contemptible by treating his onstage audience with a degree of contempt guaranteed to alienate them and weaken his position (264–65).

By the time John of Gaunt warns him that he is "possessed now to depose thyself" (2.1.108), we have begun to wonder whether Richard is not daring (or perhaps begging) his interlocutors to check him, soliciting punishment even as he tries to see how much he can get away with. However flippant his utterances are in these scenes, they are edged with anger that seems directed as much toward himself as toward his interlocutors. This verbal aggressiveness appears in the play's very first words:

Old John of Gaunt, time-honored Lancaster,
Hast thou, according to thy oath and band,
Brought hither Henry Hereford, thy bold son,
Here to make good the boist'rous late appeal,
Which then our leisure would not let us hear,
Against the Duke of Norfolk, Thomas Mowbray? (1.1.5–10)

Richard begins with a stately parade of verses, one end-stopped line stepping slowly after the other, each of the first three lines further decelerated by qualifying phrases enclosed in commas. A string of blunt monosyllables identifies the addressee by place of birth ("Old John of Gaunt," that is, John from Gaunt, or Ghent). These are rhythmically organized to accentuate "Old . . . Gaunt," so that they lean on the association of age with weakness or impotence. They're followed by the resonant polysyllables of the first qualifier, the ducal title, "time-honored Lancaster." The shift upward from "Old" to "time-honored" gives the expression of respect for seniority a wicked bite—makes it puffier, more suspect as a mystifying euphemism, because it appears to countervail the snide allusion to senility.[16] Richard's second qualifier, "according to thy oath and band," quietly turns a purely rhetorical and ceremonial question into an admonitory nudge: "Have you lived up to your promise?" Young Bolingbroke has been troubling the king's peace, and old Gaunt will be held responsible for his boisterous boy's good behavior.

Finally, Richard's explanation for ignoring the previous request (the "late appeal") is so bizarre that several editors rewrite it: They insist that "our leisure" in line 9 must mean want or lack of leisure. But given his obvious pleasure in ceremonial trash-talking, why can't he mean what he says—"we chose not to let official business or unruly youngsters interrupt our leisure, our play time." This is both plausible and hilarious as a sequel to his insistence on the promptness, the obedience, he expects from Gaunt: "We expect you to hop to it when we give an order. We, on the other hand, will attend to these matters when we aren't busy doing something less important." In short, "Look how Bad we are. And what are you going to do about it?"

These lines foreshadow what will soon become evident: Richard is not only a tart and witty practitioner of the politics of oratory. He's also an expert ceremonial trash-talker whose occasional mimicry of the way his interlocutors deploy the resources of the genre suggests more than a touch of cynicism. He goes out of his way to offend those by whom he has cause to suspect he is threatened, and his obvious contempt for Gaunt seems linked to the latter's refusal to stand up to Richard's bullying.

Richard continues to push and bully until he finally succeeds in arousing organized resistance to his conspicuously arbitrary displays of power and violations of his subjects' rights. In current parlance, he has an "attitude": Whatever trouble he gets is trouble he asks for. To recognize this is to view his apparently radical change of behavior in act 3, scene 2 with suspicion. After returning from Ireland he refuses to take action and instead flaunts his helplessness and luxuriates in self-pity. But since we know that he is a knowing accomplice in his undoing even as he loudly proclaims himself an innocent victim, we have a hard time taking his self-representation as a betrayed Christ-figure at face value.

It has been argued that Richard "sincerely believes his downfall to be solely the work of traitors, and is sincerely sorry for himself."[17] If so, he must be remarkably stupid. We can save him from this by imagining that the speaker of Richard's words in act 3, scene 2 remembers no less than we remember about the same speaker's performances in act 1, scenes 1, 3, and 4, and act 2, scene 1. Then it will be easier to read or hear the royal victim's protestations of outrage as acts of parody, easier to imagine that he glories not only in expressing self-pity but also in displaying it, and by "it" I mean not self-pity per se but its expression.

Once we grant Richard the minimal self-awareness of his seemingly calculated campaign to get himself victimized, it becomes obvious that his hyperarticulate flights of menace and lament in act 3, scene 2 and after are self-discrediting provocations. They seem intended to embarrass those who are foolish enough to continue encouraging him to stay the course when he and they know it is a course he has thoroughly discredited. At least from the moment in which he directs them not to "mock . . . my senseless conjuration" (3.2.23), he seems obsessed, exhilarated, by a histrionic project guaranteed to try their dignity as well as their patience.

In these scenes he throws himself into high-decibel mimicry and mockery of a bad-faith role we're all familiar with because it is a cultural readymade, a well-formed strategy of self-representation anyone can perform: The victim's discourse pithily expressed in Lear's self-pitying rationalization, "I am a man / More sinned against than sinning" (3.2.59).[18] This rationalization obviously defends against the speaker's apprehension that he may be more sinning than sinned against.[19] Various versions of the victim's discourse are defensively aired by Gaunt and York, and Richard's parody may be directed against all those who have countenanced his crimes and disclaimed responsibility for their passivity or nonresistance.

On another level, the parody may be directed against the hapless, helpless figure of Poor Richard depicted in the chronicles. Then Shakespeare's Richard could be making fun of Holinshed's Richard.[20] For anyone who finds allusions to—and not merely echoes of—the chronicle account in the play, this could contribute to a critique of the simplistic morality of that account.

The play's critical relation to the chronicle is evident in the most important of Shakespeare's departures. Poor Richard doesn't have much to say for himself in Holinshed.[21] *Richard II* corrects this in a way that suggests a correlation between haplessness and inadequate opportunities for self-representation. Shakespeare's Richard "does nothing but talk and talk and talk," John Halverson complains, but he goes on to make a striking suggestion: The "astonishing eloquence [that] seems to have been Shakespeare's invention" is "the verbal equivalent of Richard's beautiful physical appearance"; "none of his sources credits the king with a reputation for fine speech, although they do regularly mention his handsome features and dress."[22]

More forcefully, there is not only equivalence but also displacement, as if Shakespeare saw in the narcissism of fine appearance a less sensitive and nuanced medium of self-expression than the narcissism of fine speech—as if the performer's dressing himself up in speech can do more justice to the complex erotic charge of his investment in the media that represent him to himself and others. Critics have always observed that Richard is in love with the sound of his own speech, and I have been trying to bring out the elements of self-parody, self-critique, and self-loathing that constitute the richness of such love.

In this connection it's significant that the play virtually ignores a side of Richard Holinshed associates with his fine appearance: his participation in "the filthie sinne of leacherie and fornication" that "reigned abundantlie" in his court.[23] Shakespeare redirects attention from Richard's pleasures in sex to his pleasures in speech and from sexual aggression to verbal aggression. Where the chronicle associates Richard's misgovernance and fall with luxurious self-indulgence, the play associates it with luxurious self-representation.

Shakespeare thus replaces Holinshed's royal victim with a more complicated figure. His Richard seems to go out of his way to get himself victimized, and he then blames his victimization on others. It is as if the author of *Richard II* tries to give an old story a new twist, and decides to do this by having the character himself give the story of his decline and fall a new twist—as if Richard enters the play already knowing he had been—would be—deposed and decides to rewrite his story by preemptively taking his deposition into his own hands.[24]

This is not to deny that Bolingbroke is a usurper and regicide. But it radically alters the received story because if indeed Richard is actively complicit in his own undoing, if he is the usurper's silent partner or seducer, if he contributes more aggressively to his deposition than Bolingbroke knows, the portrayal of Bolingbroke also gets more complicated. He remains a usurper and regicide, but he also, in a strange way, becomes Richard's victim.

In the discussion that follows, I try to show that Richard entertains the idea of getting deposed well before it becomes a clear and definite option for Bolingbroke, who is neither consistently nor decisively committed to usurpation until Richard forces him to commit himself in act 3, scene 3. Though Richard doesn't move to abdicate until act 4, scene 1, when he adopts Bolingbroke as his heir, he drops hints from the very beginning that suggest he finds his cousin impressively qualified to serve as his usurper, and he proceeds to goad and in effect seduce him into performing that service.

Richard's contrariness is evident in the episode that opens the play. His cousin, Henry Bolingbroke, has accused Thomas Mowbray, the Duke of Norfolk, of treason and requested that the king let him justify the charge in trial by combat. In this judicial ritual, God is supposedly the umpire who picks the winner and thus reveals the truth. Richard's opening words suggest that he has already dragged his heels in the matter. He orders the duel to begin but then tries to persuade the participants to back off, and when they refuse, he reschedules it for a later date. On the second occasion he again intervenes and prevents the duel, but only after acting as if he will let it happen. Then he chastises the would-be combatants as disturbers of the peace and banishes them, Mowbray for life and Bolingbroke for ten years, subsequently reduced to six. What does he stand to gain by stopping the duel and banishing the combatants?

According to the specific conventions of trial by combat, if Bolingbroke were to win it would be God's way of declaring Mowbray guilty. As we learn in act 1, scene 2, Richard's guilt and Mowbray's complicity in the murder of Gloucester are already assumed. They don't have to be made evident to Gaunt, the Duchess of Gloucester, the Duke of York, or, presumably, Bolingbroke. Were Mowbray to be defeated, he would be disgraced. Dead or alive he would officially carry the blame he unofficially shared with Richard. But if he were to win, he would redeem his honor by "proving" Bolingbroke a liar, and he would thus be protecting Richard.

It has been suggested that if Bolingbroke were defeated, Richard would "be open to Mowbray's blackmail."[25] Yet Mowbray's behavior in the play makes this unlikely. His denial of the murder charge is cunningly phrased. He insists that he did not slay Gloucester, "but to my own disgrace / Neglected my sworn duty in that case" (1.1.133–34). Even as "sworn duty" bounces the accusation toward Richard, Mowbray fixes apologetically on his own insubordination. There is no indication that he had blackmailed Richard before, and he is careful here. He appears heavily invested in the discourse of honor, and the general pattern of behavior summed up in act 4, scene 1, by Carlisle's report of his "holy" death abroad makes it seem unlikely that victory over Bolingbroke would incline him to blackmail Richard.

I conclude that Richard stops a fight by which he would be protected, officially "cleared," no matter who won, and that he stops it in a manner calculated to anger and dishonor the two combatants. This hardly seems motivated by political self-interest. Furthermore, Bolingbroke, the appellant, is on the face of it the more dangerous of the two. Why then does Richard banish Mowbray for good but give Bolingbroke some encouragement to return from exile?

These moves reveal Richard's interest in not being protected either by Mowbray's victory or by Mowbray's judicial assumption of guilt if Bolingbroke were to win. In short, Richard seems to want to keep open the possibility—and maintain control of—his self-destruction. But why? Why does he pursue self-deposition, and what is it that keeps Bolingbroke from yielding to Richard's seduction until the middle of the play?

As depicted in act 1, scene 4, and act 2, scene 1, Richard's abuse of his royal office may be unconscionable, but it is not unconscious. He knows very well what he is doing when (as everyone assumes) he orders Gloucester's death, milks the "royal domain" to support both his Irish war and his unrestraint (1.4.43–52), and expropriates Bolingbroke's inheritance (2.1.160–62, 209–10). He knows, in short, that he has abused both the office and the idea of kingship. If he accepts the dogma that the king is God's deputy, he knows equally well that God did not choose to—or lacked the power to—prevent him from using his divine office to commit "murders, treasons, and detested sins" (3.2.44). He intends these words to characterize those who, like "this thief, this traitor Bolingbroke," will be exposed and guiltily "self-affrighted" by the light of the returning sun-king (3.2.47–53). But his terms of accusation apply to himself.[26]

The diatribe against Bolingbroke is rhetorically excessive and self-delighting but savage and bitter in tone. It wickedly flashes a lining of mockery mixed with self-mockery. For Richard has already shown himself to be—and heard himself called—a thief of his subjects' property (and his uncle's life).[27] It is as if he enjoys hinting to his supporters and sycophants that he is speaking of his depravity and theirs, and that the God who lets his deputy do what Richard does must be willing to let him get away with murder. Thus if he was ever wedded to the idea that the occupant of the throne was morally constrained or uplifted by the sanctity of divine kingship, he has already divorced himself from it.

The energy with which he mocks the rhetoric of sanctification testifies less to cynicism than to the bitterness of an apostate, an ex-believer. When, for example, he invokes the assistance of stones and angels, Richard's utterance vibrates with a range of parodic and sarcastic tones, as in the statements following the diatribe against Bolingbroke:

> Not all the water in the rough rude sea
> Can wash the balm off from an anointed king.
> The breath of worldly men cannot depose
> The deputy elected by the Lord.
> For every man that Bolingbroke hath pressed
> To lift shrewd steel against our golden crown,
> God for His Richard hath in heavenly pay
> A glorious angel. Then, if angels fight,
> Weak men must fall, for heaven still guards the right. (3.2.54–62)

The principle of nonresistance is broadly parodied: The idea that the ruler's subjects should not resist is replaced by the idea that they couldn't possibly do so. The lines leave open the possibility that although only the Lord has the authority to depose an anointed king, he may delegate that to his deputy—who may bring it about by his own nonresistance, as Richard suggests when (in 3.2.36–62) he reduces the Bishop of Carlisle's plea for action (3.2.27–32) to an argument for remaining inactive and leaving the good fight to heaven.[28]

By such mordant utterances Richard conveys the sense that if he was once convinced of the dogma that the monarch is the Lord's deputy and therefore secure from "worldly men," he no longer believes it and now condemns himself for having believed it. The more pressing question for Richard is whether it is by divine will that he has been able to get away with all he has been accused of, and, if so, what this says about the power of that divine will or about his relation to it. Since at several points in the first two acts he cheerfully demonstrates his lawlessness (1.4.43–52 and 59–64; 2.1.209–10), his subsequent appeals to the rhetoric of divinely ordained kingship in acts 3 and 4 can hardly be accepted at face value. There aren't enough clues in his language to indicate whether he is defying or slandering God, trying to prove that God is helpless to stop him or that he legitimizes knavery.[29] But there are many clues that although Richard may deem himself beyond forgiveness he is interested in punishment and is prepared to subject any conviction of invulnerability to a serious test.

In Ernst Kantorowicz's political reading of the play, Richard becomes "a traitor to his own immortal body politic and to kingship such as it had been to his day." He is therefore complicit in the destruction not only of his "body natural" but also of "the indelible character of the king's body politic, god-like or angel-like."[30] My point is that awareness of this betrayal is inscribed in Richard's language, that it is the source of his self-contempt and of his sarcastic use of Christian rhetoric. What we hear in such utterances as Richard's diatribe against Bolingbroke (discussed above) is not merely poetic effusion or arrogance. Rather it is a diffuse contempt aimed both at the ideology of kingship and at his own performance as king—contempt for an institution powerless to restrain his abuses. He despises those around him who, if they don't actually believe in the ideology, continue to invoke it, especially when they want to excuse or justify the inaction that lets him go on abusing and slandering it.

Richard's contempt is inscribed in the mocking irony of his setting himself up as Christ (4.1.167–75), coming down as Phaeton the usurper of the sun-god's chariot (3.3.178–79), and playing the role of a Faustus forced to stage-manage his own secular damnation. His conspicuous disregard of defensive measures, indeed, his going out of his way to antagonize powerful enemies and give them the advantage, is the familiar symptom or index of a desire to seek the punishment one feels one deserves. The advantage of inducing others to cut him down to size is that he can blame them while enjoying the savor of his victimage. The disadvantage is that such a strategy can only increase his self-contempt. This spiraling oscillation—between contempt for self and contempt for others, between the impulse to aggression against oneself and the impulse to aggression against others—

is inscribed in Richard's rhetoric and politics. It patterns the course of his behavior and the trajectory of his career. It motivates the perverse project his skillful management of which argues considerable finesse: to get himself deposed, pick out a likely candidate for the job, give him the motive and the cue to action, reward him with the title of usurper, and leave him with a discredited crown.

The first item in this schedule was announced early in the play by Gaunt: "[Thou] art possessed now to depose thyself" (2.1.108). But Richard's appreciation of Bolingbroke's qualifications finds its way into his language in the opening scene:

> How high a pitch his resolution soars! (1.1.109)

> Were he my brother, nay, my kingdom's heir,
> As he is but my father's brother's son,
> Now by my sceptre's awe I make a vow:
> Such neighbor nearness to our sacred blood
> Should nothing privilege him. (1.1.116–20)

This display of evenhandedness has another side, a side that appears when Richard first calls Mowbray and Bolingbroke "to our presence" in words which momentarily suggest that the opposing knights will confront him rather than each other:

> Face to face,
> And frowning brow to brow, ourselves will hear
> The accuser and the accused freely speak. (1.1.15–17)

Like the nefarious dangling participle manuals of style always warn about, the parallel adverbial phrases unsettle the meaning. They are attracted as modifiers to "ourselves will hear" before they reach their rightful destination as descriptions of the way the opponents will speak. An oddly pluralized royal plural ("ourselves" rather than "ourself") encourages this diversion: If only for a second, it depicts Richard self-divided into two opponents before the image is twice recomposed, successively modulating into phantasms of Richard versus the others and of Bolingbroke versus Mowbray.

The central scenario of the play is epitomized in the oscillation between Richard against himself and Richard against the others. At this point, the syntactical confusion in the utterance registers the scenario as no more than a pressure on language. It is a sequence of accidental flickers, nothing so clear as an intention of the speaker. The scenario moves a little closer toward the intentional status of a possible (and nasty) pun in act 1, scene 3, during the preliminaries to the duel. Richard concludes his response to Bolingbroke's ceremonial leave-taking with a smartly turned couplet, "Farewell, my blood—which, if today thou shed, / Lament we may, but not revenge thee dead" (1.3.57–58). The obvious message is that if Bolingbroke loses he will have unjustly—by the logic of judicial combat—shed the lineal blood his kinsman shares, so that there can be no royal redress. But the statement also lets "if you kill me" (shed my blood) be heard in it, and this subversive hint is generated by the lines preceding the couplet:

> We will descend and fold him in our arms.
> Cousin of Hereford, as thy cause is right,
> So be thy fortune in this royal fight. (1.3.54–56)

The speech rhythm accentuates the will to descend; the image of embrace, reinforced by the odd reference to "royal fight," darkly figures the desire coupling Richard and Bolingbroke in their dance toward deposition and regicide—and toward the subsequent regime of Henry IV, during which the usurper gradually comes to feel the embrace as a moral stranglehold. Of course, the compelling power of these insinuations can only be felt by readers and auditors who know the whole story. But as I suggested at the beginning of this chapter, the whole story of the Henriad is in principle already known since the tetralogy dramatizes a narrative enshrined in Tudor historiography. It's thus plausible to assume some familiarity with it on the part of at least some of the audiences for whom the plays were written. Or, to put it a little more rigorously, the plays presuppose and therefore construct—and will most richly reward—such an audience.

The effect of retrospective foreboding is again produced by Richard's language after he stops the fight and pronounces the sentences of banishment. In a puzzlingly gratuitous gesture he commands both nobles to perform the following ritual:

> Lay on our royal sword your banished hands.
> Swear by the duty that you owe to God—
> Our part therein we banish with yourselves—
> To keep the oath that we administer:
> You never shall, so help you truth and God,
> Embrace each other's love in banishment,
> Nor never look upon each other's face,

Nor never write, regreet, nor reconcile
This louring tempest of your home-bred hate,
Nor never by advised purpose meet
To plot, contrive, or complot any ill
'Gainst us, our state, our subjects, or our land. (1.3.179–90)

At this point nobody expects Bolingbroke and Mowbray to dishonor their professions of mutual enmity by forming an alliance. Why, then, does Richard so carefully give specific instructions about the sorts of things the exiles are not to do? More than a display of apprehensiveness, the speech carries the weight of an insult. It seems intended to rankle, as does the order that joins the two together in a symbolic tableau of cooperation. But it also actualizes and stabilizes the flickering image (evoked at 1.1.16) of Richard and the two nobles "frowning brow to brow" as if the latter were in league against him.

Richard's parade of prohibitions winds eerily, riskily, toward the status of an invitation. As he lists the sorts of things they might well do if they are willing to overcome their scruples and homebred hate when abroad, the prohibitions begin to sound like suggestions, proposals, or dares. "Our part therein we banish with yourselves," that is, "you are now free to dissociate us from God. If you are dishonorable enough to join forces, no obligation to our part in the divine kingship need stand in the way of your returning to lay banished hands on our royal sword, crown, and body." My paraphrase is intended to accentuate what I detect as a wry acridity of tone in Richard's utterance. He delights in flaunting his control of ritual speech and action to the point of frustrating and antagonizing the participants, and ultimately of arousing resistance to his high-handed exploitation of sovereign privilege.

Richard brings this self-subverting strategy to a first climax in act 2, scene 1, when he noisily seizes Bolingbroke's inheritance, dismisses in one airy couplet the Duke of York's long, impassioned protest, then blithely announces that he is placing the country in the shaky hands of that very protester while he dashes merrily off to Ireland (2.1.209–23). All this is staged for the benefit of Northumberland and the other peers who are standing by. Richard seems eager to invite and incite the uprising that is already in motion and that only awaits the "first departing of the king for Ireland" (2.1.290). When he returns from Ireland in act 3, scene 2, his success in mobilizing aggression against himself enables him to step comfortably into the victim's role he has prepared.

Someone else is also standing by in act 2, scene 1, and quietly watching Richard behave as if possessed to depose himself—so quietly, indeed, that critics often ignore her presence. The Queen speaks one line at her entrance and is addressed once just before leaving when Richard briskly bids her be merry as he marches her offstage (2.1.223–24). Critics who puzzle over her strange and haunting rhetoric in act 2, scene 2 often write as if she makes her first appearance in this scene, even though Bushy begins the scene by reminding her—and therefore the audience—of Richard's parting injunction when he says she promised the king she would "lay aside life-harming heaviness" (2.2.2–4). We should take this as a cue to try—as the saying goes—to feel her pain by imagining what she may have observed or felt or thought in 2.1. Her foreboding in 2.2, her presentiment of giving birth to the monster, the "nothing," with which her "inward soul . . . trembles" (2.2.5–12, 28–40, 62–66), is expressed in language so dense and tortured as to be conspicuously evasive. What is it that she simultaneously hints at and resists? What does she flinch from as if trying not to acknowledge the (no)thing she knows, not to utter the name of the woe she bears? It must be more than the bad news Greene delivers (2.2.41–61), even though she calls Greene "the midwife" who helps her soul bring "forth her prodigy" (2.2.62–66).

Following the uncanny force of the words that express her anxiety, the news of political danger seems anticlimactic; if Bolingbroke is her "sorrow's dismal heir," the sorrow she gives birth to must be Richard.[31] But what could that mean? In what sense is Richard the "woe" that she so tortuously insists is "nameless," the "grief" that haunts and impregnates her speech, the "unborn sorrow" she would like, perhaps, to abort? These lines suggest an answer:

I know no cause
Why I should welcome such a guest as grief,
Save bidding farewell to so sweet a guest
As my sweet Richard. (2.2.6–9)

That wistful and wishful (and perhaps already nostalgic) "sweet" may register her continuing loyalty and love against the grain of what she has just observed in act 2, scene 1. Richard's departure for Ireland troubles her less than the exchange of guests in which the sweet Richard has been displaced in her "inward soul" by the bitter Richard who, she now suspects, has willed to get rid of himself because he is possessed by and reduced to the self-loathing of despair.

The Queen balks at calling her "prodigy" Richard's child, for the nothing she grieves over is the void produced by his refusal to confront or let her share his "life-harming heaviness." Instead, she speaks of an "unborn sorrow ripe in Fortune's womb" and thence transferred to hers. The name of the "nothing [that] hath begot my something grief" and of the "something [that] hath the nothing that I grieve" is the bitter Richard. She can receive it as his child only "in reversion"—that is, she can't inherit as her own the despair Richard withholds until his intercourse with Fortune produces the "dismal heir" who will finally help him fulfill his deepest wish: to "be eased / With being nothing" (5.5.40–41).[32]

What, is my Richard both in shape and mind
Transformed and weakened? Hath Bolingbroke
Deposed thine intellect? Hath he been in thy heart?
The lion dying thrusteth forth his paw
And wounds the earth, if nothing else, with rage
To be o'er-powered; and wilt thou, pupil-like,
Take the correction, mildly kiss the rod,
And fawn on rage with base humility,
Which art a lion and a king of beasts? (5.1.26–35)

With these words of spirited chastisement the Queen finally has her say. But her words say more than she may intend. She intends to rebuke him for being a cowardly lion who doesn't even put up a show of angry resistance to being overpowered. But since "rage / To be o'er-powered" can mean "desire to be overpowered," the rebuke also describes the self-flagellation of the lion who flatters his rage by treating his downfall as his "correction." And whatever she intends by her questions about Bolingbroke, "Hath he been in thy heart?" suggests between Richard and his adopted son the kind of intimate attachment she has been denied. Bolingbroke has replaced her as Richard's partner. And when she, in her final words, refuses to take responsibility for killing Richard's heart or letting him kill hers (5.1.97–100), she signals her reluctance to let him do to her what he is doing to Bolingbroke and himself.

Richard's passive-aggressive scenario of self-deposition is more consistent and decisive than his rival's answering scenario of usurpation. Of the two protagonists, Bolingbroke initially shows more respect for the ideology of kingship than Richard. Whatever happens later, he enters the judicial process in act 1, scene 1 as a reformer intent on making those who wield or influence authority clean up their act. Though his three accusations clearly have Richard for their target, he has enough respect for the protocols of deference and piety to redirect them toward Mowbray. There is no reason to doubt that when he claims to be weeding out the sycophantic "caterpillars of the commonwealth," he is at least in part genuinely concerned to preserve the kingship from corrupt practices, practices that jeopardize respect for the system of lineal inheritance on which all the major players depend. The guilt and remorse that haunt him from the end of the play until his death in *2 Henry IV* are hardly those of the hard-edged Machiavel Bolingbroke has sometimes been taken to be. Rather, they're the signs of a tender conscience. He is aware that the trials he undergoes as king and as father may be God's punishment for his "mistreadings."[33] In this he understands his predicament in traditional terms. That is, he is an orthodox reader of his story; he speaks and behaves as if he were in Holinshed's chronicle.

The irony is that unbeknown to himself he is in a very different kind of story, one in which the royal victim has in effect selected his victimizer, appointed his usurper, and co-opted him into seizing a discredited crown. Bolingbroke's is the story of a character who at first isn't sure—or doesn't want to know—where he is going. Until Richard actively maneuvers him—and all but locks him—into the project of usurpation, he vacillates between gestures that threaten rebellion and gestures of restraint, loyalty, and obeisance. From the end of act 1, scene 3 through act 3, scene 3, he seems diffusely aggressive, ready for anything, but inconsistent as to the precise course he will choose. He jumps abruptly forward with imperious gestures and then nervously backtracks into deferential postures. What follows is a survey of some of the episodes and passages that support this portrayal of Bolingbroke.

1. The Duchess of Gloucester may find Bolingbroke more forceful and direct than his father in seeking to avenge her husband's murder. But in fact the son hesitates no less than the father to "lift / An angry arm against . . . [God's] minister" (1.2.253–54). Whatever he intimates or insinuates about Richard, his arm is expressly lifted only against a rival peer he treats as a thug whose misdeeds are damaging to Richard and the crown. His preliminary self-description is a careful, even labored, effort to make this clear:

> First—heaven be the record to my speech!
> In the devotion of a subject's love,
> Tend'ring the precious safety of my prince,

And free from other misbegotten hate,
Come I appellant to this princely presence—
Now, Thomas Mowbray, do I turn to thee;
....
Thou art a traitor and a miscreant,
Too good to be so, and too bad to live,
Since the more fair and crystal is the sky,
The uglier seem the clouds that in it fly.
Once more, the more to aggravate the note,
With a foul traitor's name stuff I thy throat,
And wish, so please my sovereign, ere I move,
What my tongue speaks, my right-drawn sword may prove. (1.1.30–46)

After pledging allegiance to Richard and turning to Mowbray, Bolingbroke's shift from blank verse to a parade of rhymed couplets garnished by a poetic comparison produces a florid scent of artifice and cliché. "Rhyme is the most conspicuous example in the play of formal verse, formal in the sense of verse which is overtly not a rhythmical version of ordinary speech,"[34] and is thus a signifier of speech that is preformulated rather than spontaneous utterance.[35]

To break out in rhymes often signifies the speaker's desire to represent himself as an actor performing a role before an audience he desires to impress. In Bolingbroke's case, it is as if he had memorized and now recites the lines to be spoken by a participant in the culturally prescripted ceremony of ordeal by combat. The rhymes accentuate his effort to show effortless mastery of verbal violence and abuse, obligatory features in the "chivalric foreplay"[36] building up to the combat. They accentuate the calculated redundancy by which he labors to drive his message home. Above all, they accentuate his desire to impress on Richard, on the other participants or bystanders, and on himself, the high seriousness, the righteous indignation, with which the loyal subject performs the appellant's role in the formal ceremony of accusation.

Nevertheless, the success of this performance was placed in question even before Bolingbroke entered and spoke. After Richard's opening exchange with Gaunt, he turns to summon the two participants with the utterance in which he visualizes their demeanor. Two conspicuously enjambed lines propel him impatiently past his addressee, Gaunt, and toward the challenge he anticipates. At that point, the quickening pace is brought to a sudden halt by the play's first rhymed couplet and by the resonantly redundant literary cliché it delivers:

Face to face
And frowning brow to brow, ourselves will hear
The accuser and the accused freely speak.
High stomached are they both and full of ire,
In rage deaf as the sea, hasty as fire. (1.1.19–23)

The lilting rhythm of self-assured and self-delighting rhetoric projects a speaker who obviously enjoys visualizing the ritual display of aggression and imagining the passion it symbolizes—enjoys it so much that, as fluent blank verse gives way to the end-stopped couplet, the description verges on parody, as if neither the ceremonial charade nor its participants (including the speaker) can be taken too seriously.

The couplet is itself a complex speech act: Does it describe the opponents' disposition? Or is it a self-fulfilling stage direction prescribing the appropriate behavior? The mood is indicative, but the sense is imperative. "Deaf as the sea, hasty as fire": Since these analogies of unruly nature are clichés of rulebound art, the couplet simultaneously commands and mocks a rage that will be as artificial and theatrical as the language that invokes it. Richard not only flaunts his mastery of ceremonial instruments and his power over the conduct of the event; he also treats them with contempt. Thus even as he sets the stage for Bolingbroke's performance, his preemptive mockery frames it in a reception-context that makes the appellant's tone of righteous indignation both predictable and a little shrill—and makes Bolingbroke seem ingenuously to follow Richard's stage direction. This tonal contrast reinforces the sense that Richard is jaded and Bolingbroke callow. And indeed it accords with our general impression of the latter's political ineffectiveness in the first act. There is nothing especially brilliant in his opening maneuver. He is easily finessed by Richard, with Gaunt's help, and sent packing abroad.[37]

2. Something other than callowness, righteous anger, or the investment in ritual performance throws the shadow of a doubt over Bolingbroke's own sense of his project: his repeated recourse to the motif of the expiatory journey threaded through the Henriad. What Bolingbroke refers to as his "ceremonious" leave-taking prior to entering the lists against Mowbray is very strange: He wishes to kiss his "sovereign's hand" and genuflect before him, "For Mowbray and myself are like two men / That

vow a long and weary pilgrimage" (1.3.48–49).[38] This is uttered just after he proclaims Mowbray a traitor "To God of heaven, King Richard, and to me. / And as I truly fight, defend me heaven" (1.3.39–41). Why should he assimilate the prospect of judicial combat to an expiatory journey to the Holy Land unless he views his appeal no less than Mowbray's alleged treason as in some way an offense to his God, his King, and himself? It may not be possible for him to believe that heaven will defend him if it is not Mowbray against whom he "truly" fights—if his appeal is directed beyond Mowbray toward Richard, and, more perilously, more darkly, beyond Richard toward his own father.[39] Such motives can only contaminate his ritual obeisance to Richard and, in turn, be further contaminated by its falsity.

3. Some critics sensitive to the complexity of Shakespeare's portrayal have described Bolingbroke as the prototypical political climber: "the man who will go further than his rivals because he never allows himself to know where he is going"; the exemplar of the "tacit vice" of opportunism, the duplicitous ability to induce others to clarify and fulfill the purposes of which one keeps oneself only "vaguely aware."[40] His language represents a speaker who sometimes betrays anxiety about where he is going—where he finds himself desiring or tempted to go. To Gaunt's advice that he dull the pain of exile with idyllic rationalizations and fantasies, he protests, "O no, the apprehension of the good / Gives but the greater feeling to the worse" (1.3.299–300). The words gesture toward meanings beyond the rejection of Gaunt's half-baked recipes for grief management. To imagine the good you desire but can't have, Bolingbroke remonstrates, only makes you feel worse. What if the good is kingship? Or what if it is virtue—loyalty, piety, respect for legitimate authority? What if "apprehension" means not only the imagination of the good but also the act of reaching for it and taking it ("here, cousin, seize the crown")? And, since "to apprehend" means not only "to imagine" and "to take" but also "to fear" (to be apprehensive), what if one fears the desire to reach for the good and fears the consequences of taking it?

If, however, he should be fearful of the desire to take the good, will he feel worse for having suppressed the desire? I'm far from claiming that Bolingbroke audits the full range of meanings tangled in the suspension of his utterance. My claim is that all these meanings are relevant to desires and anxieties that repeatedly obtrude themselves in his language. They betray a moral irritability, a desire for justification, a fear of his susceptibility to the very opportunism critics accuse him of. In this respect, the resonance of "the apprehension of the good / Gives but the greater feeling to the worse" echoes through the long corridor of the Henriad. It is an uncannily prophetic motto of Bolingbroke's ever more precarious journey through the declivities of his own conscience.

4. The first unguarded manifestation of apprehensive desire occurs in one of the play's cloudier moments. In act 2, scene 1, after Richard has laid claim to Gaunt's patrimony and departed, Northumberland confides to Willoughby and Ross that Bolingbroke is on his way home from Brittany with several peers and a small army in "eight tall ships" (2.1.277–85). In act 2, scene 3, shortly after he lands, Bolingbroke insists to Berkeley and York that the reason for his illegal reentry is "personally" to "lay my claim / To my inheritance" (2.3.134–45) because he has been denied the normal channels of legal representation by which an heir reclaims property that reverts to the crown.

York warns Richard not to violate this procedure (2.1.186–208), but Bolingbroke's complaint (2.3.112–35) shows that Richard ignored the warning. The problem is that according to Northumberland's announcement, Bolingbroke set sail from Brittany before the events in act 2, scene 1 transpired. Perhaps, as Peter Ure suggests, Shakespeare may have "telescoped the various events" in this episode "in the interests of dramatic timing."[41] Perhaps readers and auditors aren't expected to grasp legal complexities that are only hinted at in passing.[42] Perhaps they aren't being asked to worry about the inconsistency between Bolingbroke's asserted motive for returning and the fact that he couldn't have had that motive when he mustered his forces and left Brittany (since Gaunt had not died yet). And if they do notice the inconsistency, perhaps they will chalk it up to Bolingbroke's hypocrisy and opportunism.

My own view is that in act 2, scene 3 Bolingbroke behaves as if he worries both about the inconsistency and about a moment in which "the apprehension of the good" led to a brief and diffuse act of opportunism.[43] For despite the aggressive embarkation Northumberland reports, Bolingbroke seems careful, even diffident, in his dealings with those who greet him on his return. His response to Northumberland's windy sweet talk (2.3.2–20) is curt.[44] He shows himself to be concerned with the way he is perceived, addressed, and flattered or criticized. In thanking the nobles for their support, he is careful to keep his promises vague.

Bolingbroke thus seems to resist—without entirely discouraging—the push of an incipient rebellion of nobles who would obviously like to see him go all the way. Ironically, they have the same designs on Bolingbroke that Richard has. This unwitting complicity will, with Bolingbroke's help, turn against him in *1 Henry IV* after he has become king. Above all, he takes the opportunity offered by Berkeley's cool and York's censorious remarks in act 2, scene 3 to back away from any appearance of ambition greater than the desire to recover his rightful inheritance.

However wild or undefined his intention may have been on setting sail before Richard seized his patrimony, the seizure gives Bolingbroke a solid ground of defiance and grievance.[45] Against York's double charge that he is "a banished man" who has returned "before the expiration of thy time" to threaten his king (2.3.107–11), Bolingbroke's demand for legal justice reproduces the logic of York's protest against the seizure. Richard jeopardizes his own position as well as his cousin Bolingbroke's in violating the principle of lineal succession: "If that my cousin king be king in England, / It must be granted I am Duke of Lancaster" (2.3.123–24). Within these limits, Bolingbroke's sense of grievance is morally justified, and he can represent himself to himself as a man more sinned against than sinning. Richard's problem, then, will be to make Bolingbroke transgress those limits and reach for more than his own.

5. My response to Bolingbroke's language agrees with the opinion that throughout the play he "is genuinely trying to say what he means."[46] But what he means, what he intends to do, is often far from obvious—his speech is marked by moments of confusion and indecisiveness that suggest it is not always obvious to him. When he sentences the flatterers to death in act 3, scene 1, he goes back, in effect, to square one and blames them for all royal misdeeds just as he had blamed Mowbray in act 1, scene 1. This time, however, he is more careful to dissociate the misdeeds from Richard and represent the king himself as the victim of the flatterers' corrupt practices.

He is equally careful to control public reaction to the death sentences by a painstaking explanation most of which is devoted to the flatterers' victimization of him. Thus he and Richard are in the same position: Whatever he does on his own behalf he also does on Richard's, preserving both the king and the crown from the sources of corruption. However, the pressure behind this strenuous exercise in self-exculpation betrays itself in the introductory comment with which he justifies the death penalty: "To wash your blood / From off my hands, here in the view of men / I will unfold some causes of your deaths" (3.1.5–7). As Phyllis Rackin points out, in act 4, scene 1, when Richard associates "his betrayers with Pilate, the biblical archetype for a futile attempt to deny guilt . . . is prefigured here."[47]

But in Bolingbroke's case the allusion slips out against the grain of the speaker's stated intention. It hints at the futility of his attempt to persuade himself that he is not guilty of an action aimed at weakening rather than (as he claims) safeguarding Richard's position.

The solicitude Bolingbroke shows for the Queen immediately after his indictment of the flatterers (3.1.36–39) is part of the same pattern. It may be dismissed as another politic gesture intended to impress or placate his audience. But that does not prevent it from being at the same time a gesture of good faith he performs for his own benefit—or, more darkly, a preemptive washing of the hands by one who, like Macbeth, may be shaken by his apprehension of the good.

6. It is an apprehension Bolingbroke struggles to control in act 3, scene 3, against the mounting pressure of Richard's disturbing acquiescence. Even the impatient Northumberland tries to slow down the process when Richard accuses him of backing an effort to seize the crown (3.3.101–20). But Richard sardonically and melodramatically persists in offering the lure of deposition.

Bolingbroke's one long speech early in the scene (3.3.31–67) registers his uncertainty. It begins with a calculated alternation between reassurance and threat, expressly confined to the demand that his banishment be repealed and his lands restored. But as he continues, he momentarily loses control of his imagery and has to rein it back in:

> Be he the fire, I'll be the yielding water;
> The rage be his, whilst on the earth I rain
> My waters—on the earth and not on him. (3.3.58–60)

The runover line that pauses on and then passes through its ear-pun (rain/reign) enacts a loss of balance but stumbles awkwardly back to its feet. Two lines later, after Richard shows himself on the battlements, Bolingbroke is still stumbling: Richard, he says, appears

> As doth the blushing discontented sun
> From out the fiery portal of the east
> When he perceives the envious clouds are bent
> To dim his glory and to stain the track
> Of his bright passage to the occident. (3.3.63–67)

As Bolingbroke continues to develop the figure of elemental warfare, his words attribute questionable motives to the envious clouds that represent his own intention.

The parley between Richard and Northumberland that follows goes on for more than a hundred lines before Bolingbroke speaks again. During the remainder of the scene, which Richard monopolizes, Bolingbroke is allowed only five brief utterances. In the second of these he commands obeisance to the king, and in the third he protests once more that "I come but for my own" (3.3.195). But Richard immediately denies him this fallback position: "Your own is yours, and I am yours, and all" (196). Bolingbroke still resists: "So far be mine, my most redoubted lord, / As my true service shall deserve your love" (197–98). Richard brooks no further resistance. He pushes Bolingbroke into a corner and forces him to take all:

> Cousin, I am too young to be your father,
> Though you are old enough to be my heir.
> What you will have I'll give, and willing, too,
> For do we must what force will have us do.
> Set on towards London, cousin, is it so? (3.3.203–7)

That is, "what I will give, you'll have, for do you must what force will have you do"—convey Richard to London to prepare for the next phase of deposition. Bolingbroke surrenders: "Yea, my good lord" (3.3.208). I imagine this to be uttered weakly, with resignation. For this is the turning point of the play. The die has been cast by Richard, and Bolingbroke has lost the moral struggle. And now commence the "inward wars" of the future King Henry IV.

7. "Here, cousin, seize the crown" (4.1.181): Like this duplicitous speech act, the inverted rite of discoronation shows Richard having it both ways. He reenacts the self-deposition he has helped bring about, thereby publicly demonstrating his active relinquishment of the crown. At the same time he forces Bolingbroke to reenact his usurpation. He thus publicly dramatizes the act of illegal seizure while presenting himself to his audience as the usurper's Christlike victim.

Shortly after this he begins to shift from the victim's to the sinner's discourse and to perform an act of degradation aimed as much at the crown as at himself. What he proposes to remove from his person and offer Bolingbroke is a debased crown, a gift that has poison in it. Perversely staging and savoring both the pathos of victimization and the power of the self-deposing sinner, he stigmatizes Bolingbroke as a usurper even as he denies him the manly pleasure of being able to claim that he won the throne without Richard's help.

Bolingbroke's disadvantage in his competition with Richard had been established at the beginning of act 4, scene 1, before Richard's entry. The return to the question of Gloucester's murder invites a contrast with Richard's brash management of the trial by combat in the opening scenes. The battle of the gages is a comic and soured replay of those scenes. This contrast reflects poorly on Bolingbroke, who sits quietly through most of the scene and—unlike Richard—doesn't intervene in the volatile factionalism that bodes ill for future stability. The epidemic of gage-throwing reaches a thudding climax when Aumerle runs out of gages and Bolingbroke is once again (as in 1.1 and 1.3) frustrated, this time by the shadow of Mowbray, the news of whose holy death abroad prevents another attempt to resolve the Gloucester question.

8. At the end of act 5, scene 3, after having pardoned Aumerle for his part in the conspiracy planned by Richard's supporters, Bolingbroke threatens "the rest of that consorted crew" with death, but, as he twice suggests (5.3.140–42), carrying out the threat is contingent on finding the conspirators. The next scene begins with Sir Pierce Exton quoting words uttered in his direction by Bolingbroke—"Have I no friend will rid me of this living fear?" (5.4.2). Exton decides that he has just been invited to kill Richard.

There is some textual confusion as to whether or not this brief colloquy is a continuation of act 5, scene 3, with Exton having been present during at least part of that scene. Such a possibility has a substantial impact on our response to Exton's decision, which is expressly voiced as his interpretation of Bolingbroke's words:

> he wishedly looked on me,
> As who should say "I would thou wert the man
> That would divorce this terror from my heart"—
> Meaning the king at Pomfret. (5.4.7–10)

Other accounts of this episode—those of Hall, Holinshed, and Samuel Daniel—clearly signal Bolingbroke's intention to have Richard put to death secretly so that, in Daniel's words, he would not "seeme to wil the act."[48] But Shakespeare muddies things up by placing Exton's remarks in the immediate vicinity of Bolingbroke's worry about the conspirators, and then appointing Exton the sole interpreter of Bolingbroke's "ambiguous instigation."[49]

This juxtaposition makes it more plausible that Exton may have misconstrued a request to get rid of the conspirators (who are at liberty while

Richard is safely in prison).[50] Nevertheless, the instigation remains ambiguous, and the question is how to interpret the ambiguity. Some see the episode as consistent with the representation of Bolingbroke's "deviousness": "Without explicitly avowing his intention," he gets someone else not only to do his dirty work but also to articulate the purpose he leaves unexpressed. This is another example of his refusal to allow himself "to know where he is going."[51] Making a slight but significant change in this strong reading, I add that for Bolingbroke such a refusal is no longer possible. After Richard has denied him the fallback position in act 3, scene 3, and teased him in act 4, scene 1, with "Here, cousin, seize the crown," he knows where he is going and where he has gone. The words with which he pardons Aumerle in act 5, scene 3 poignantly betray his own sense of moral precariousness ("I pardon him as God shall pardon me," 5.3.130). Thus the motivational haziness or terseness characteristic of his language after act 3, scene 3 is indicative less of political deviousness or even of moral self-protection than of his fear of where he finds himself going.

"Have I no friend will rid me of this living fear?": Whatever Bolingbroke intends to say, the living fear of danger from others has come by this time to mirror the living fear of danger from himself. Were Bolingbroke to utter the wish Exton extrapolates from his glance ("I would thou wert the man / That would divorce this terror from my heart"), the mood would be counterfactual: that is, "if only you could; but you can't," for nobody else, least of all a political supernumerary like Exton, could assure him that "God shall pardon me."

Regardless of what he may have intended Exton to hear or do, the upshot in act 5, scene 6 is that Bolingbroke seems once again to lose control of the situation. The effort to wrap things up and assume high moral ground signified by the parade of rhymed couplets with which he pardons Carlisle in the final scene (5.6.24–29) is rudely interrupted by Exton's melodramatic entry and announcement: "Great king, within this coffin I present / Thy buried fear. Herein," he adds, angling for his gratuity, "all breathless lies / The mightiest of thy greatest enemies, / Richard of Bourdeaux, by me hither brought" (5.6.30–33). He gets no thanks from the great king, who oddly identifies Richard's plight with his own when he blames Exton for having "wrought / A deed of slander with thy fatal hand / Upon my head" (5.6.34–36). This is uncanny: It is as if Richard has penetrated Bolingbroke's conscience, possesses it, and now speaks through him. To hear this ghostly intrusion is to hear something startling in Exton's simple and direct reply, for it voices precisely the protest Bolingbroke would be justified in making to Richard: "From your own mouth, my lord, did I this deed" (5.3.37).

Surrounded as he is by supporters, Bolingbroke is not politically embarrassed by Exton's entrance. Yet perhaps even the supporters who brought in a harvest of rebel heads would shy away from the ultimate crime of regicide. The evidence on this score is not decisive because the play's emphasis is elsewhere. In Bolingbroke's rejoinder to Exton it remains fixed on the continuing intrusion of uncanny Ricardian overtones:

> They love not poison that do poison need,
> Nor do I thee. Though I did wish him dead,
> I hate the murderer, love him murdered.
> The guilt of conscience take thou for thy labor,
> But neither my good word nor princely favor.
> With Cain go wander thorough shades of night,
> And never show thy head by day nor light. (5.6.38–45)

As we listen to this bitter reproach, we may hear Bolingbroke's malediction on himself as well as on Exton. Since sending Exton off with Cain recalls his own comparison in act 1, scene 1 of Gloucester's murder to that of sacrificing Abel, he now finds himself involved in the same kind of kin-murder he had accused Richard of. But it is Richard whose voice usurps the grammatical first person, and his despair that speaks through Bolingbroke's words and condemns both himself and Bolingbroke. "Here, cousin, seize the crown": And so he did, and now he resurrects his buried fear and receives his reward, or sentence. "Hath Richard / Deposed thine intellect? Hath he been in thy heart?"

3. *Richard's Soliloquy*

Richard II, Act 5, Scene 5, Lines 1–166

"Enter Richard alone," and he tells us first what he has been trying to do, "studying how I may compare / This prison where I live unto the world," and then why he "cannot do it": "because the world is populous / And here is not a creature but myself" (5.5.1–5). Nevertheless, he continues bravely,

I'll hammer it out.
My brain I'll prove the female to my soul,
My soul the father, and these two beget
A generation of still-breeding thoughts,
And these same thoughts people this little world,
In humors like the people of this world,
For no thought is contented. (5–11)

These thoughts/people compose into a social hierarchy of three classes, each with its own form of discontent: "The better sort, / As thoughts of things divine," are troubled by moral "scruples"—self-doubt—as they sophistically take advantage of contradictions in scripture ("set the word itself / Against the word," 11–14). Perhaps this leads to the desperation of "Thoughts tending to ambition" that "do plot / Unlikely wonders" and, when they fail, "die in their own pride," which in turn leads "Thoughts tending to content" to rationalize their acceptance of their miserable lot as "fortune's slaves." In the third and longest of the three descriptions, the speaker's impatience comes through most sharply. His contempt flares up at those who "find a kind of ease" by comparing themselves to "silly beggars," thus "Bearing their own misfortunes on the back / Of such as have before endured the like" (29–30).

With one exception (the personal reference to "my ragged prison walls" at line 21) these increasingly bitter reflections have the ring of general cynical wisdom. Yet the speaker summarily incorporates them in a self-portrait—"Thus play I in one person many people, / And none contented." He goes on to describe his vacillation between the thoughts of kingship and of beggary as if his actual changes of fortune were the consequences of his wishes and reflections (30–38).

In act 4, scene 1, Richard disingenuously uses the two-buckets figure to highlight his dominance in the perverse game of "Here, cousin, seize the crown." He implies that he, the tear-laden down bucket, controls the upward motion of the empty bucket he describes in an image more applicable to himself than to Bolingbroke ("The emptier ever dancing in the air," 4.1.182–87). Similarly, as the soliloquist reviews the actual changes of status he recently suffered, he resituates them in the floating present tense of fantasy, and depicts his thought and desire as controlling the seesaw between kingship and beggary. It is both a superficial evasion and a profound truth for the already deposed king to imagine himself operating both ends of the seesaw, as he does when he says "by and by [I] / Think that I am unkinged by Bolingbroke, / And straight am nothing" (5.5.37–38).

From this glimpse of the truth of self-deposition, he turns and wings away on the redundant whir of a generalizing jingle:

> But whate'er I be,
> Nor I, nor any man that but man is,
> With nothing shall be pleased till he be eased
> With being nothing. (5.5.40–41)

This not only recalls the desire to "find a kind of ease" he had just implicitly disparaged in his reference to the self-demeaning flattery of "Thoughts tending to content." It *illustrates* and *enacts* that desire. It bears the marks of a biting recoil from the flattery of the victim's discourse, and so the conclusion of this exercise in "the generation of still-breeding thoughts" circles back like a boomerang from human nature—any man that but man is—to the speaker.[1]

"Enter Richard alone." Until now he has always directed his eloquence—whether sardonic or self-pitying—toward others. This is the play's first and only soliloquy. Do we infer from this that he suddenly becomes aware of the audience offstage and moves forward to address them? He begins his speech with a verb phrase in the present perfect tense: not "I am studying" but "I have been studying." Does this mean that he assumes his fans in the theater audience have been wondering what he's been up to since they last saw him, and that he considerately brings them up to date? Maybe he thinks they think he spends his time offstage working out the poetic comparisons he is famous for, and are eagerly waiting for the progress report he now shares with them (or at them).

Maybe, then, this is an example of the convention of extradramatic address frequently used in Tudor drama before Shakespeare, especially by such figures as the Vice in the morality plays. Yet Anne Righter argues that by Shakespeare's time soliloquies were distinguished from addresses to the audience and tended to be contained within the dramatic fiction: "It was understood that almost all speeches of this kind were overheard by the spectators as the result of stage conventions, not through conscious intent on the part of the speaker."[2] In other words, it was understood that although the actor knows he is playing to the audience in the theater, the character doesn't know he is a fictional character being performed by an actor onstage.

If the presence of the theater audience to the actor reminds us of its absence to the character, we become aware that the soliloquizing character-as-actor is deprived of the very conditions he needs in order to resemble the performer or role-player he desires to be. He may be his own audience by default. The contrast may then establish the missing audience as the object of the speaker's anxiety or desire. Of course an actor may play a character who performs as if he is an actor playing roles before his onstage audience, and Richard is famous for this. The soliloquy is a special case of performative behavior, and it poses a problem: Since, in contrast to the actor, the character is by convention unaware of the theater audience he appears to address, whom does he address? Is he imagining or constructing the audience he wants to be heard by, the audience he wants to persuade or be judged by, an audience that may include (or consist entirely of) himself?

Righter quotes a wonderful example of a moment of hesitation between extradramatic and dramatic address performed by the Vice in an earlier play, *Kyng Daryus* (c. 1565). After he "opens the performance by hailing the audience in what seems to be the old manner . . . he deliberately and rather slyly withdraws this initial recognition of the spectators" in the following lines:

> But softe, is there no body here?
>   Truly, I do not lyke thys gere;
> I thought I should haue found sum bodie.[3]

"Enter Richard alone" and teasingly runs up the question of the audience like a flag in his statement that "here is not a creature but myself."

Although he attributes his failure to the difference between the populous world and the empty prison, the emphasis on enforced isolation suggests an additional obstacle. Accustomed as he is to public speaking, he finds it hard even to elaborate a figure of thought when there is no audience of flatterers or adversaries for him to dominate with his superior rhetorical firepower.

Lois Potter speculates that if Richard has been "playing a power game where he loses in order to win," the soliloquy shows "his realization that you can't play these games by yourself."[4] But he tries anyway. "The people of this world" may have shut him out but they can't shut him up. He will now replace the missing audience with himself, will divide himself into the auditor or receiver or mother and the speaker or sender or father of his comparison ("My brain I'll prove the female to my soul"), will posture for his own approval or disapproval as if checking his performance in a mirror.

But hasn't he always done that? "Enter Richard alone" is the phantom stage direction I am tempted to slip behind the one that heads the play's opening scene ("Enter King Richard, John of Gaunt, with other Nobles and Attendants"), for even in Richard's acts of dialogue he seems always to be talking and listening to himself. What he has been saying to himself throughout the play is a variation or illustration of what he says in this soliloquy. He has "been studying" since act 1, scene 1. The problem he poses for himself is stated portentously enough to justify the amount of study he suggests he has given it, since "This prison where I live" can be—and has been—taken as a reference not only to his literal incarceration but also to his self-imprisoning state of mind.[5]

If he succeeds in persuading himself that he has overcome either or both of these prisons, he will have risen above his isolation and victimization. On the one hand, he will have proved his self-sufficiency to himself and, on the other hand, he will have asserted his resemblance, his connection, to the world. Yet both that project and its failure are mocked by the desperate and violent futility, the melodramatic pathos, of the image he uses to illustrate the "Unlikely wonders" plotted by "Thoughts tending to ambition":

> how these vain weak nails
> May tear a passage through the flinty ribs
> Of this hard world, my ragged prison walls,
> And, for they cannot, die in their own pride. (5.5.19–22)

To the extent that Richard finds himself in a prison and world he recognizes as partly—perhaps largely—the effects of self-incarceration in despair, he stands before himself as his own jailer. This is what makes fantasies of escape "Unlikely wonders." Among the indications that he bitterly recognizes this bitter truth about himself is the awkward redundancy of lines 9–10, in which he says he will "people this little world" with thoughts that are "In humors like the people of this world" because both thoughts and people are discontented.

Apart from the fact that this assertion displays the bad humor of the speaker ("no thought [of mine] is [ever] contented"), the emphasis on resemblance seems arbitrary. But when we take into account the effect of the redundancy, which collapses the two phrases—and the worlds they refer to—the focus on discontent becomes plausible. It amounts to an acknowledgment by the speaker that the subjects he creates as soliloquist are doubles of those he created as king.

Potter brilliantly suggests that the personified thoughts are "unsympathetic listeners getting ready, yet again, to mock his senseless conjuration," and she adds that "of course the unsympathetic listener is also a self-projection."[6] Thus, now and always, whether alone or in public, for him to listen to himself thinking or speaking is to divide "one person" into "many people," none of them ever "contented." The soliloquy not only demonstrates but intensifies his sense that since, as Wolfgang Iser puts it, "he cannot reconcile himself with any of these roles, and therefore has to act them all, he enhances the dissatisfaction with his own nothing—a nothing from which only death can liberate him."[7]

"Enter Richard alone" and marks his awareness of his dilemma by representing the act of soliloquy as a monstrous act that is at once self-dividing, self-confining, and self-coupling. Shifting apparitions of escape, suicide, and caesarean trauma converge to register the confusion and impotence of the "still-breeding thoughts" produced by what he depicts as the intercourse between his soul and brain. The conflicted senses of "still-breeding" dramatize the causal relation between frenetic activity and futility: "always breeding" and "still-born" (breeding "still," or dead, thoughts).

However strained or strange this figure of self-coupling and generation is, it is charged with meaning by its inclusion in, its allusion to, a network of apprehensions that pervade the play and manifest what may be called the Bad Seed Fantasy, or paedophobia (fear of children). The precariousness of generational continuity is suggested by the glimmers of several troubled father/son relationships. Gaunt quietly betrays his son in act 1, scene 3; York loudly contemns his in act 5, scenes 2–3; and Bolingbroke worriedly mentions his "unthrifty" son in act 5, scene 3.

In the deposition scene York announces that Richard has adopted Bolingbroke as his heir (4.1.108–13). This makes it possible for Richard legally to resign the crown by designating his cousin as his "son." Such a strategy comically exemplifies one of the troublesome properties of sonship that produce paedophobia: Fathers are expected to raise their sons not only to perpetuate the paternal image but also to replace the mortal father, and replacement may sometimes take the form of displacement or deposition.

"Time broke in a disordered string" (5.5.46). Richard's phrase provides an apt figure of the tensions and surrogations that untune the genealogical string of patriarchal succession. Prominent among the Henriad's projects is its exploration of the failure of paternal authority, and the impact of this failure not only on social and political behavior but also on the fears and desires that motivate such behavior. Like so many phrases in the play, Richard's "disordered string" chimes with an earlier expression used by another speaker: "He that hath suffered this disordered spring / Hath now himself met with the fall of leaf" (3.4.48–49). This is the gardener, describing Richard's folly in the terms provided by his analogy between care of the state and care of gardens.

Even before his assistant proposes the analogy of garden to kingdom, the gardener rakes politiculture into horticulture by translating the anxiety of fathers into an arboreal figure of self-endangering virility:

> Go, bind thou up young dangling apricocks
> Which, like unruly children, make their sire
> Stoop with oppression of their prodigal weight. (3.4.29–31)

The bizarre pun on "dangling apricocks" together with that key word of the *Henry IV* plays, "prodigal," turns apricots/sons into limp penile figures. It produces a caricature of anxiety that rubs off on the gardener as a pompous representative of youth-hating oldsters: If Richard had "cut off the heads of too fast-growing sprays / That look too lofty," he could have kept the crown. The gardener subordinates his critique to the unruly spray of examples that happen to be available in his horticultural analogue. His discourse thus illustrates the unruliness he criticizes.

In the best commentary on representations of the nothing that is despair, not even death can liberate the ambitious sinner who tries vainly to get rid of himself and dies in his own pride. Kierkegaard describes "the sickness unto death," the self-loathing of the sinner despondent over his sin, in terms that assimilate it to the dark side of what might be described as the Christian version of narcissism: "A person in despair . . . despairingly wants to be . . . a self that he is not. . . . He would be in seventh heaven were he the self he wants to be . . . , but to be forced to be the self he does not want to be, that is his torment—that he cannot get rid of himself."[8]

4. *On the Continuity of the Henriad*

1

Since I am hardly the first to argue that the four plays of the Henriad should be read as a single text, I'll begin by distinguishing my sense of its singleness from that of other critics who insist on its "artistic integrity," "thematic unity," and "organic" wholeness.[1] These critics advance divergent accounts of the patterns holding the Henriad together even as they agree on its structural or sequential coherence. They tend to be academic interpreters and armchair readers rather than theater-centered interpreters.

There are three reasons why I don't find their claims and accounts persuasive. The first is that no one arguing for the unity of the Henriad has seriously confronted the objections of theater-centered critics who insist that the unifying features picked out by academic critics defy the conditions of performance. The occasional literary critic mentions this problem only to dismiss it.[2] These objections are nevertheless substantive, and to confront them involves confronting basic assumptions that underwrite theater-centered attacks on armchair interpretation.[3]

The second reason is that accounts of the unity of the Henriad tend to treat either *Henry V* or its protagonist or both as flawed in some way. It's often hard to determine whether what those accounts find problematical is a praiseworthy effect of the text or a blameworthy defect in the author or an indecisive combination of the two. The third reason is related to the general theoretical weakness inherent in appeals to thematic or esthetic "unity," "artistic integrity," and "organic wholeness." These terms hover uneasily between evaluative and descriptive status. "Integrity," for example, denotes a virtue as well as the state of being whole, or intact. It glances toward criteria of esthetic value and autonomy that have been convincingly discredited.

The question of the unity of the Henriad has exercised some of its most important interpreters. My concern is not with unity or integrity per se, and if I invoke the singleness of the text, I do so in terms not of structure but of dynamic transformation. To illustrate these alternatives, on the one hand E. M. W. Tillyard locates the unity of the Henriad in a series of static contrasts (of style, character, and action) and a "network of cross-references" that boil down in his account to an uninterpreted list of anticipations and echoes. Tillyard premises that "Shakespeare knew what he was doing from the start and deliberately planned" the Henriad as a "single organism."[4] On the other hand, D. A. Traversi states that although the Henriad is a "closely integrated series," the continuity of its argument "does not . . . imply that the four plays were originally conceived as a single unit, but simply that the later terms of the series recognized the existence of the earlier."[5] I want to explore a stronger version of Traversi's thesis: The later terms are radically modified by their relation to the earlier terms, which are in turn modified by that modification.

For me, what makes the Henriad a single text is that it unfolds a process of continuous revision. Earlier textual moments persist like ghosts that haunt and complicate later moments. The most highly charged currents of meaning circulate through the sequence of four plays in such a way that if you disconnect any one play from the others and read it independently you short those currents out.

This is especially true of the language and motivation of the three kings. They are hooked up in series so that if one of them goes out the others do too. Richard's power charges up Henry, whose resistance to it charges up Harry. Harry's resistance increases Henry's and Richard's power, just as Henry's increases Richard's.

To unplug any play from its tetralogical source is to impoverish the power of its drama and the resonance of its language. *Henry V* suffers most from disconnection, as the critical record testifies, and much of what follows will be directed not so much toward a new view of Harry as toward a new way of conceiving the interpretive problems his language poses when the Henriad is read as a single text.

2

The practice of stage-centered reading pursued in this study takes theatrical performance into account while responding to the demands and opportunities peculiar to close reading. No approach develops out of thin air, and mine is situated at the center of a complex network of ongoing negotiations with other critical approaches and their practitioners. It owes much more to their imaginative, responsive, and generative encounters with Shakespeare than the references scattered throughout my text and footnotes can adequately indicate.

The debt deepens when I consider how much I've learned in the struggle to transfer my predecessors' insights from their interpretive frameworks to my own. If in what follows I seem more intent on harrying them than thanking them, that can only increase both their generosity and my gratitude. I'll now perform this double service by describing six types of reductionism they have taught me to avoid.

1. *Theatrical* reductionism restricts the interpretive possibilities inherent in the reader/text relation according to criteria more appropriate to the playgoer/performance relation. Theater-centered critics are concerned primarily with the actability or performability of plays and interpretations. They don't give high priority to the Henriad as a continuous text. The reductive effect produced by diminishing the links among the plays or ignoring their interactivity is especially noticeable—as one might expect—in theater-centered treatments of the last two plays in the sequence.

2. *Metatheatrical* and *metadramatic* reductionism insists that whatever else the plays are about their most important and interesting themes are reflexive. That is, they are ultimately about theatricality, or mimesis, or role-playing, or language. The *metapoetic* version of this reduction shifts the focus of reflexivity to the author: the plays are about the artist's struggle with his material.[6] Since this concern tends to be coupled with attention to the artist's development it edges into another category,

3. *Developmental* reductionism: Its basic premise, "later is greater," adversely affects plays dated earlier in the chronological canon. So, for example, it is argued that *Julius Caesar* and *Hamlet* deal more adequately with "tragic" themes imperfectly treated in *Henry V*.[7] Another form of developmentalism finds its way into psychoanalytic reductionism.

4. *Psychoanalytic* reductionism, or, to be more precise, Freudian reductionism. The Freudian interpreter uses epigenetic (developmental) schemes of explanation, with their focus on the repression, displacement, and so on,

of oedipal and preoedipal relations, as if these relations and their fictional subjects were natural rather than constructed. The plays are sometimes evaluated according to the adequacy with which those schemes are represented: One of the reasons given for the superiority of *Hamlet* to *Henry V* is the mother's presence in the former play and her absence in the latter.

5. *Ethical* reductionism channels interpretive energy into the project of judging whether and explaining why characters—Henry V, for example—are good or bad. This is a kind of voyeurism. It is reductive because it ignores the plays' central concern with the internal dramas of conscience, self-judgment, self-evasion, and self-esteem.

Ethical critics worry more about what they think of characters than about what characters are shown to think of themselves. Yet the desire and danger of self-judgment are inscribed in both the interlocutory and the discursive registers of the characters' language. It has been too easy for critics to find reasons for praising or blaming, liking or disliking Harry, and though my own practice betrays the same tendency, I try to minimize it in two ways: first, by trying to distinguish between what I think of Harry and what he thinks of himself, and second, by bracketing out the former and isolating the latter as the more relevant object of interpretive concern.

6. *Historical* reductionism occurs whenever an overall diachronic scheme is imposed on the tetralogy in a manner that encourages disregard of effects that don't fit the scheme. For example, the movement from *Richard II* through *Henry V* has been characterized as "a passage from the Middle Ages to the Renaissance and the modern world," from "feudalism and hierarchy to the national state and the individual," and from the failure of weak King Richard II to the triumph of strong King Henry V.[8] This is the familiar story of disenchantment in which religious attitudes toward history and politics give way to secular and humanistic attitudes.

Whether this pattern is treated as a fall from a sacramental to a Machiavellian conception of kingship, or as the emergence of a triumphant Renaissance humanism, or as some combination of both, the story positions the three kings in a politico-historical context that narrows the framework of explanation. It obscures the extent to which their interlocutory politics and psychological warfare produce sequences of plot that compose a larger story. I say *a* rather than *the* larger story because disenchantment may not be the only story, and, in the form outlined above, it may have lost some of its cachet. There are two reasons for this, one connected with a new emphasis emerging in recent studies of *Richard II* and the other with my own reading of Harry's career through the tetralogy.

Recent accounts of *Richard II* don't question the disenchantment thesis so much as complicate it and rearrange the relation of the sequence of plays to the sequence of "historical" changes. In effect, they move the sequence of changes forward in time so that, from the opening lines of *Richard II*, we encounter a community already disenchanted with the feudal and medieval ritualism to which everyone pays lip service. Chapter 2 in this study emphasizes the extent to which the first play and its titular character question or demystify the traditional ideology. The pressure of this demystification can be felt in reinterpretations of the other three plays, especially in the controversies that center on the moral assessment of Harry and the esthetic assessment of *Henry V*.

My response to these controversies—and this is the second reason why I think the disenchantment story needs to be changed—is to treat with utmost seriousness the importance that Harry's question "May I with right and conscience make this claim?" has *for him*.[9] I'll argue that the cause behind his claim to the French throne is morally dubious, if not reprehensible. When we trace the cause back to his first appearance and soliloquy in *1 Henry IV*, we see that it leads him to make war more in his own than in the national interest.

Harry asks his subjects to risk their lives for reasons that might not stand up at the bar of his own conscience. Thus his language betrays the pressure of his need to persuade himself, and not merely the world, that his cause is just. His frequent appeals to God spring less from the desire to give himself political legitimacy and his war religious sanction than from concern for his ethical probity and spiritual welfare.

This view of Harry calls for a modification of the disenchantment scheme. The historico-political approach to the tetralogy traces the passage out of the declining ritualism and religious ideology of medieval kingship. The psycho-political approach I'm proposing traces increasingly strident appeals, cresting in *Henry V*, to God, to religion, and to the scenario of salvation and damnation we associate with the Morality Play tradition.

Both Henry IV and his son rehabilitate religious motifs to guarantee more efficient guilt management. Consider, for example, Henry's longing for Jerusalem, Harry's enactment of the Prodigal Son parable, the Puritan parodies Falstaff aims at Harry, and the persistent if varying use the royal protagonists make of the imagery of Christ's betrayal and sacrifice. All these point to the abiding desire for the punishment, justification, absolution, and forgiveness that only God can give.

This movement reaches a climax in the fourth act of *Henry V.* The fear of damnation and the desire of salvation embedded in the language of the Chorus and of the first scene register by their very hyperbolic quality how much Harry has at stake in the battle ahead of him. As he moves through the Henriad from Shrewsbury to Westminster to Agincourt the need for personal justification becomes more critical and hence more dependent on religious as well as secular validation. His express reliance on God increases in direct proportion to his famous victories at home and abroad.

The "mirror of all Christian kings" has won loud applause for the splendor of his Renaissance humanism and loud catcalls for his lurking Machiavellianism and his skill in shifting responsibility. But in recent decades the irritability of his filial and Protestant conscience has begun to excite the attention it merits. Thus my story of disenchantment will be crossed by the no less familiar story of Protestant reenchantment.

That story centers on both the intimacy and the vividness of the subject's dialogue with himself and God. Shakespeare represents spiritual warfare in the conflict of discourses that animates the language of the three kings and Falstaff—in the dialectical and self-regenerating struggle of the sinner's discourse with the discourses of the victim/revenger, donor, hero, and saint. Such a configuration of discourses, grounded in the sinner's desire for self-recognition and judgment, is historically specific—is, in a word, Protestant—and accounts for the drive toward religious reenchantment that pulses through the Henriad. Given this reading, it should be clear what I find wrong with the final category of reductionism, political reductionism.

6. *Political* reductionism. To begin with an example, the thesis of Sigurd Burckhardt's striking and original essay on the Henriad is that Shakespeare deployed "two mutually inconsistent . . . models of succession," primogeniture and combat, in a relation of complementarity.[10] Burckhardt shows how the disenchantment process corrodes the legitimacy of the traditional belief system. But his analysis remains at the level of political structure. Of the encounter over the crown between Henry IV and Harry in *2 Henry IV* (4.5), he observes that "even under primogeniture succession seemed to be by combat."[11] This is offered as a strictly political comment on the bloody transmission of the crown from the time of Richard II to that of Henry VII. But it doesn't do justice to the way the episode represents the more pervasive theme that dominates the tetralogy: the combat

between father and son that frustrates all their attempts at reconciliation or atonement.

Another form of political reductionism appears in the wave of commentaries associated with cultural materialism and New Historicism. The project of politicizing and de-estheticizing interpretation too often leads advocates of "political Shakespeare" or "alternative Shakespeares" to adopt new rules of evidence that restrict the scope of close reading. Their narrow focus on the Thing they call "power" prompts them to construe legitimation in purely political terms as the effect of successful manipulation of the resources of idealization. Their reliance on selective citation and paraphrastic foreshortening deprives them of the interpretive resources that would enable them to unpack a theme that interests many of them, the theme of self-legitimation.

For example, Jonathan Dollimore and Alan Sinfield locate Henry V's problems not in the struggle to protect his conscience from the ethical contradictions inscribed in his language but in his struggle with the vulnerability of power. They attribute this struggle to the transitional character of "the Elizabethan state" reflected in the history plays:

> What really torments Henry is the inability to ensure obedience. . . . Not surprisingly, he has bad dreams. The implication [of his soliloquy on ceremony] is that subjects are to be envied . . . because as subjects they cannot suffer the king's fear of being disobeyed and opposed. Henry indicates a paradox of power only to misrecognize its force by mystifying both kingship and subjection.

For Dollimore and Sinfield this is the "sub-text" of the speech in which Harry reaches "the height of his own program of self-legitimation."[12] But they confuse a subtext with a displacement. What really torments Harry is not a failure in political legitimacy. What torments him is fear of a failure in moral legitimacy.

When proponents of the New Politicism of the 1980s isolated the representation of power, ideology, and strategies of legitimation, they ignored the politics of interlocutory and psychological conflict. It may well be true that the Henriad is about the legitimization of misrule, that its hero is a figure of carnival, and that its major conflict is between different conceptions of political order. What it demonstrates may indeed be that "legitimate order can only come into being through disruption."[13]

Nevertheless, to restrict attention to these themes is to reduce the moral struggles of the Henriad's royal protagonists—their psychological warfare with each other and with themselves—to Shakespeare's critique of ideology. I don't mean to imply that such a critique (whether "Shakespeare's" or the critic's) can't or shouldn't be explored, only that in New Politicism it tends to be the product of too soft or fast or blurry a reading of the text.

The chief obstacle to the idea of the unity and tetralogical continuity of the Henriad is posed by theater-centered interpretation. This practical perspective is not vulnerable to the charge of reductionism. It puts a different set of aims into play. Because its proponents are not engaged in a polemic against reading, the problem they have in staging the tetralogy offers the strongest obstacle to my emphasis on the Henriad's unity.

3

Anthony Quayle notes in the foreword to *Shakespeare's Histories at Stratford 1951* that his production of the complete cycle was only the second on record since Shakespeare's time. Quayle, who was director of the Shakespeare Memorial Theater at the time, goes on to argue forcefully for the advantages of cycle presentation:

> We well knew that each play was strong enough to stand theatrically on its own feet, and that economic necessity for many years had forced them to do so; but the more we studied the more we felt that this practice of presenting the plays singly had only resulted in their distortion, and that their full power and meaning only became apparent when treated as a whole. It was not only that many of the characters lived and developed through several of the plays; it was not only that literary and dramatic echoes reverberated backwards and forwards through the text of all four; it was because what appeared to be puzzling psychological inconsistencies when the plays were treated singly disappeared when they were considered as a whole, and became clear as purposeful and masterly writing.[14]

The co-authors of this volume, Dover Wilson and T. S. Worsley, agree with Quayle on the specific differences produced by the cycle conception. Personal dramas are more effectively contained within the larger political story. The "star vehicle" aspects of such roles as Richard, Hotspur, and Falstaff preempt less attention from the cycle's political scenario and morality design.

As Worsley sees it, Richard's "personal tragedy" yields to his function as "the last of the kings who is claiming the Divine Right."[15] Bolingbroke becomes more important from the beginning of the tetralogy, and he is a more complex figure in the *Henry IV* plays. The unfolding of the Prodigal Son drama clarifies Falstaff's role and just deserts as the Prince's "Tempter."[16] Finally, the portrait of Harry becomes more understandable because the "long sweep" allows the apparent inconsistency between Prince Hal and Henry V to be resolved in the heroic king's favor.

Because Wilson and Worsley are sensitive both to the demands of the theater and to the practical obstacles that beset serial presentation, their assessments of Shakespeare's intention are cautious. Wilson thinks "it would be going too far . . . to suppose that he planned the four plays from the beginning as one historical masterpiece in serial parts." He assumes instead that Shakespeare added "links . . . to give them a measure of unity and coherence."[17]

Although Worsley supports and develops this rationale, the production failed to convince him that the plays were designed for performance in cycle. In his opinion "the most probable way in which the plays came to be written" was "that they *happened* one after the other": Because *Richard II* was successful, Shakespeare wrote another history play in which he "developed a better chronicle method," then responded "to the public's demand for 'More!', particularly more of Falstaff," with a much weaker sequel, and finally met "a different demand from the audience" with *Henry V*.[18]

I think both the occasion of the Wilson-Worsley volume and the volume itself testify to the justness of Worsley's verdict. For if Quayle's is only the second cycle performance recorded since Shakespeare's time, and if "the economic and organizational difficulties in the way of presenting the cycle as a whole are so formidable,"[19] and if Shakespeare was as smart a practical theater man as everyone says, it stands to reason that he would not have written *for* the theater a sequence the overall meaning of which depended on conditions of performance it was not likely to receive *in* the theater. From this, however, we don't have to conclude that such a sequence didn't get written, only that it didn't get written *for*—or at least not exclusively *for*—the theater.

To put it barbarically, whatever it got written for, whatever it was intended for, *it got written as writing.* And as writing it can be read as well as staged. A single phrase buried in Quayle's foreword points to the alternative that is thrown away by the theatrical orientation of the volume as a whole: "Literary and dramatic echoes reverberated backwards and forwards through the text of all four" plays.[20]

I'm not sure what the aural metaphor means in the temporal context of theatrical performance. Could we anticipate or identify a forward reverberation or "pre-echo" before it is registered as an echo that reverberates backwards? But the figure makes good sense if we imagine "the text" stabilized in a material inscription that makes all parts of it accessible in any or all moments of reading.

It's conceivable that the Henriad lends itself to a mode of interpretation radically different both from those that guide the staging of the plays and from those generated by a theater audience. But it's also conceivable that such a reading makes enough dramatic and theatrical sense to open itself to performance.

When reading the Henriad I don't think of it as a dramatic poem. Nor do I conceive of it as the blueprint for a film or video performance. Nor do I approach it as a system of signs whose referent is to be visualized in some extratheatrical context of actual experience.

What I visualize or imagine while reading are the conditions, the conventions, and the positional relations—relations among actors, characters, and audience—of Elizabethan theater as Shakespeare uses it. This includes, for example, the conventions that govern staging, scene division, and role performance. It includes the choreography of violent action, the variations of prose and verse, and the forms of interlocutory relationship (soliloquy, dialogue, eavesdropping). These offer themselves to the armchair interpreter as *theater effects* that help interpret the performances of fictional speakers.

Text-centered reading is in this respect as parasitical on theater-centered reading as it is on theater itself. It should always take account of the ways any theatrical interpretation reflects the interests, values, powers, dangers, and privileges that are embedded in the very structure of theatrical relationships as they were institutionalized and performed in Shakespeare's time—and as they are represented by his texts. His plays are clearly written *for* theater, and aspects of the theatricality with which this purpose invests them are often thematized as constituents of their meaning.

At the same time, Shakespeare's texts are just as clearly underdetermined by their theatrical purpose. Tension between theatrical and textual perspectives vibrates throughout the tetralogy. The themes binding the four plays together are so finely woven into the language of the Henriad community that they respond best to the sort of literary excavation on which theater-centered critics frown because it violates the constraints and opportunities peculiar to performance.

It's unlikely that the Henriad as a whole will come to occupy a place in Shakespeare's repertory similar to the *Ring* in Wagner's. Practical theater people have much more reason than theater-centered critics to give the individual plays primacy as self-contained producible units and to interpret each play as much as possible on its own terms. The trouble is that as the tetralogy unfolds, this strategy tends to be self-defeating. The rich interplay of shadow and light becomes more intense, the motivational drama more powerful, in the last two plays precisely because of their position in the sequence.

In strictly theatrical terms, *2 Henry IV* and *Henry V* have less independence, lose more in being isolated, than the first two plays. Because this especially troubles *2 Henry IV*, it has neither had a distinguished theatrical career nor been appreciated by those whose criterion is the self-contained play. And because it is less clear in the case of *Henry V*, that play has attracted more theatrical and literary attention. Until recently, however, both its advocates and its detractors have judged *Henry V* on the dubious basis of interpretations that presuppose its independent status.

Both of these plays—*Henry V* more subtly but no less certainly than *2 Henry IV*—are haunted by "the nature of the times deceas'd."[21] Since those times are depicted in the first two plays, a more comprehensive burden is placed on both the theatergoer and the literary interpreter. And since the tetralogy is not readily available as a theatrical unit, viewers of the last two plays will at least have to have read the first two in order to respond to the full power and drama of *2 Henry IV* and *Henry V*.

But the problems go beyond this relatively mechanical level. For the third and fourth plays not only presuppose the material of the first two. They represent and continually revise that material. This sends us back and forth between the earlier and later plays in order to determine (1) how the characters' motives and interests affect their memory, and (2) how the themes and emphases of the earlier plays are affected by their development in the later plays.

So, for example, when *Richard II* is viewed in the light of the whole tetralogy, the relation between Gaunt and Bolingbroke is retroactively situated in the thematic center in such a way as to belie its peripheral appearance in the first play. This happens because strains that were damped down by the ritual surface of the play and by the focus on Richard are exposed and repeated and exacerbated in later plays.

It's hard to stage the psychopolitical thematics embedded in the rhetorical texture of the language that carries the Gaunt-Bolingbroke conflict, especially since the silent king's silence about it remains unbroken. Yet the failure to ground the tetralogy in this conflict may contribute to the misunderstanding that attends the traditional theatrical view of *Henry V*. Consider, for example, the brief and genuinely perceptive outline of the tetralogy Sally Beaumann gives in assessing the importance of Anthony Quayle's 1951 production:

> No company had ever embarked on an exploration of all four plays, attempting to trace their continuing themes, their poetic structure, and their development of characters. The workings of Richard II's curse had never been followed through; the contrasting of three kings, one anointed, one a usurper, one attempting to merit kingship, had never been examined. Their central story, the expiation of guilt and Hal's transformation from renegade boy to the mirror of all Christian kings, had never been given by one company on one stage. The intricate subplots of the plays, the way in which actions throw ahead of them long shadows, the continuing revenges of sons for fathers—these could never be fully appreciated when they were played singly, or out of sequence.[22]

Beaumann blames the critics' "traditional preconceptions" and stargazing tendencies for their failure to appreciate a cycle that was a box office success and that had much influence on subsequent productions of Shakespeare's histories.[23] But if you give her final sentence the weight I think it deserves, it produces a significantly different emphasis.

Although she censures critics who found Michael Redgrave "insufficiently moving and sympathetic" as Richard—"few questioned the degree to which Richard *should* be sympathetic"[24]—Beaumann accepts the flat contrast between the anointed king and the usurper. Yet her statement points in another direction: Even as he actively courts deposition, Richard may be "insufficiently moving" because he works so hard at moving himself and his subjects with his play, *The Tragic Deposition and Death of King Richard*. He goes so far as to select and seduce his usurper. This throws an odd light on the increasing corrosiveness of the "inward wars" that afflict Henry IV and that he manages to bequeath to Harry in the uneasy language of the atonement scene. As a result, Harry's language in *Henry V* betrays the cost of his "transformation" from a "renegade" to a king who never stops trying not only to merit kingship but also to expiate guilt.

Shakespeare builds into his text a critical thesis about theater in particular and theatricality in general. In writing *for* theater he also writes *against* theater, and he represents this ambivalence in his dramatic fictions. However much difference there is between the conspicuous theatricality of *Richard II* and that of *Henry V*, it works in both plays to raise moral questions about the projects of Richard and Harry—questions about the motives informing self-presentation, self-justification, self-doubt, and self-evasion.

Although Shakespeare's texts proclaim their ability to do justice to theater, they question the ability of theater to do justice to them. This questioning thematically informs the depiction of royal actors who, in staging themselves, simultaneously delight in their political performances and fail to be fully persuaded by them. A theatricality that is reflexively ironic is entirely within the limits of theatrical production. But as the plays often suggest, it may demand a modesty and temperance that go against the grain of the performer's sensibility.

Finally, if we assume that earlier plays in the sequence get rewritten by later plays, and if this assumption alters our sense of the tetralogy as a whole, then sequence has to be violated. It may be the only alternative in performance, but reading is more versatile. This doesn't mean that sequence has to be thrown out the window, only that its role in the reading process needs to be more carefully situated.

We recall that Anthony Quayle and his company found in their study of the plays "that literary and dramatic echoes reverberated backwards and forwards through the text of all four."[25] But how could this reverberation be touched off unless we could "listen" backward from the last play to the first while "listening" forward from the first to the last? The direction of reading can't be confined to the linear sequences of dramatic narrative and theatrical performance. We have to practice a kind of omnidirectional reading that doesn't ignore linearity but, on the contrary, consistently interrogates its contribution to the drama.

5. *Falstaff and Harry*

Throughout the two *Henry IV* plays, from his very first appearance in the second scene of part 1, Falstaff knowingly collaborates with Harry on the scenario titled "The Rejection of Falstaff," which is the subplot of "The Return of the Prodigal Son." Harry's resounding "I know thee not, old man" near the end of part 2 fulfills the scenario he entertained in the "I know you all" soliloquy that concluded the second scene of part 1. But Falstaff had already anticipated the scenario, alluding to it several times during the conversations leading up to this soliloquy.

Consider, for example, his sanctimonious parody at act 1, scene 2, lines 88–92:

> O thou hast damnable iteration, and art indeed able to corrupt a saint: thou hast done much harm upon me, Hal, God forgive thee for it: before I knew thee, Hal, I knew nothing, and now I am, if a man should speak truly, little better than one of the wicked. I must give over this life, and I will give it over: by the Lord, and I do not I am a villain, I'll be damned for never a king's son in Christendom.

Substituting "Falstaff" for "Hal" in this passage makes it clear that the sentiments he utters in the first person are those he attributes to Harry. They indicate his awareness that Harry will sooner or later run bad humors on the knight, and that the rejection of Falstaff will be necessitated by a Puritan impulse to self-purgation in the prince.

Falstaff impersonates Harry's response to his report that "an old lord of the Council rated me the other day in the street about you" (1.2.81–82), and this suggests that he already anticipates Harry's famous "I do, I will" (2.4.475) and his more famous "I know thee not, old man" (*2 Henry IV*, 5.5.47). He knows from the beginning both that he has been chosen to play the role of Harry's misleader and that his misrule must have an end.

He also recognizes the particular version of the Prodigal Son story that will best accommodate not only Harry's political needs but his moral needs as well: the naïf victimized by misleaders. That he knowingly, ironically, accepts this role turns out to be motivated by his own need for the judgment he seems so enthusiastically to flout, and thus to ask for. His very assumption of the role in the second scene of part 1 sharpens the challenge and the risk by giving Harry both the moral advantage and the chance to misuse it.

This is why it is more than a simple desire for preferment that occasions Falstaff's excited rush toward the royal presence in act 5 of part 2. Everything about the episode vibrates uneasily with the desire to bring his carnival to a conclusion, to make himself "bait for the old pike" (3.2.308) and get his comeuppance. This orgiastic prospect spurs him to transgression and provocation: "Let us take any man's horses—the laws of England are at my commandment" (5.3.131–33).

His plan to greet the king "stained with travel, and sweating with desire to see him" is explicitly voiced as a histrionic fantasy: "To ride day and night, and not to deliberate, not to remember, not to have patience to shift me . . . thinking of nothing else, putting all affairs into oblivion, as if there were nothing else to be done but to see him" (5.5.20–26). Given his previous knowing assessments of Harry, it isn't likely that he thinks the newly crowned king will appreciate his "zeal . . . to see him," his "earnestness of affection," his "devotion" (14–18). If he is in a state of "inflammation" similar to the one he mockingly ascribed to the "operation of sack" in the soliloquy at 4.3.97–112 it must be because he has prepared himself for the long-deferred expulsion or sacrifice that will end the "ling'ring act" (1.1.156) of his carnival.

This is not to deny that Falstaff's behavior in the scene *displays* hope of advancement. That hope rides on the rhetorical surface of his excitement. But the message conveyed by the totality of his utterances and actions up to this point is that he wants to put both his hope and Harry to the test. He wants to see how far Harry will let him go. He probes for the limits of transgression and exposes himself to the danger of the rejection and punishment he half looks forward to.

Falstaff's actions are further confused by another motive: He knows the king needs a public occasion, a ritual of exorcism, to dramatize his reformation, and he cooperates in providing it. Yet even as he yields to the temptation to offer himself up to Harry, he continues Being Bad. For if Harry shifts responsibility in calling Falstaff his misleader, Falstaff's provocation gives him the opportunity to do that and makes the king appear solely responsible for the rejection the two had been conspiring to bring about from the start. It is in the context of this discursive tug of war that we can begin to appreciate the ethical constraints on Harry and the meaning of his response to it.

"I know thee not, old man. Fall to thy prayers. / How ill white hairs become a fool and jester" (5.5.47–48). These words signal Harry's rejection not only of Falstaff but also of the knowledge of what really went on between Falstaff and himself. The rejection is sharpened by the generic appellation, "old man," which Harry's subsequent words interpret in a religious context (the biblical Old Man or unregenerate nature) so that "old man" becomes synonymous with "my former self."

Similar connotations reverberate later in Canterbury's scary characterization of the king's violent conversion: "Consideration like an angel came, / And whipp'd th' offending Adam out of him" (*Henry V*, 1.1.28–29). "I know thee not" asserts the reality of Falstaff's sinfulness as a rake by so forcefully and publicly rejecting it even as it also asserts the validity of Harry's conversion. This seeming knowledge may keep Harry from submitting to an unknown or half-known fear of himself, but it does so by a strategy that must reactivate the fear, since he is at this very moment falsifying the hope he aroused—the hope of his corruptibility.

Without such seeming knowledge he could win the crown of England but could not ensconce himself on the throne of his self-esteem. Therefore, he rejects the ironic Falstaffian voice that refuses to sanction the knowledge and that stubbornly reminds him that he was a falsifier of hopes. Yet even here the traces of guilt and his need to manage it are registered in the sentence he passes on Falstaff.

Harry has been criticized for the harshness of his treatment of Falstaff, for the narrowing of his sensibility, and for the sacrifice of humaneness demanded by the royal office. Yet given the severity of his rhetoric, the sentence he imposes is surprisingly light:

> When thou dost hear I am as I have been,
> Approach me, and thou shalt be as thou wast,
> The tutor and the feeder of my riots.
> Till then I banish thee, on pain of death,
> As I have done the rest of my misleaders,
> Not to come near our person by ten mile.
> For competence of life I will allow you,

That lack of means enforce you not to evils;
And as we hear you do reform yourselves,
We will, according to your strengths and qualities,
Give you advancement. (5.5.60–69)

Because "I banish thee, on pain of death" sounds so threatening, the actual terms of banishment specified two lines later seem surprisingly lenient by contrast. They produce the effect of a feint toward strict justice countered by a gesture of clemency. The sentence is proclaimed in words that express the speaker's full assurance in his moral superiority. But what he brandishes is a carrot, not a stick.

I view this maneuver as an act of moral self-protection. The motivation behind it may be suggested by comparing a section of Harry's first soliloquy in *1 Henry IV* with the declaration that precedes the passage quoted above:

So when this loose behavior I throw off,
And pay the debt I never promised,
By how much better than my word I am,
By so much shall I falsify men's hopes;
....
I'll so offend, to make offence a skill,
Redeeming time when men least think I will. (Part 1, 1.2.203–12)

Presume not that I am the thing I was;
For God doth know, so shall the world perceive,
That I have turn'd away my former self;
So will I those that kept my company. (Part 2, 5.5.56–59)

Since these two passages represent a promise and its fulfillment, they dramatize the singleness, the integrity, of the speaker's purpose over time. Thus they contradict the assertion that he is not the thing he was.

Harry knows he never *was* but only *played* the prodigal. He knows he was and therefore remains the misleader of his misleaders and the falsifier of the hopes he falsely planted in others. That this is not something he has been able conveniently to forget is evidenced by the continuing traces of anger and violence his language betrays from the time of his interview with his dying father to the end of *Henry V*.[1]

Henry V as a whole reflects the consequences of Harry's need to produce and maintain a ten-mile trouble-free zone around his conscience. This may be sensed in the language with which he protests to the French ambassadors that "we are no tyrant but a Christian king," whose passion "is as subject to his grace / As is our wretches fetter'd in our prisons" (1.2.242–43), an odd analogy that exposes his dim view of his passion. The anger he directs toward Henry, Falstaff, and the French is rooted in the self-purging fury with which he "scours [the] faults" of others while persisting in his famous disclaimers of responsibility. These signs of anxious concern for moral solvency indicate his abiding suspicion that he may be more sinning than sinned against.

Harry's tempered rejection of Falstaff is a defensive maneuver of self-exculpation, part of a pattern in evidence from their first appearance together in the second scene of *1 Henry IV*, and a pattern all but articulated in the soliloquy concluding that scene.[2] Near the end of the scene Harry reluctantly agrees to the ingenious plot proposed by Poins after Falstaff leaves. The plot is ingenious because Poins shifts the emphasis from theft to a practical joke on the thief, and he thus offers the cautious Prince both moral protection and a chance to baffle his misleader. So it is to be expected that the Prince, who seemed just a few minutes earlier to be in his element as Happy Hal the Corinthian wit cracker, would appreciate Poins's thoughtful concern for his fears and scruples.

Yet when Poins exits, the speaker left alone on stage shows no sign of gratitude:

> I know you all, and will awhile uphold
> The unyok'd humor of your idleness.
> Yet herein will I imitate the sun,
> Who doth permit the base contagious clouds
> To smother up his beauty from the world,
> That, when he please again to be himself,
> Being wanted he may be more wonder'd at
> By breaking through the foul and ugly mists
> Of vapors that did seem to strangle him. (*1 Henry IV*, 1.2.190–98)

This is our first glimpse of Harry as Henry burning off the mist of Hal, and it is marked by his first shift from prose banter to the ritual formality of blank verse. The shift produces the odd effect that, just when he could be expected to speak what he feels, not what he ought to say, he sounds like he is making a speech, rehearsing a preformulated scenario, before an audience. Dr. Johnson thought the soliloquy artful because it "keeps the prince from appearing vile in the opinion of the audience," and this comment becomes more interesting if we redirect it toward the only opinion and audience of which the soliloquist can be aware.[3]

It used to be thought that Shakespeare wrote this speech to reassure the audience about Harry: He is very different from his genuinely rakish counterpart in *The Famous Victories*. This is reassuring only if we overlook one simple point: The difference resides in Harry's *pretending* to be the counterpart. Harry-haters make much of the motives and moral implications of the pretense, and the prince's defenders join battle on this point.

A committed meliorist like Dover Wilson argues that such a speech in Shakespeare's time was a convention whose "function was to convey information to the audience about the general drift of the play, much as a prologue did." Wilson therefore finds it absurd to "charge him with meanness . . . for not communicating to Falstaff what Shakespeare makes him, for technical reasons, tell the theater."[4] A more cautious meliorist like William Empson devotes his long essay on Falstaff chiefly to dogging Wilson. He doesn't deny "that the placing of this soliloquy is meant to establish Hal as the future hero as firmly as possible." But he fails to see "that it does anything (whether regarded as a 'convention' or not) to evade the obvious moral reflection, obvious not only to the more moralizing part of the audience but to all of it, that this kind of man made a very unreliable friend."

Empson nevertheless ends up on Wilson's team. "The basic point of Henry's first soliloquy, saying that he will be more admired later because he is despised now, is not a cynical calculation to betray his friends but a modestly phrased reassurance that he is learning how to be a national king." In any event the story of his "useful development"—which Empson views as a justification of Falstaff's tutelage—does "not need us to suppose that Henry was very good to start with."[5]

This position is a little wobbly because Empson, no less than Dr. Johnson and Wilson, assesses the speech primarily in terms of its effect on the audience. Presumably he means that Harry's "modestly phrased reassurance" is directed at "us," the audience to whom the unsettling "moral reflection" is "obvious." But everything becomes more interesting once we redirect attention from the audience in the theater to the auditor in the speaker.

The speech as a whole reveals intense ambition. It also reveals an equally intense desire for personal (not only royal) legitimacy. The speaker wants to maintain self-esteem while winning the esteem of others. But the terms in which Harry conceives of his scenario confront that desire with a problem.

To cite one example, his promise to imitate the sun is poised between a condescending emphasis on the one-sidedness of the conflict and a censorious emphasis on the culpable violence of those he calls "the base contagious clouds," "the foul and ugly mists / Of vapors." Since these antagonists are trying to strangle the sun-prince, they will deserve what they get after he has finished using them as a screen.[6] The terms of the nature image he chooses enable him illogically to suggest that the clouds are doing to the sun-prince what he is actually planning to make them do. But the image subverts itself because mists and vapors are raised—upheld—by the sun before being burned off, as they will be when the carnival moves from Eastcheap to Westminster.[7]

"If all the year were playing holidays," the prince continues,
To sport would be as tedious as to work;
But when they seldom come, they wish'd-for come,
And nothing pleaseth but rare accidents. (199–202)

This utterance seeks the reassurance of proverbial wisdom in the tone of the earnest explainer who carefully rehearses its adversative logic ("But when . . .") as if to make sure he gets it right.[8] He means to tell himself that when he leaves his carnival among the base contagious rioters, "when this loose behavior I throw off," the reformation he plans to stage will so glitter "o'er my fault" as to surprise and delight the world at large like an unexpected holiday. Since he wishes that holiday for himself and is currently playing holidays all the year, he may also be saying that he finds this preliminary Falstaffian carnival tedious but necessary to the achievement of that goal.

But *does* he find it tedious or is he only telling himself that in order to justify upholding (and enjoying) it for a while? And does he also mean to tell himself that the ugly Falstaffian mists he raises and hides behind will be sacrificed as scapegoats in preparation for the real carnival?—the carnival briefly savored at Shrewsbury, ritually inaugurated at the end of *2 Henry IV*, and extended through *Henry V*? Does he already anticipate violently dispelling those mists as just punishment for their attempted thievery of "the day's beauty"? (1.2.25). For surely the touch of anger flaring forth at lines 192–94 of the soliloquy responds to the Actaeonic provocation of Falstaff's earlier comment, his association of the future king with "our noble and chaste mistress the moon, under whose countenance we steal" (1.2.28–29).

Obscure motives and unruly impulses lurk under the probable intentional surface of Harry's language. They make its bottom hard to discern. They cloud it with uncertainties that resist penetration now and may possibly resist it later. But beating under that surface is the pulse of a restrained violence intensified by deferral and building toward a moment of release.

This pulse quickens during the remainder of the speech, which already tangs with the foretaste of carnival:

So when this loose behavior I throw off,
And pay the debt I never promised,
By how much better than my word I am,
By so much shall I falsify men's hopes;
And like bright metal on a sullen ground,
My reformation glittering o'er my fault,
Shall show more goodly, and attract more eyes
Than that which hath no foil to set it off.
I'll so offend, to make offence a skill,
Redeeming time when men think least I will. (203–12)

The positive question, "What does he mean to say? What is he trying to tell himself?" needs to be supplemented by its negative, "What is he trying not to mean? What is his language saying that he doesn't want to hear?" Does he want to hear himself saying what I hear him saying when he plans to "falsify men's hopes"? For no matter what we suppose the utterer to intend, the utterance is open to Stephen Greenblatt's paraphrase: "to exceed . . . and . . . also to disappoint . . . expectations, to deceive men, to turn their hopes into fictions, to betray them."[9]

I imagine that Harry would prefer to have his speech read back to him by Alan Dessen, who endorses him as "a notable and crucial exception" in a world where everyone else "readily finds reasons not to pay their debts or keep their vows." Harry "pays all his debts, even those he never promised," and Dessen thinks this is fine.[10] This reading would protect Harry from Leonard Tennenhouse's judgment on him: He is Shakespeare's "most memorable figure of misrule," and his career proves that "legitimate order can only come into being through disruption."[11] Tennenhouse doesn't venture an opinion as to whether Harry's language may be troubled by the same insight, but the possibility that it may—that Dessen's idealization might not make Harry entirely comfortable after all—is what I find most compelling in Shakespeare's portrait.

It's often said that Harry is falsifying hopes or causing disappointment by playing the rake. But that isn't what *he* says. He says he will falsify hopes by reforming. This implies that when his loose behavior deceives men, he counts on their hoping he will come to no good end, will remain corrupt, so that he may suffer for his evil ways. Falstaff isn't the only intended victim of the imposture. The vagueness of the phrase "men's hopes," even as it defends against the specific identification of victims, gestures beyond the tavern.

One of the provocations behind the soliloquy is Falstaff's report that "an old lord of the Council rated me the other day in the street about you" (81–83). The plural form of "men's hopes" no doubt muffles a reference to Harry's father. But it also embraces the Establishment in general: "Old," "lord," and "Council" index the three aspects—generational, social, and political—of authority targeted by "the paradigm of prodigal rebellion," which, as Richard Helgerson (whose words these are) has shown, expressed central cultural tensions in sixteenth-century England.[12]

The deception or betrayal Greenblatt mentions has a more insidious dimension: Falstaff's hopes and Henry's will be falsified in contrary ways, but in both cases the falsification *presupposes the planting of false hopes.* He assumes or hopes that he can deceive them into hoping for the worst so that he can show them up for the ill-wishers they are.

The aggressive and self-justifying cynicism of the epithets "base contagious" and "foul and ugly" is transferred to the word "hopes" and suggests the same disclaimer of responsibility for the false impression he plans to encourage. From this standpoint, what he owes them is not only the reformation that will pay off the debt incurred by profligacy. He also owes them the disappointment that will reward or punish them for their false hopes.

I have put the harshest construction on the soliloquy, have ascribed sentiments to it that we might expect to hear from Iago, Edmund, and Richard III. And perhaps because the soliloquy lacks their peculiar verve, their self-amused or self-loathing delight in speaking evil, I have made it seem even more unpleasant. But I do this to bring out the problem that confronts a speaker who has good intentions, who is confident that he can overcome the handicap he gives himself and win the world's esteem, but who would also like to assure himself that he is worthy of his own esteem. Otherwise it would not be a problem.

More than three decades ago, Joseph Porter developed an interesting and original approach to Harry's moral dilemma. In his fine experimental application of speech-act theory to the Henriad, Porter argues that it makes a difference whether we take the soliloquy (A) as a statement of intent ("My intention is to throw off this loose behavior, falsify men's hopes, etc.") or (B) as a promise ("I promise to throw off this loose behavior, falsify men's hopes, etc."). With (A), Porter claims, "Hal is autonomous—he has a plan which he deigns to state; and this fits with the picture of him as a sort of hypocritical schemer. With (B), however, Hal is placing himself under an obligation to act in a certain way—he is being morally responsible."[13]

This is a valuable distinction, but the notion that falsifying hopes is being morally responsible strikes me as a little weird. I would modify Porter's (B) as follows: Harry places himself under an obligation to *play-act* in a certain way. He promises to perform in such a manner as to persuade the world that when he pays the debt he will have become morally responsible. This implies that he assumes he is already morally responsible, even now, as he contemplates falsifying hopes.

Given the very different implications of (A) and (B), Porter thinks it important to decide what kind of "illocutionary act" Harry performs.[14] I think it is more important for *Harry* to decide what sort it is, and to decide that it is (B) even though it may be hard for him to avoid at least suspecting it is (A), since the two kinds of speech act Porter picks out are entangled with each other in the utterance. The problem his soliloquy confronts him with is identical with the one that will attend his claim to France in the second scene of *Henry V* (1.2.96): "May I with right and conscience make this claim," or play out this scenario?

Harry is no fox. Right and conscience are important to him. But since he obviously enjoys the language that expresses his power, autonomy, and theatrical ability, it may also be important for him to disarm his conscience by acknowledging this pleasure in terms that will enable him to deal with it. Thus he attenuates his awareness of hypocritical intention (A) by transforming it into the promise to reform (B). And the threat of (A) is further forestalled by the complex figure that concludes the soliloquy and begins at line 207, "And like bright metal. . . ."

The puns and images in these lines reconceive the promise in esthetic and heroic terms: a precious display, a theatrical triumph, and an honorable encounter. When I visualize the bright metal with which he plans to pay off the debt, I think first of a coin, a royal medallion struck off to commemorate the anticipated victory. After that, I think of a sword, and then my eye is attracted to the alliterating filament threaded through the sullen ground: *falsify-fault-foil-offence.*

The last two words strike off another image: dueling.[15] The undertone of violence persists, but changes to a less devious, more forthright image, and one that characterizes the soliloquy as a whole, the image of aggression controlled and blunted: not an ambush or robbery or unequal assault by the almighty sun, but a dream of honor that goes Hotspur one better. Harry will redeem his "banish'd honors" in a battle of wits, a test of skill undertaken with foils rather than rapiers. And his honor will be increased by giving all odds to the enemy. Putting on loose behavior will mobilize a royal troop of ill wishers against him and make the underdog's single-handed victory more admirable. The rationale of the Crispin's Day speech already glimmers on the horizon: "The fewer men, the greater share of honor"; "if it be a sin to covet honor, / I am the most offending soul alive"; "we few, we happy few" (*Henry V,* 4.3.22, 28–29, 60).

What Harry seeks, however, is not mere Hotspurian honor but the justification that will confirm his sense of probity. The structural pattern of his confirmative activity in all three plays is to exchange bad humors or bad conscience for good. This moral economy confronts him with a problem: How can he respect the respect of those he aims his virtues at if the validating audience he depends on consists of those he plans to deceive? Won't the very success of his strategy keep alive the fear it's designed to bury? Won't the double-edged glitter of his benign intentions perpetually renew the sullen ground of the fault that foils them? The language of his soliloquy both suggests and responds to a suspicion that the scenario is morally reprehensible—not merely because it is hypocritical but because it implicates him in the bad faith of scapegoating others and disclaiming responsibility for it.

I agree with Ernst Kris that Harry's paramount concern is moral solvency, and that his playing the rake is both a comment on the bankruptcy of usurpation and a defense against it.[16] But the line of argument developed above suggests a strategic function closer to home: He invests moral capital in the Prodigal Son role in order to minimize risk, for to pretend to a form of wickedness he knows himself unaffected by doesn't jeopardize his self-esteem. It may temporarily work to divert himself as well as others from the suspicion of a more profound culpability. And if the device proves not to persuade him, he will have to depend all the more on the validation he receives from the world on that glorious day when, after a single encounter or change of status, the issue will be resolved for all time.

To dream of a onetime future reformation may blunt the fear that reformation is something he needs now and always. The melodramatic form of the noble change he purposes has the look of a fail-safe device calculated to burn off any mists of self-doubt the scenario trails behind it. Thus what disturbs the Harry-hating critics of *Henry V* is already present early in *1 Henry IV*. My formulation differs from theirs in identifying the problem with Harry as Harry's problem with Harry: Shakespeare represents Harry as a potential Harry-hater and centers on his struggle for moral (not merely political) legitimacy.

Behind his capers with the Corinthians in Eastcheap then, is the desire articulated in the soliloquy: to cut his moral losses in the long term by playing the prodigal in the short term. The strategic value of Harry's commitment to Corinthian pleasures is that it responds to both sides of his dilemma. On the one hand, it lets him avoid a degree of voyeuristic detachment that could jeopardize his self-esteem and confront him with the danger of thinking himself a princely hypocrite. Given his plan for an eventual disengagement that will falsify hopes, we can understand why Harry should be in earnest about the importance of being Hal and of enjoying his idleness as genuinely, perhaps ingenuously, as he can.

Yet on the other hand, this submission must be tempered by the maintenance of a critical attitude toward his fellow Corinthians, since, if he plans to falsify their hopes, he will have to justify it to himself. His way of preparing for this justification is continually to put them down in jokes and wit play that target their cowardice, their dishonesty, and their license. These are the culpable misleaders he plans to hold responsible for his "loose behavior" after he throws it off. Their misrule is permanent and real, while his is temporary and make-believe.

Nothing in this interpretation of Harry's soliloquy would surprise the speaker who emerges from my reading of Falstaff's language. His sense of Harry's project and of his own relation to it is suggested from the beginning, conveyed by such teasingly indirect means as the puritan parody I discussed above. It peeps forth with equal diffidence in act 2, scene 2, when he complains about the removal of his horse:

> I am accursed to rob in that thief's company; the rascal hath removed my horse and tied him I know not where. . . . Well, I doubt not but to die

> a fair death for all this, if I scape hanging for killing that rogue. I have forsworn his company hourly any time this two and twenty years, and yet I am bewitched with the rogue's company. If the rascal have not given me medicines to make me love him, I'll be hanged. It could not be else, I have drunk medicines. Poins! Hal! A plague upon you both. (10–21)

This is ambiguous for two reasons. First, as David Bevington points out, though Poins is the obvious referent of the complaint, "much of what Falstaff says about the rascal's bewitching company applies no less aptly to Hal."[17] Second, until the outburst at the end, we can't be sure what kind of speech act it is, and this will be determined by the way it is staged. The speaker could utter or mutter these words to himself. He could say them loudly enough to indicate that he wants to be overheard, and those to whom the words are directed could be either offstage or visibly within earshot. If he aims his vexation at potential eavesdroppers, he could do so simply to register a complaint, but he could also do it to keep the game in play by telling his persecutors what they want to hear.

It becomes clear as he continues—and even clearer if we note the echoes of the previous scene with Gadshill and the Carriers—that Falstaff is *performing* the victim's discourse. He exploits its dialectical turnings and lets his rhetoric alternate between the specious probity of injured innocence and the villain's compensatory bluster:

> I'll starve ere I'll rob a foot further—and 'twere not as good a deed as drink to turn true man, and to leave these rogues I am the veriest varlet that ever chewed with a tooth; eight yards of uneven ground is threescore and ten miles afoot with me, and the stony-hearted villains know it well enough. A plague upon it when thieves cannot be true to one another! . . . A plague upon you all, give me my horse and be hanged! (2.2.21–30)

When a speaker echoes the words and sentiments uttered in an episode from which he was absent (in this case, 2.1), it usually means that he is inscribed in the same discourse. Here, Falstaff inscribes the discourse and inscribes himself in it. He allows himself to be set up. He pretends to be an unwilling victim. He feigns indignation at the faithlessness of thieves. These moves elucidate the underlying complicity and self-deception inherent in the intertwined discourses of the victim-revenger and the villain. Falstaff parades himself as an example of what he mocks.[18]

The structure of eavesdropping in this performance may be complex, but it is clarified by the sense David Bevington conveys of its staging. During his account of the textual difficulties that make for indeterminate stage directions he speculates that since Harry "comes forward to torment Falstaff about his horse . . . he presumably overhears with Poins the soliloquy of comic grumbling that Falstaff directs at them. Conventions of darkness on the Elizabethan stage allowed the audience to suppose that Falstaff could not see those who tease him and overhear his complaint."[19]

Falstaff, then, listens to them listening to him and lets them know it. The speech is itself a kind of eavesdropping performed by someone who rustles conspicuously behind the arras. What he says is not "I love him" but "he has made me love him. It's his fault. He has bewitched me, seduced me, misled me, victimized me. He is indeed able to corrupt a saint." This is another piece of innuendo by mimicry. It continues Falstaff's proleptic parody in act 1, scene 2, of the purposes Harry subsequently reveals in the "I know you all" soliloquy.

If he submits "with comic grumbling" to the project he mimics, a project which (the mimicry suggests) will victimize him sooner or later, is it because he believes what he says—"I am bewitched with the rogue's company"? Believes it about Harry? About himself? Is he expressing what he thinks Harry feels, or what he thinks Harry pretends to feel? What he himself feels, or what he pretends to feel?

Is he—and this is a possibility the Shakespearean soliloquy always promotes—eavesdropping on himself as well as on the others? Is he testing his ability, his desire, to believe the sentiments he utters? Testing his ability and desire to deceive himself and justify yielding to the affection he knows will undo him? And if the innuendo by mimicry is intended for Harry's ears, is he prompting Harry to listen to him listen to Harry so that Harry will understand "I know you all" has been overheard? And, understanding that, will perceive that Falstaff perceives "I know you all" supplies the real force, the real meaning, behind the comic colting/uncolting of Falstaff?

At this point we can do little more than sift aimlessly through these questions because they encode the unresolved condition and ongoing interrogations of the bond between Falstaff and Harry. They represent questions I imagine Falstaff continually to ask himself, and to ask Harry, and to ask Harry to ask himself; questions asked through the safely indirect medium of practical jokes and wit wars, questions that aren't yet answerable, questions with darker implications that Falstaff glances at and then carefully throws away by his comic performance of the victim's discourse.

The spectacle of Falstaff colted and uncolted reduces those implications and thereby controls them. But they are very much alive in the fireworks of the soliloquy. Yet although their latent power casts a shadow, the comic energy that drives his talk saves the day. It enables Falstaff and Harry to go on colting and testing each other, sounding each other out, circling about each other.

6. *A Horse Named Cut*

1 Henry IV, Act 2, Scene 1

> By heaven, methinks it were an easy leap
> To pluck bright honor from the pale-faced moon.
>
> —*1 Henry IV,*1.3.199–200

> Speak terms of manage to thy bounding steed.
>
> —*1 Henry IV,* 2.3.50

If for no other reason, act 2, scene 1 of *1 Henry IV* can claim our attention because it introduces that noble piece of insulation, the horse—not quite in the flesh, but objectified in speech as the object of the speakers' concern. It is introduced in a manner that raises questions about both its pedigree and its effectiveness. It is neither a steed nor a bounder but a poor honest ailing "jade." After Hotspur's Pegasean rhetoric in the preceding scene (1.3.197–200), the opening dialogue of act 2, scene 1 strikes an antithetical low note by introducing us to a Shakespearean version of contemporary truck-stop culture.[1]

Transition and contrast are established in the first utterance: "Heigh-ho! An it be not four by the day I'll be hanged; Charles' wain is over the new chimney, and yet our horse not packed. What, ostler!" Kittredge's suggestion that "*Charles' wain* means 'the wagon or chariot of Charlemagne'" and "is a corruption of *carl's* (churl's, countryman's) *wain*" provides a link between Hotspur's airborne fantasies and the earthier instrumentalities they so strenuously exclude.[2] But the reference to time also recalls the opening words of act 1, scene 2: "Now, Hal, what time of day is it, lad?" This echo sets the stage for another contrast: between the superficially careless escapism of the Eastcheap holiday ("What a devil hast thou to do with the time of the day?," 1.2.6–7) and the inconvenience to which transporters of food are exposed in a politically and economically unstable world where the price of oats matters and sharp practices are the order of the day.

Not one but two horses are mentioned in the scene (Cut and Gadshill's "gelding"), and their nominal references link them together as fellow victims of the knife. "I prithee, Tom," says the First Carrier, "beat Cut's saddle, put a few flocks in the point; poor jade is wrung in the withers out of all cess" (5–7). "Cut" names either a curtal or a gelding, but since "horse" begins to creep toward figurative status, the difference fades between symbolic castration (a docked tail) and the real thing. The fact that Gadshill twice calls his mount a "gelding" (33, 94) speaks to Cut's condition. Does it speak to the Carriers'? To Gadshill's? To the Chamberlain's? To anyone else's?

When the dialogue continues, the emphasis of the Second Carrier's complaints against the ostler is on the effects of exposure to damp humors. First he grumbles that Cut, whose withers are galled by the weight and friction of the packsaddle, is subject to further miseries: "Peas and beans are as dank here as a dog, and that is the next way to give poor jades the bots" (8–9). Poor Cut is threatened with infiltration by maggoty worms that breed in the dank earth and the fodder she bears—or conversely, the horse generates the worms as a result of the dank fodder that carries worm-breeding earth into its stomach.[3] The dankness turns the Second Carrier's thoughts to fish:

> I think this be the most villainous house in all London road for fleas, and I am stung like a tench. (13–14)
>
> Why, they will allow us ne'er a jordan, and then we leak in your chimney, and your chamber-lye breeds fleas like a loach. (18–20)

Horses and men need better armor, better boots. They fail to "hold out water in foul way" (83). Gadshill concludes the scene by calling the chamberlain a "muddy knave" (95), and the epithet condenses all the previous references to earthy dampness. It is against such muddy or mundane uncertainties, insufficiencies, irritations, and suspicions of chicanery, that men saddle up or think to protect themselves by making their saint, the commonwealth, their boots (79–82).

Cut's hard usage soon rubs off on the Carriers. As it becomes clear that their gall is inscribed in his withers, he begins to slip from his literal mooring and vanish into the figural mist, where the beast represents its master.[4] This conventional symbolism is enforced by the occupational name, "Carrier," which assimilates the horse's function to the man or the man's to the horse.[5] The commonplaces exchanged by the Carriers belong to the jargon of the victim's discourse. They tell us less about the speakers' "objective" circumstances than about their condition as they represent it to themselves: the condition of those who bear not only the goods of others but also the ills that accompany the burden. Their dependent status exposes them to dishonest ostlers, miserable accommodations, overworked horses, fleabites, and highwaymen. This self-representation betrays the conventional symptoms of apprehensiveness: expressions of impatience and suspicion, and such outbursts of compensatory bluster as "'twere not as good deed as drink to break the pate on thee, I am a very villain. Come, and be hanged! Hast no faith in thee?" (28–30).

This scene can be very funny in performance, partly because of its skewed echoes of the scene it follows. All four of its speakers are themselves sitting ducks for social parody, even as they generate an underclass comment on the aristocratic style and political substance of the Percies. The script encourages actors to ramp up their gulling of the characters they play, the roguish braveries of Gadshill and the Chamberlain no less than the rustic tribulations of the Carriers. It invites spectators to enjoy the theatrical vulnerability of the typical characters it serves up as sacrifices to the pleasurable collusion between performers and audience.

Yet to think in terms of "typical characters" and "social types" may be to approach the peculiar richness of this theatrical moment with the wrong categories. For the speakers are neither individuated nor stabilized by their roles in the drama. What the actors embody by their presentations are not so much characters as speakers, and not so much speakers as positions in a particular language game. In the dialogue between the Carriers, for example, it doesn't matter which speaker says what lines. Their relation to the language they speak is essentially a pastoral one. That is, the dialogue "gives us . . . personal sentiment without personal reference" because in the representation of socially or dramatically insignificant speakers, the latter may serve as mere models of complex if familiar attitudes.[6]

The Carriers are thus more the objects than the subjects of their discourse. They are *carriers* in the same way horses or fleas are carriers, and in the same way that a woman in the Henriad is a carrier: They are bearers of the meanings of others. If the attitudes they exhibit seem to be reduced or simplified versions of those apparent in major characters, the versions reveal the basis of such attitudes in socially constructed forms and conventions of discourse.

In this respect, act 2, scene 1 is an obvious candidate for the pastoral function William Empson and others have discussed in their analyses of double or multiple plots. It's also pastoral in another sense, the sense implicit in the full range of meanings imparted by the Greek prefix, *dia-*: *through*, *with*, and *against*. The pastoral dialogue of the Carriers speaks *through* its speakers and binds them together. It also *speaks apart* from them, since they are only its carriers, and the primary object of attention is the dialogue itself. Finally, their speaking *together* is at the same time a competitive or dialectical speaking *at variance*.

There are discernible moments of pastoral debate in act 2, scene 1. But what binds the speakers together is the form of utterance Bronislaw Malinowski called "phatic communion": Its primary function is that of "binding hearer to speaker by a tie of some social sentiment or other."[7] In more positive terms, phatic communion is a form of language use that works to reaffirm the sentiment, and thus to reify or naturalize the circumstances giving rise to it. It is, for this reason, conspicuously citational. Displaying knowledge of an authorized stock of lexical, rhetorical, and syntactical formulas is like giving the password that not only signifies membership in a particular community discourse but also validates that discourse.

In the case of the Carriers, what speaks through them and binds them together is Shakespeare's representation of the victim's discourse. In performance- or stage-centered reading the representation is further mediated—and therefore interpreted—by the actors' performance. This double mediation generates a variety of possible responses. We can choose to uphold or to blur the distinction between presentation and representation. In either case, we can emphasize one at the expense of the other. If we avail ourselves of the voyeur's privilege, we can laugh *with* the actors and *at* the Carriers; if we suspend it, we can laugh with the actors and *with* the Carriers. For both actors *and* characters perform the discourse.

Let's test these general observations by closing in on the fleabite sector of the Carriers' dialogue:

> SEC. CAR. I think this be the most villainous house in all London road for fleas, I am stung like a tench.
>
> FIRST CAR. Like a tench! By the mass, there is ne'er a king christen could be better bit than I have been since the first cock.
>
> SEC. CAR. Why, they will allow us ne'er a jordan, and then we leak in your chimney, and your chamber-lye breeds fleas like a loach. (2.1.13–20)

The first thing to notice is the obvious affection the speakers have for the rhetorical expressiveness the discourse puts at their disposal. Since Harry and Falstaff also notice this about each other, we can use their terms to describe it. The Carriers enjoy (at)tiring themselves "in base comparisons" (2.4.246) and "the most unsavory similes" (1.2.77). And they enjoy competing in the skills of complaint.

Consider, for example, the effect produced by interposing a pause after "London road" in the first utterance: The abrupt descent from the reinforced superlative ("most villainous" and "all") to "fleas" hyperbolizes the aggravation. The pause draws attention to the hyperbole and, after that, "like a tench" explodes. The First Carrier repeats it as if to savor it and take its measure, and then counters it with an upward hyperbole that one editor glosses as "kings have the best of everything," even fleabites, and in this department, at least, the Carrier is the peer of princes. The other Carrier insists on his bathetic category and leads his aetiology back down to it.

A speaker brought into being by such phrases as "I am stung like a tench" and "your chamber-lye breeds fleas like a loach" deserves our attention on several grounds: for the calculated baseness and consistency of his comparisons; for the exaggerated misery embodied by his poor fish—the tench is spotted, that is, born flea-bitten, flea-bitten by nature and forever; and above all, for his mastery of consonantial expectoration. His "tench" and "loach" are phonetically as well as piscatorially cospecific. Both allow strings of minor dental or palatal explosions to climax in a major sneeze.

The facial expressions generated by the pattern of phonetic changes easily materialize around the little parable of the loach. We can chart the trajectory of the Second Carrier's righteous indignation. It moves from the open liquid glide inaugurated by its first word through an echoing chain of oppositional clenches as the softer "l" hits a wall of consonants. Finally it succumbs to the rounded pucker and plosion that transform "leak" into "loach."

The phonetic and rhetorical pleasures of this passage are inseparable from the repugnance the language not only expresses but also imitates in a series of plosives that onomatopoetically enforce the speaker's attitude toward the problem of evacuation. These bursts of punctuated and dramatically expelled air condense a mouth around them as their efficient cause, and a body around the mouth to relieve itself of bad humors, and a mind or soul within the body to make the process formally meaningful and finally satisfying by venting air in unsavory similes. Such is the breath of Carriers.

In the parable of the loach, the predatory fleas are offspring of their prey. Like Lear's barbarous Scythians they make their generation messes (*King Lear*, 1.1.116–17). The parable illustrates the cycle of complicity that binds knave and gull symbiotically together, and this bond gets dramatically activated by Gadshill's breezy entrance. At first, however, the Carriers acquit themselves with roguish panache. When Gadshill asks for the time, they tell him the wrong time (compare the "two o'clock" of line 32 with the "four by the day" of line 1). When he asks for a lantern, he is twice rebuffed: "Nay, by God, soft! I know a trick worth two of that, i' faith"; "Lend me thy lantern, quoth he! Marry I'll see thee hanged first" (35–39). This crackling and competent show of diffidence seems justified, and commentators praise the Carriers for their shrewdness.

Whether Gadshill is represented as *being* clumsy (because he enjoys his villainy and their suspicion) or only trying to seem so (to divert their attention from the major-league information he seeks) may be as moot as it is insignificant. Nevertheless, when he pops the money question with a bluntness calculated to reinforce suspicion, the Second Carrier's defensive reply turns out to be less cagey than it appears:

> GADS. Sirrah carrier, what time do you mean to come to London?
> SEC. CAR. Time enough to go to bed with a candle, I warrant thee; come, neighbor Mugs, we'll call up the gentlemen, they will along with company, for they have great charge. (40–45)

The knave is apparently put down by the prospective cat's-paw, who is careful to note that the gentlemen are well convoyed. Yet at the same time he supplies Gadshill with a hint—an estimated time of departure—and his concluding words offer an incentive.

The intelligence gathered a moment later from the Chamberlain who is in cahoots with Gadshill adds more detail but no new information (52–59). The Arden editor cites the Carrier's opening retort as an example of "evasive rustic wit" (Arden, 39), but the wit fails the speaker before the end of the next clause. Turning away to shut the rogue out, he shows him his back. This may possibly be why, just before the First Carrier leaves the stage, he is baptized "Mugs."

The *OED* lists several Elizabethan possibilities for the common form of this name, but the one to which my reading of the passage makes me partial is a dialect word meaning "a breed of sheep having the face completely covered by wool." This yields a lovely cognominal equivalent to "come, neighbor Mugs": "Come, fellow Sheep." And in the next scene, at the very moment in which Gadshill's work bears fruit, this companionly gesture is recalled by the victimized Traveller's "Come, neighbor, the boy shall lead our horses down the hill," which is shortly followed by Falstaff's "Down with them, fleece them!" (2.2.75–76, 82).

"Who does the wolf love?," Menenius asks in *Coriolanus*, and the tribune Sicinius replies, "The lamb" (2.1.6–7). The two meanings of the syntactically ambiguous question—"whom does the wolf love?" and "who loves the wolf?"—converge in the lamb to register the ambivalence and reciprocity that binds the victim's discourse to the villain's. By providing a transitional point of contact between these discourses, the interchange between the Carriers and Gadshill gives us a comic glimpse of what lies just beneath the plaintive surface of the victim's discourse: his own contribution to the galls and pinches, the rubs and fleabites, to which his circumstances expose him. Victimization has its pleasures, chief of which is the delight in mastering the expressive conventions of the discourse that represents it.

If there is reciprocity and complicity between the lamb and the wolf, if—as in *Coriolanus*—the roles are not only symbiotic (that is, co-parasitic) but also interchangeable, shouldn't we expect to find subversive traces of this interdependence in the villain's discourse? We can begin with the already noted fact that although Gadshill struts his knavery like "a very villain," his performance is bracketed within two references to his gelding. Does the villain's discourse also ride and gall the withers of a "horse" named Cut?

Gadshill boasts with self-delighting swash of his connections to invisible powers of evil in high places (65–86). But his little battle of wits with the Chamberlain is perforated on both sides by diffidence and the push of an uneasy machismo. Shakespeare wonderfully manages the shiftiness of tone, part bravado and part guardedness, that characterizes the thieves' discourse. Each speaker reminds the other of his falseness. The Chamberlain's jokes and retorts express discomfort over his willingness to be used, and even as he acknowledges his compliance and betrays his trust, he dissociates himself from Gadshill (62–64, 92). Thus, on entering, he replies to Gadshill's greeting with a slang citation, "'At hand, quoth pick-purse'" (46). Gadshill takes it as a reference to his own handiness and promptly throws it back: "That's even as fair as 'At hand, quoth the chamberlain': for . . . thou layest the plot how" (48–51).

After receiving the tip he came for, Gadshill starts up another series of references to hanging—already overworked as epithets by the Carriers and as jokes by Harry and Falstaff in act 1, scene 2—and then delivers his major aria:

> GADS. Sirrah, if they meet not with Saint Nicholas' clerks, I'll give thee this neck.
>
> CHAMB. No, I'll none of it, I pray thee keep that for the hangman, for I know thou worshippest Saint Nicholas, as truly as a man of falsehood may.
>
> GADS. What talkest thou to me of the hangman? If I hang, I'll make a fat pair of gallows: for if I hang, old Sir John hangs with me, and thou knowest he is no starveling. Tut, there are other Troyans that thou dream'st not of, the which for sport sake are content to do the profession some grace, that would (if matters should be looked into) for their own credit sake make all whole. I am joined with no foot-landrakers, no long-staff sixpenny strikers, none of these mad mustachio purple-hued maltworms, but with nobility and tranquillity, burgomasters and great onyers, such as can hold in, such as will strike sooner than speak, and speak sooner than drink, and drink sooner than pray—and yet, 'zounds, I lie, for they pray continually to their saint the commonwealth, or rather not pray to her but prey on her, for they ride up and down on her, and make her their boots.
>
> CHAMB. What, the commonwealth their boots? Will she hold out water in foul way?
>
> GADS. She will, she will, justice hath liquored her: we steal as in a castle, cock-sure: we have the receipt of fern-seed, we walk invisible. (60–86)

To begin with the reference to "Saint Nicholas' clerks," the joke behind this popular piece of impiety is on the wayfarers, children, and schoolboys who pray for protection to what must really be the devil in disguise, since the prayers of so many of them are answered by the appearance of Old Nick's disciple, the highwayman. But, of course, what the devil's clerk says of his victim—"there is a devil haunts thee in the likeness of" a guardian spirit (2.4.441)—applies to him as well and proclaims his own state of danger. The show of impiety in the villain's discourse flaunts the risk-taker's defiance of vulgar fear; therefore, it registers the sense that a risk is being taken and there is something to fear.

To put oneself at risk, to savor the fear and outface it, is part of the game. Gadshill, for example, can't resist the little extra bounce of confidence he can give his brag by executing the pun on "Nicholas" (= "necklace" = "noose") that exposes his neck to the Chamberlain. Since the Chamberlain predictably consigns it to the hangman, I find the irritability of Gadshill's response a little surprising. On the face of it, "What talkest thou to me of the hangman?" translates into "Don't be ridiculous": He is protected by too weighty a figure not to escape hanging ("break the gallows") should he be caught. But like a string of firecrackers, the repetitions of "hang" go off in a manner that betrays his touchiness. And the reference to Falstaff is not merely defensive. Gadshill is warning that if he is caught he will peach and incriminate Falstaff. But why should he get caught unless someone peaches on him? His neck is indeed at the Chamberlain's disposal.

The prospect of betrayal, the villain's vulnerability to the villains he depends on, infects the whole of the great chain of robbery from king to rebels to thieves, and from the prince to Falstaff to Poins to Gadshill to the Chamberlain. The chain is only as strong as its weakest link. What supports it, what the villain's discourse rides on, is represented by the figure of a horse that has been cut and galled.

The fear of hanging, the image of an elevated body that suddenly drops toward earth (sometimes from a horse) and goes limp, gives focus to the pervasive anxiety that nourishes the villain's bravado. Hanging, in addition, suggests emasculation in a pointedly ironic form, since it may produce—as an exception to the limpness of the rest of the corpse—an erect penis that, like the supplementarity of a priapean dildo, symbolizes the power it wants. The symbolism can serve to characterize the particular tension in the remainder of Gadshill's speech between swaggering rhetoric and staggering syntax. The speech represents a speaker who is spurred forward in rising euphoria by the sound of his own words. "Let me taste my horse," cries Hotspur (4.1.119), and the taste of the language Gadshill rides excites him until he can scarcely manage the reins.

The topics and code words that parade the desperado's wickedness are trotted out in repetitions or variations: Once Gadshill has heard himself say them, he can't get enough of them. Yet the speech also registers defensiveness, as if sneering at the gallows somehow entails keeping his interlocutor in his place. Thus, by his arch nondivulgence of secrets, he hints at credentials that elevate him not only above the law but also above the

Chamberlain: "Tut, there are other Troyans that thou dream'st not of, the which for sport sake are content to do the profession some grace, that would (if matters should be looked into) for their own credit sake make all whole" (68–72).

The awkward stack of relative clauses in this baggy utterance projects the strained effort of a speaker trying hard to belabor his auditor with the concealed identity of the fast company he keeps. Especially in the second clause, which aspires to hit off that company's presumed tone (cool, condescending, disengaged), Gadshill is out of it. Since this scene continually reminds us of its plot-fellow, the second half of act 1, scene 2, we know that he has it all wrong, and that if the terms in which he states Harry's motives are correct, they are so in a manner he dreams not of. Anyone who listens to Gadshill with ears primed by Falstaff's "the poor abuses of the time want countenance" (1.2.151–52) understands that the enthusiasm with which he boasts of his access to the overmighty bespeaks the awe and dependence of the undermighty. As he continues, this enthusiasm gradually picks up warmth and speed.

The gait of Gadshill's long final sentence (72–81) is at first mired in the compound epithets with which he savors his dissociation from riffraff. He discharges an alliterating string of epithets each more gorgeously stuffed than its predecessor: "I am joined with no foot-landrakers, no long-staff sixpenny strikers, none of these mad mustachio purple-hued maltworms" (72–74). Whether this effusion is appositive or conjunctive is impossible to determine, and of no importance except to signal the speaker's shaky control of his syntax. The primary effect is one of redundancy produced by his desire to go himself one better. But in representing a speaker who explores and displays his skill in amplification, the language at the same time portrays a speaker who protests too much. The "mad mustachio" bravery he so grandly scorns characterizes his "purple-hued" performance more than the "nobility and tranquillity" of "such as can hold in" (74–76).

After Gadshill dismisses the riffraff, his language moves into a rhythmic canter that registers the pulse of the power on which the speaker rides: "with nobility and tranquillity, burgomasters and great onyers, such as can hold in, such as will strike sooner than speak, and speak sooner than drink, and drink sooner than pray" (74–77). But what is rhetorically an exhilarated approach to climax is syntactically an appositional quagmire. As he gives the sentence its head, it sinks into a pit of recursive clauses that dim the prospect of closure.

He is saved by stumbling across the *pray/prey* pun (78–81) that lets him pull up and start off in another direction so that he can discharge his sequenced rhetorical assault on the commonwealth, which he first canonizes, then feminizes, and finally despoils, representing "her" as the victim of a gang rape. Notice that the calculated irreverence of his trope is an attempt to impress on the Chamberlain *their* reckless abuse of power—the wickedness of the nobility with which he is joined—and to communicate his admiration of it. By this verbal appropriation and heightening of their depravity he shows himself worthy of their acceptance, their fellowship, and this claim is ratified when he shifts to the first-person plural, "we steal."

The Chamberlain seems impressed less by his interlocutor's pretensions than by his tropes. He breaks Gadshill's stride when he takes "boots" away from him, and though Gadshill tries to roll with the pun, he acknowledges the theft by switching from "ride" to "walk." The Chamberlain's tart rejoinders are too much for Gadshill, who testifies to the truth of Feste's "By swaggering could I never thrive," where the dominant meaning of "swagger" is infected by the recessive sense contained in "swag"—to sway, reel, stagger (*Twelfth Night,* 5.1.388). His crazy horse pants excitedly ("She will, she will") toward the haven of tyrant, voyeur, coward, and thief: invisibility.

Gadshill's assault on the saint reproduces and sharpens the implications of the abuse of Saint Nicholas, and the repetitions of "hang" triggered by that reference are matched here by the clustered repetitions of the *pray/prey* homophone together with its pronominal feminine object. The rape of Saint Commonwealth gives the ultimate fico to the fear and prospect of hanging. At the triumphant conclusion of his ride from "the ridge of the gallows" to the downtrodden "boots"—or, continuing Harry's image, to "the foot of the ladder" (1.2.37–38)—Gadshill funnels the thrill of political, legal, and religious violation into that of sexual violation. The figure draws into its orbit Falstaff's reference to stealing under the countenance of "our noble and chaste mistress the moon" (1.2.25–29) and Hotspur's imagined violation of the same mistress (1.3.199–205). These three passages are variations of the same fantasy of preying *on* what one should pray *to*, doing violence to the object of desire or devotion, the source of protection or justice or honor. This vision of freedom from restraint by or dependence on any power but one's own is "out of all cess." Its extravagance betrays the fear and weakness—the fear of weakness—that give rise to it, for what else could prompt an image in which the one-sided and savage abuse of the victim ("ride up and down on her") combines with the desire for the added advantage of invisibility?

I have been trying to show how this polarity in the villain's discourse is textually represented by the tension between rhetorical bluster and syntactical uncontrol. In the exchange that concludes the scene, we glimpse an image of this tension that returns to and deepens the symbolism implied in the First Carrier's reference to Cut:

> GADS. Give me thy hand, thou shalt have a share in our purchase, as I am a true man.
> CHAM. Nay, rather let me have it, as you are a false thief.
> GADS. Go to, *homo* is a common name to all men: bid the ostler bring my gelding out of the stable. Farewell, you muddy knave. (90–95)

Gadshill on his gelding: the contiguous mention of the castrated horse oddly skews the grammar-book citation. *Homo* is defined not in terms of false against true but in terms of man against horse, and not merely horse but unmanned horse. The convergence of the knife, horse, and gender figures grounds the feckless display of verbal aggression in the fear of being cheated, betrayed, hanged, undone—the fear that motivates those who "will strike sooner than drink" and who dream of "walking invisible."

Within the traditional coalescence of man with horse, itself potentially subversive, is the even more subversive coalescence of horse with woman. Joel Fineman brilliantly observed that the "lust for maleness" is an "exquisitely female lust."[8] On this logic it is the woman or gelding within that moves the villain to seek more maleness, and every time he parades his lust for maleness he reaffirms his sense of its absence. What bears him toward manly endeavors and away from his fear of being psychologically gelded, effeminized, is the fear itself. So there can be no escape. The villain's discourse rides on and reanimates the victim's discourse it flees from.

In a familiar iconographic tradition the horse symbolizes social, moral, or psychological aspects of specifically male *virtù*—nobility, chivalry, courage, anger, passion, and so on. But the passages discussed above give this symbolism a defensive and gynephobic spin that testifies to the anxieties, the vulnerabilities, by which it is motivated. Such anxieties are scarcely alleviated by another tradition that endangers homosocial masculinity from within and thus makes the horse a Trojan horse.

This tradition, as Stephen Booth observes, exploits the "obvious . . . likeness between equestrian and sexual activity."[9] One or both of these activities is always standing in the wings of language ready to intrude itself, as when the Hostess in part 2 tells Doll and Falstaff to stop bickering and reminds Doll that "one must bear, and that must be you—you are the weaker vessel, . . . the emptier vessel." Doll's response completes the transformation of "bear" from "put up with" to "be poured into," "bear the children of," and "carry the weight of": "Can a weak empty vessel bear such a huge full hogshead?" (*2 Henry IV*, 2.4.58–62). As objects of use and abuse, and as beasts of burden, woman and horse are side by side in Harry's "this sanguine coward, this bed-presser, this horse-back-breaker" (*1 Henry IV*, 2.4.237–38) and in Hotspur's "a tired horse, a railing wife" (3.1.154), where they are made to bear the onus of things that have to be borne.

The logic of these transgressions makes it difficult for the man to free himself from the power of woman by displacing his desire to his horse. Woman joins horse in the male's currency—or armory—of rhetorical self-definition. But Shakespeare criticizes the invidious cultural practice of using textualized woman in gynephobic discourse. He does this by inventing such spirited figures as Rosalind, Portia, Helena, Viola, Desdemona, and others (including Hotspur's wife), who would have been standing rebukes to that discourse had the representation of women not been complicated by Elizabethan casting conventions.

The fact that males not only invent women's parts but also play them and speak through them reaffirms the discourse: The ideal woman for a man is a woman constructed and played by immature, unmanly, and subordinate males. Not even the paragon of Venerean womanhood, who deserves least to be manned, can claim equal rights. Some squeaking Cleopatra boy undoes her. Despite these constraints, however, such squeaking transvestism is ambiguous enough to retain an edge of danger: The boy/woman confronts men with an image of the weakness and feminization they fear.

7. *Hydra and Rhizome*

A rhizome as subterranean stem is absolutely different from roots and radicles. Bulbs and tubers are rhizomes. . . . Even some animals are, in their pack form. Rats are rhizomes. Burrows are too. . . . The rhizome itself assumes very diverse forms, from ramified surface extension in all directions to concretion into bulbs and tubers. When rats swarm over each other. The rhizome includes the best and the worst: potato and couchgrass, or the weed. Animal and plant, couchgrass is crabgrass.

—Gilles Deleuze and Félix Guattari, *A Thousand Plateaus*

Hydra[1] . . . A multifarious source of destruction that cannot be eradicated by a single attempt.
Hydra[2] . . . A many-headed monster . . . growing back two heads for each one cut off.

—*American Heritage Dictionary*

Hydra . . . A genus of Hydrozoa . . . [whose] name was given it by Linnaeus (1756), in allusion to the fact that cutting it in pieces only multiplies its numbers.

—*Oxford English Dictionary*

The camomile, the more it is trodden on the faster it grows.

—Sir John Falstaff

Hand-pulling may be a perfectly good way of removing some weeds, but this isn't true of crabgrass if it's an established growth—hand-pulling actually pulls buried crabgrass seed into sprouting position.

—*Sunset Introduction to Basic Gardening*

> The human mind is not adapted to interpreting how social systems behave. Our social systems belong to the class called multi-loop nonlinear feedback systems. . . . Actions taken to alleviate the difficulties . . . can actually make matters worse. . . . In fact, a social system tends to draw our attention to the very points at which an attempt to intervene will fail.
>
> —Jay Forrester, "Counterintuitive Behavior of Social Systems"

1

"And yet new *Hydraes* lo, new heades appeare / T'afflict that peace reputed then so sure." So Samuel Daniel in the third of his *First Foure Bookes of the Civile Wars*. The editor of the New Arden *1 Henry IV* notes in his comment on Henry's opening speech that "the irony of Henry's deluded hopes is present" in Daniel's image.[1] "Head" in various senses crops up all over the text of the play, but the Hydra itself does not appear until act 5, scene 4, after the raging Douglas has killed two of Henry's decoys at Shrewsbury ("The king hath many marching in his coats") and confronted what he takes to be a third:

DOUGLAS.
Another King. They grow like Hydra's heads:
I am the Douglas, fatal to all those
That wear those colors on them. What art thou
That counterfeit'st the person of a king?
KING.
The King himself, who, Douglas, grieves at heart
So many of his shadows thou hast met,
And not the very King. . . .
DOUGLAS.
I fear thou are another counterfeit,
And yet, in faith, thou bearest thee like a king. (5.4.24–35)

Daniel's "heades" are rebellious factions and their armies, whereas Douglas's are kings. Henry's tainted succession jeopardizes that distinction, and Douglas's language makes the most of the uncertainty that results.

In this chapter I try to connect the generation of Hydra heads with the transgression of the official lines of battle. The Hydra will become a figure of the continuous process of displacement from the discourses at war *within* language to the interlocutory, military, and political conflicts that unfold in narrative time and theatrical space. I begin with a glance at act 5, scene

3, the scene of displacement that surrounds the first mention of the Hydra in *1 Henry IV.*

Thinking that Sir Walter Blunt, the second royal counterfeit, is Henry, Douglas says, "Some tell me that thou art a king," and, after he kills Blunt, "A borrow'd title hast thou bought too dear" (5.3.5, 23). Regardless of what the speaker may intend, his comments target Henry's illegitimate possession of the title he "borrow'd." They brighten the eye of the ethical reductionists in search of the ironic little nuggets of Henry-bashing they assume that Shakespeare salted away in odd textual corners unbeknown to the guilty king himself. But they can also convey a more interesting message if we take them as clues to the lurking presence of the sinner's discourse in Henry's own language—clues, that is, to the Henry-bashing of which Henry himself seems capable, and desirous, and afraid. They may then remind us of the anxiety that motivated him in act 1, scenes 1 and 3 to behave in a manner guaranteed to provoke his supporters to insurrection.

In the political economy of the Henriad the Northumberland rebellion would dissociate Henry from his allies in usurpation and make him more legitimate. But in the ethical and psychic economy the rebellion would create a faction that could uphold Richard's cause and administer his and God's revenge on Henry's mistreadings. Worcester's complaint is self-interested, but it accurately characterizes the relation of Henry's private war to the factious Hydra heads of public war:

> We were enforc'd for safety sake to fly
> Out of your sight, and raise this present head,
> Whereby we stand opposed by such means
> As you yourself have forg'd against yourself. (5.1.65–68)[2]

From the political standpoint, Douglas's military victories could only help continue the succession of counterfeit kings and help the Hydra to another head. But they give Henry temporary relief from his private war. They divert him from the conflict between the sinner's discourse and the discourses of the victim/revenger and generous donor that he mobilizes against it. To achieve the objective of the sinner's discourse he needs eventually to lose, not win, the public war.

The effect of the royalist victory at Gaultree in *2 Henry IV* is a strange deflation of Henry's morale that seems only to hasten his death. At the end of *1 Henry IV* he is on the verge of defeating the rebels, but under conditions not calculated to let him resolve his private war. Douglas accommodates him by embodying the threat of public war in the convenient narrative form of a physical encounter. But the more dangerous battlefield to which the private war is displaced is that of Henry's interlocutory struggles with his "nearest and dearest enemy" (3.2.123).

In act 3, scene 2, Henry attacks his son with the example of Hotspur, whose "more worthy interest to the state" he oddly ascribes to the martial energy that makes Harry Percy politically unstable. Henry especially admires him for having

> Discomfited great Douglas, ta'en him once,
> Enlarged him, and made a friend of him,
> To fill the mouth of deep defiance up,
> And shake the peace and safety of our throne. (3.2.114–17)

Henry goes on to praise Hotspur and criticize Harry in a manner that testifies to the success of the latter's perverse plan to influence "men's hopes"—lower their opinion of him—by displaying "loose behavior" (1.2.203–6). Harry's response to his father is at once a promise and a deferral of the reformation that will glitter "o'er my fault" (1.2.208):

> I will redeem all this on Percy's head,
> And in the closing of some glorious day
> Be bold to tell you that I am your son. (3.2.132–34)

But not yet: Henry will have to wait until his son is ready and thinks the time is ripe to falsify men's hopes.

Harry's acerb mimicry of his father's opinion, "This gallant Hotspur, this all-praised knight, / And your unthought-of Harry" (3.2.140–41), suggests that his challenge to Hotspur will also be a challenge to Henry. And when he later offers to meet Hotspur in single combat at Shrewsbury, the terms of the challenge he aims at Hotspur glance at the king:

> Yet this before my father's majesty—
> I am content that he shall take the odds
> Of his great name and estimation,
> And will, to save the blood on either side,
> Try fortune with him in a single fight. (5.1.96–100)

Although Percy is the obvious antecedent of "he" in line 97, "he" veers momentarily toward Henry.

The king's response is politic: "So dare we venture thee," he begins, arrogating some of Harry's daring and venturing to himself. He then adds what at first appears to be only a counterfactual objection: "Albeit, considerations infinite / Do make against it" (5.1.101–3). But he goes on to ignore

Harry's offer, and at line 103 he turns to Worcester with his own stratagem for saving blood. When the prince, eager for his chance, predicts that "it will not be accepted, on my life" (115), Henry foils his son's scenario by unwrapping his backup plan: "Hence, therefore, *every* leader to his charge" (118).[3]

Falstaff's comment to Harry two lines later crystallizes the ambiguity of this interchange and anticipates the second moment of father-son conflict: "Hal, if thou see me down in the battle and bestride me, so; 'tis a point of friendship." The "point" flashes in scene 4. After Harry presents himself in full regalia as "the Prince of Wales . . . / Who never promiseth but he means to pay," he beats Douglas away from his endangered father, and he then shows top-class behavior by making conspicuously little of his accomplishment:

> Cheerly, my lord, how fares your grace?
> Sir Nicholas Gawsey hath for succour sent,
> And so hath Clifton—I'll to Clifton straight. (5.4.43–45)

This gives Henry a chance to delay Harry long enough to lavish thanks on his savior. He takes, but doesn't exactly seize, the opportunity. His thanks are carefully measured out in terms that remind Harry of what he owes while limiting his own obligation:

> Stay and breathe a while:
> Thou hast redeem'd thy lost opinion,
> And show'd thou mak'st some tender of my life,
> In this fair rescue thou hast brought to me. (46–49)

Harry responds with an outburst that effectively lays claim to a larger share of gratitude:

> O God, they did me too much injury
> That ever said I hearken'd for your death.
> If it were so, I might have let alone
> The insulting hand of Douglas over you,
> Which would have been as speedy in your end
> As all the poisonous potions in the world,
> And sav'd the treacherous labor of your son. (50–56)

Warding off Douglas's "insulting hand," Harry replaces it with something close to an insulting speech. Henry can meet this thrust only by turning abruptly to other matters—"Make up to Clifton, I'll to Sir Nicholas Gawsey" (57)—and hurrying off.

Douglas's role and fate symbolize the subordination of the public to the private war. As Stephen Booth remarks, Douglas is a parody of Hotspur, and he provides a service similar to the one Harry expects from Hotspur: "Percy is but my factor . . . / To engross up glorious deeds on my behalf" (3.2.147–48).[4] In the economy of honor Douglas fulfills the demand for a General Chivalric Factor, a feared and famous warrior whose sole function seems to be to get beaten so that the victors may become even more feared and famous.

His win/loss ratio in the play is mediocre: He kills two or three royal decoys (only one onstage) and threatens the king. But he is captured twice and sent flying once by Harry, who later reports his humiliating last stand, or stumble: When Douglas saw "the noble Percy slain, and all his men / Upon the foot of fear," he

fled with the rest,
And falling from a hill, he was so bruis'd
That the pursuers took him. (5.5.19–22)

This makes poor Douglas a pawn in the next move of the private war. "I beseech your Grace," Harry continues, "I may dispose of him," and Henry replies, "With all my heart" (23–24).

Does the king hear "dispose" as "put away"—as an offer to imprison or execute the man who endangered his life? If so, the prince's response is unexpected:

Then, brother John of Lancaster, to you
This honorable bounty shall belong;
Go to the Douglas and deliver him
Up to his pleasure, ransomless and free:
His valors shown upon our crests today
Have taught us how to cherish such high deeds,
Even in the bosom of our adversaries. (5.5.25–31)

Another show of top-class behavior; another insult to the king whose person and decoys were the only apparent objects of Douglas's "valors."[5] The gesture recalls, mimics, and responds to Henry's praise of Hotspur for having captured and "enlarged" Douglas (3.2.114–17). In imitating Hotspur, Harry both competes with him and replaces him as the king's adversary.

"I'll so offend to make offense a skill" (1.2.204): The offensive skill of this gesture—freeing Douglas—ambiguates Harry's final line, his last words in the play, and gives them a resonance that sustains the father-son conflict beneath the comedic resolution of the public war. Descriptions that focus on the war but ignore the family feud don't quite ring true: "*1 Henry IV* is designed toward the release of combat. We watch the opponents quarrel; lay their plans, gather their forces; march toward Shrewsbury and fail in last-minute negotiations, until by Act v, scene iii, we are ready for that discharge of tension which of itself seems to create a sense of order."[6] Burckhardt misses the extent to which the public war provides a medium of displacement for the struggle between Henry and Harry and for the private war within each.

Those "inward wars" are conspicuously latent, conspicuously damped down by the forward push of the public war. But they invest the speakers' language with performative energy. They drive the narrative forward and motivate the sequence of public actions that constitute the "history" that the Henriad represents. I use the term "performative" to denote what a speaker's language is doing apart from what he may be doing with it. This objective force can be explored even when the language doesn't provide the evidence for deciding whether the strings of action it produces appear to be intended or unintended.

From my reading of the performative aspects of language, I derive a sense not only of the speaker's contribution to the dramatic or "historical" plot but also of the *scenario* that motivates that contribution. The scenario is what the speaker wants to happen, but "wants" in the register of desire: It is what he wants whether he knows it or not. I try to elicit the scenarios of Henry, Harry, Hotspur, and Falstaff by exploring the private war within each, and I trace their patterns of convergence or collision as they gear into the action of speech and event—into the interlocutory and narrative sphere to which inner conflicts are displaced.

The relation between the private and public wars resembles that between latent and manifest content in Freudian analysis. The public war appears as the anamorphic projection or representation of the private war. The contradictions, ambiguities, fissures, and dislocations of the private war persist beneath the smooth resolution of the public war.

This approach to the Henriad has more explanatory power than one that is content to describe closures, symmetries, and antitheses, and then show that they are problematized. For example:

> Loose ends are apparent at the end of *1 Henry IV*, to be sure, for history is open-ended even in a play that achieves brilliant closure. After all, even *Henry V* concludes, for all its triumphs in war and marriage, on a reminder of the failures of Henry VI that are to follow in the course of history. In *1 Henry IV* rebellion is never wholly quelled, and the introduction of the Archbishop of York in 4.4 is a reminder of unfinished business. . . . The uneasy relationship between Hal and his father attains a moment of trust appropriate to Hal's emergence as his father's son, but there is unfinished business here too. The actions in *Part 2* that involve repetition—the second rebellion of the Percys, the second long tavern scene, the second interview of father and son—all arise from the perception that what seemed so easy of solution is in fact deeply problematic.[7]

But what makes it problematic? To attribute failures and loose ends to the open-endedness of history is to ignore their source in the texts of the Henriad.

The closure of *1 Henry IV* is brilliant because it is already problematic, and its easy solution is inadequate. I don't merely mean that it is circumstantially inadequate, which is obvious: The final scene falls away from the conclusive certainty of Henry's opening line, "Thus ever did rebellion find rebuke," to the provisionality of his final sentence, "Rebellion in this land shall lose its sway" *if* the troops press on; therefore, "Let us not leave till all our own be won." Rather, I mean that this military project is traversed by the contradictory desires that divide Henry's scenario against itself and that are elliptically registered in the first line of his concluding speech: "Then this remains, that we divide our power." Harry's freeing of Douglas adds bite to this irony, especially when the king says, "Myself and you, son Harry, will towards Wales" (5.5.39). Teaming up with Harry is one way to keep his power divided and continue the private war in which Harry's function is "to punish my mistreadings" (3.2.11).

When the division is alluded to in *2 Henry IV*, the relation between latent conditions and manifest circumstances has decisively altered. Hastings follows his report that the king's divisions "are in three heads" with this assessment: "So is the unfirm King / In three divided, and his coffers sound / With hollow poverty and emptiness" (1.3.70–75). This is meant as a comment on the king's military circumstances, and as such it is false. But the statement also contains an unintended description of the king's ethical condition, and as such it is true.

The rebels continually misjudge situations and talk themselves into losing—almost, indeed, as if their need to lose is their hidden ethical agenda. Everywhere, the manifest circumstances of *2 Henry IV* fail to contain its latent grief. The pressure of the sinner's discourse challenges both the repeated claims of victimization and the assertive displays (whether serious or comic) of villainy. In saying this, I'm not criticizing the play but stating its theme. Until Harry takes over in act 5, the apparently casual ramble through tableaus of social misrule and political disorder composes into a "rude scene" (1.1.159) which shadows the unseen grief that produces it.

A. R. Humphreys rightly notes that the fluent energies of the play's language are "more important, dramatically, in that the narrative content is not greatly compelling."[8] What actually happens in castle, tavern, palace, battlefield, and country orchard is conspicuously anticlimactic. The manifest circumstances of emplotment and narrative are *represented* as inadequate displacements of the latent grief.

2

The Hydra that presides over *2 Henry IV* isn't mentioned until act 4, scene 2, line 38. But it is prepared for by several anticipatory allusions. The first appears in Rumor's Induction: She gleefully claims to specialize in the wholesale distribution of "smooth comforts false, worse than true wrongs" (40).[9] She describes herself as a pipe

Blown by surmises, jealousies, conjectures,
And of so easy and so plain a stop
That the blunt monster with uncounted heads,
The still-discordant wavering multitude,
Can play upon it. (Induction, 16–20)

With characteristic shiftiness Rumor selects an image that traditionally—under Platonic influence—represents at once a psychic and a political source of disorder. She links the monster to the psychic referent in line 16, then redirects it outward to hoi polloi in the appositional clause. The source of false report is displaced first from Rumor's own uncounted tongues to the general apprehensiveness and mistrust that will plague the aristocratic leaders of faction, and then from this to their political scapegoat, the mob.

Such contagion itself rhetorically enacts the spread of false report: True wrongs are replaced by "smooth comforts false." The blunt monster is the instrument of avoidance in a moral economy produced by shifting responsibility for what Henry calls "inward wars" (3.1.107) outward to Rumor's "stern tyrant War" (Ind. 14) and downward to "the blunt monster." This is a formula for fabricating rather than eliminating new Hydras and new heads. Several lines later, one of the false reports Rumor boasts of is "that the King before the Douglas' rage / Stoop'd his anointed head as low as death" (Ind. 31–32). Her reference to the Shrewsbury episode catches the many-headed monster in a web of associated filaments that include Douglas's mention of the Hydra and the sheer mnemonic trigger "blunt." "Blunt monster" recalls "the peasant towns" (33), another reference to the blunt-headed lower class that Rumor contemptuously commandeers.

Rumor seeds potential Hydra heads throughout the play text. The Archbishop of York identifies the blunt monster with the "commonwealth," which he reduces to a "beastly feeder" and a "common dog." He cites its wavering taste in kings as a reason for taking arms (1.3.85–108). Later he argues that the king will accept the rebels' bill of grievances in order to forestall more trouble, "For he hath found, to end one doubt by death / Revives two greater in the heirs of life" (4.1.199–200)—another "smooth comfort false." The Hydra lurking under the Archbishop's figure surfaces in the next scene. There, he complains that the Court's previous rejection of the bill is part of "the time misorder'd," which "doth . . . / Crowd and crush us to this monstrous form / . . . Whereon this Hydra son of war is born" (4.2.33–38).

Rumor had anticipated that particular comfort when she took responsibility not only for false reports of peace but also for

> fearful musters, and prepar'd defence,
> Whiles the big year, swoln with some other grief,
> Is thought with child by the stern tyrant War,
> And no such matter? (12–15)

The unclarity of the image (pregnant from some other cause or not pregnant but swollen with disease?) is part of the tease. Its vagueness, its dark reaches, and its conspicuously withheld reference provoke our own "surmises" and "conjectures" about what hides behind the maddeningly noncommittal "some other grief."[10]

The Archbishop's bill of grievances and the Hydra son of war are circumstantial displacements of deep-rooted conditions. To shift the source of anxiety from grief to grievance, from inner structure to outer event, is to alienate it to some more manageable scapegoat or monster. As a personification, Rumor embodies, represents, and presides over the process by which the uncanny is domesticated—is given a local habitation, a name, a talking head. Within this thematic network, the Hydra raises *its* heads.

When it issues forth from the Archbishop's mouth, the logical implications of this figure begin to insinuate themselves subversively into the argument he is trying to make. Whether the genitive phrase, "son of war," is subjective or objective, whether "stern tyrant War" is father or son, the inherent Hydra logic—"killing" one war will generate two others—suggests something contrary to what the speaker seems to intend. So he is forced in the next line to replace the Hydra with Argus, "Whose dangerous eyes may well be charm'd asleep / With grant of our most just and right desires" (4.2.39–40). But this smooth comfort harks back to Worcester's more "jealous" (i.e., suspicious)—and truer—surmise in the preceding play: "Supposition all our lives shall be stuck full of eyes"; in other words, "Interpretation will misquote our looks" (*1 Henry IV*, 5.2.8, 13). And when Hastings proceeds to unpack the Archbishop's Hydra figure, his attempt at smooth comfort also falls prey to the monster's logic:

> We have supplies to second our attempt:
> If they miscarry, theirs shall second them;
> And so success of mischief shall be born,
> And heir from heir shall hold this quarrel up
> Whiles England shall have generation. (4.2.45–49)

As a figural embodiment, the Hydra congeals and thus conceals a destructive character only a Hercules can overcome. Hastings's language projects an endless series of quarrels, and the undesirable alternative, "mischief of success shall be born," vibrates in the many-headed meaning of "success of mischief." Reading it as "succession of mischief," we can construe the whole phrase (and not only "success") as the subject of the verb ("shall be born"). But if we construe "success" as "royal succession," the words intended to characterize the persistence that leads to success at the same time predict the Wars of the Roses and the violent operations of the "combat model" of succession.

As Hastings develops and loses control of the figure, England becomes the Hydra. Its heads are not only wars and fears but also expendable kings.

The foul and diseased "body of our kingdom" (3.1.38) thrives Hydra-like on the disorder symbolized by decapitation.

The political version of the Hydra principle was first enunciated by Richard II when he prophesied to Northumberland that

> The time shall not be many hours of age
> More than it is, ere foul sin gathering head
> Shall break into corruption: thou shalt think,
> Though he divide the realm and give thee half,
> It is too little, helping him to all;
> He shalt think that thou, which knowest the way
> To plant unrightful kings, wilt know again,
> Being ne'er so little urg'd, another way
> To pluck him headlong from the usurped throne. (*Richard II*, 5.1.57–65)

One of the first acts of the new regime is head-gathering: six freshly cut heads sent to London by Northumberland and Fitzwater (*Richard II*, 5.6.6–16).

The Hydra logic resists the intentions of those who use it to explain, visualize, and cope with the civil and political problems to which they attribute "the times misorder'd" (4.2.33). After Rumor's takeover in *2 Henry IV*, that logic expresses the desperation that underlies and erodes their hope. The Hydra's body lies concealed in the fluid medium of "some other grief." From its flourishing root system in "buried fear" and "*inward* wars" it shoots forth "new Hydraes, lo, new heades" to afflict the peace. These heads always appear in the wrong place, which is to say they appear in *place*:

> And 'tis no little reason bids us speed,
> To save our heads by raising of a head . . . (*1 Henry IV*, 1.3.277–78)

> A mighty and a fearful head they are,
> If promises be kept on every hand,
> As ever offer'd foul play in a state. (3.1.167–69)

> If we without his help can make a head
> To push against a kingdom . . . (4.1.80–81)

> And in conclusion drove us to seek out
> This head of safety . . . (4.3.102–3)

> the King hath drawn
> The special head of all the land together . . . (4.4.27–28)

We were enforc'd for safety sake to fly
Out of your sight, and raise this present head . . . (5.1.65–66)

Whether our present five and twenty thousand
May hold up head without Northumberland. (*2 Henry IV*, 1.3.16–17)

For his divisions, as the times do brawl,
Are in three heads . . . (1.3.70–71)

Think you not that the powers we bear with us
Will cut their passage through the force of France,
Doing the execution and the act
For which we have in head assembled them? (*Henry V*, 2.2.15–18)

The last excerpt is Harry's question to one of the three traitors who will soon lose *their* heads. His intention to make stern tyrant War impregnate the big year may be linked to the Hydra's second (and final) appearance in the tetralogy. This time the monster has turned and is closer to home. In *Henry IV*, part 2, the Archbishop of York blamed Harry's brother, John of Lancaster, for fomenting "this Hydra son of war" (4.2.37). In *Henry V*, the Archbishop of Canterbury marvels at the suddenness and violence of Harry's conversion:

Never was such a sudden scholar made;
Never came reformation in a flood,
With such a heady currance, scouring faults;
Nor never Hydra-headed wilfulness
So soon did lose his seat—and all at once—
As in this king. (1.1.32–37)

The reappearance of "heady" in "Hydra-headed" suggests that despite their contrary impulses the same Herculean violence may fuel both Harry's willfulness and his "currance" of reform, leaving it unclear whether the effect of scouring faults is to get rid of them or to nourish their root structure so that they can put forth more heads.[11]

Canterbury and his interlocutor, the Bishop of Ely, are trying to persuade themselves that since the king has reformed and is "a true lover of the holy Church" (23), they will be able to persuade him to forestall dispossession of Church lands in exchange for their support of his cause against France. Canterbury is obviously a worldly clergyman skilled in the art of pietistic euphemism. The strangeness and wonder in his words therefore stand out. His language of exorcistic violence so vividly betrays the hero's self-purging fury that it transgresses his apparent intention to praise Harry.

Canterbury desperately wants to believe in Harry's reformation. But the effect of his repeated "Never's," inflating Harry's "faults" to monstrous proportions (the Augean stable, the Hydra), is to stress his own incredulity. And if we remember the Prologue's heraldic image of "the warlike Harry" at whose heels, "Leash'd in like *hounds*, . . . famine, sword, and fire / Crouch for employment" (Pr. 6–8), the *cur* in the nonce word "currance" (1.1.34) strains forward to touch up the ferocity of Canterbury's image. The hidden cur externalized and idealized in the hounds waiting to be unleashed implies that some motive other than the wars of the body politic lies not only behind the bearing of "civil swords and native fire / As far as France" (*2 Henry IV,* 5.5.106–7) but also behind the rhetorical violence with which Harry will scour many faults during the course of the play, but none of them his own.

3

In my imagination I never see the Hydra's body, only its heads gnashing about like those of so many tyrannosaurs hidden from the neck down in earth, mud, or water. And if I try to imagine the body, it takes on the aspect of a densely tangled intertwining root structure creeping laterally in every direction and sending up capital shoots that work like crabgrass. It offers its enemies the wrong targets so that their efforts to curb its growth will not only fail but will invigorate the Hydra's root structure and multiply its heads.

The point about the Hydra, however, is that as a mythological pest it does not exist until someone brings it into being by desiring targets of decapitation, that is, by making heads. Decapitation is futile because it is the masked form of its opposite, capitation. The Hydra is born from the head of the decapitator.

Another name for the Hydra's hidden body, as I visualize it, is *rhizome*, the roots of which Deleuze and Guattari extend into language:

> In a rhizome . . . semiotic chains of every kind are connected . . . according to very diverse modes of encoding, chains that are biological, political, economic, etc., and that put into play not only regimes of different signs, but also different states of affairs. . . . A semiotic chain is like a tuber gathering up very diverse acts—linguistic, but also perceptual,

> mimetic, gestural, and cognitive. . . . Language stabilizes around a parish, a diocese, a capital. It forms a bulb. It evolves by means of stems and underground flows. . . . Language can always be broken down into its internal structural components, an activity not fundamentally different from a search for roots.[12]

Another name for *rhizome* might be *text.*

4

Among the various mirroring devices and "ways of recording the progress of inward 'action'" that Maynard Mack found in his groundbreaking essay "The Jacobean Shakespeare," the one that took root in subsequent criticism was the concept of "umbrella speeches," so called because "more than one consciousness may shelter under them."[13] Lear's Fool "serves, to some extent, as a screen on which Shakespeare flashes, as it were, readings from the psychic life of the protagonist."[14] Through Lady Macbeth's sleepwalking Shakespeare keeps Macbeth "before us in his capacity as tragic hero and sufferer."[15]

Some umbrellas are larger than others: Mack argues that Edmund, Gloucester, and Lear are all partly protected under the Poor Tom umbrella put up by Edgar.[16] And maybe there are choric umbrellas under which the playwright and the play as a whole—its worldview or moral order—huddle together. At least it used to be thought so, and Mack observes that he is not the first to have tried to shelter under the concept.[17]

But why it should be an umbrella remains puzzling to me. Why a manufactured defense against bad weather opened up by one character but companionably shared by another, or others? And why can't the character that is or holds the umbrella also be the "other" that shelters under it? Why can't several such speakers and umbrellas converge into one?

Mack's concept is both powerful and serviceable, but the gratuitous details of his image are distracting. It's the playwright who manufactures the umbrella and the critic who opens it up. They collaborate in producing an object the perimeter of which coincides not with individual speeches or the speeches of individual characters but with the language of the play as a whole. Individual speeches may well be defenses against textual bad weather, but what if we were to invert the image and conceive of bad weather as coming up from below?

For this image, mushrooms are preferable to the umbrellas they vaguely resemble. Mushrooms spring up like Hydra heads from the tangled dark weblike mycelium of the text, and they bear the darkness in their substance. Mushroom speeches growing from textual mycelium: an image whose time may come. But for now I'll resist its appeal in favor of another organic image more deeply rooted both in the language of the Henriad and in its genealogical themes.

In the opening lines of act 1, scene 2 of *Richard II*, John of Gaunt complains to the Duchess of Gloucester, the widow of the murdered Thomas of Woodstock, that "the part I had in Woodstock's blood" impels him to avenge his brother's murder. But he goes on to say that since he can't oppose God's deputy, who "made the fault," he leaves it to "the will of heaven" to "rain hot vengeance on offenders' heads." The Duchess retorts that he should act anyway because he and Woodstock are among "Edward's seven sons" and are as "seven branches springing from one root" (1.2.1–13). In this connection I want to register my support for the Quarto's "Woodstock's blood" in preference to the Folio's "Gloucester's blood." This is because one botanical root of the Duchess's genealogical metaphor is the (wood)stock—not in its first *OED* sense of a *lifeless* stump but in the second sense of a *living* trunk or stem. (*OED* entry 2c equates "stock" with "rhizome," and the *American Heritage Dictionary* mentions "rootstalk" and "rootstock" as synonyms of "rhizome.")

The second *OED* sense is metaphorically even less accurate than the first. Edward III is no more alive than Woodstock. It's only when his living descendants adopt the botanical fiction as a call to action that the "root" is resurrected, and the call is usually, as here, a response to some rupture or break, which itself becomes the rootstock or woodstock of the resurrective project.

Edward III is not the rootstock of *Richard II*. Woodstock, or rather his murder, is. A lifeless subterranean stump, a dead brother, a murder seeds the genealogy and text of the buried fear that gets transmitted through the Henriad.

From this progenitor no *lineal* succession can descend, or ascend, because the genealogical positions are continually being shuffled, exchanged, and reoccupied in the Henriad's symbolic economy. Brothers fill in as sons, cousins as fathers and sons, sons as cousins and fathers. The genealogical narrative, with its lineality and linearity, moves over the surface of a very different kind of structure, one that "always has multiple entrances" like a burrow, one that is "reversible, and susceptible to constant modification," one that Deleuze and Guattari at times depict less as a structure than as a vortex:

> A rhizome can be cracked and broken at any point; it starts off again following one or another of its lines, or even other lines. . . .
>
> Always follow the rhizome by rupturing, lengthening, prolonging, . . . making it vary, until it produces the most abstract and tortuous line in *n* dimensions and scattered directions. Combine the deterritorialized flows.[18]

Deterritorialized flows are textual flows. They go off the line. Reterritorializing the flows restores them to the line of events and bodies that compose into the space-time of dramatic narrative and theatrical performance. In that sense, reterritorializing protects against interpretation.

5

1. The shadow of my sorrow? ha! let's see—
   'Tis very true, my grief lies all within,
   And these external manners of lament
   Are merely shadows to the unseen grief
   That swells with silence in the tortur'd soul. (*Richard II*, 4.1.294–99)

2. . . . a plague of sighing and grief, it blows a man up
   like a bladder. (*1 Henry IV*, 2.5.327–28)

3. And who but Rumor, who but only I,
   Make fearful musters, and prepar'd defence,
   Whiles the big year, swoln with some other grief,
   Is thought with child by the stern tyrant War,
   And no such matter? (*2 Henry IV*, Ind., 11–15)

4. This tempest will not give me leave to ponder
   On things would hurt me more. (*King Lear*, 3.4.24–25)

5. They say miracles are past; and we have our philosophical persons
   to make modern and familiar, things supernatural and causeless.
   Hence it is that we make trifles of terrors, ensconcing ourselves
   into seeming knowledge when we should submit ourselves to an
   unknown fear. (*All's Well That Ends Well*, 2.3.1–6)

6. But I have that within which passes show,
   These but the trappings and the suits of woe. (*Hamlet*, 1.2.85–86)

These passages have two things in common. First, they point to a distinction and relation between "internal" and "external" representations of grief or anxiety—between what "passes show" and its expression in the passing show. Second, they mark the passing show as either an inadequate or a diversionary portrayal of what "passes show."

Their citational form reduces these six snippets to my passing show. Snippetotomy tears them from their contexts, diminishes their ability to express what lies within. Many of them rhetorically enact the problematic relation they state by parading themselves as inadequate or obscure or misleading expressions. Thus passages 1 and 6 are but the trappings and the suits of what "lies all within."

Richard II's statement in passage 1, for example, undoes itself because it is another external manner of lament. As shadows or players of his unseen grief, his words fall short: Their rhetorical embodiment falsifies that grief. Even as he appears to be harping on his victimization and loss of power at the hands of others, he enjoys flaunting his theatrical control over Bolingbroke in a manner that belies his words. But his control over both his own downfall and Bolingbroke's ethical condition is more than theatrical. His language is aflame with the searing interplay of the sinner's, the saint's, and the victim/revenger's discourses. His "still-breeding thoughts" inseminate Henry's conscience and ultimately swell with silence in his tortured soul. It's very true, then, that whether or not Richard's grief lies "all within," it *lies*.

Falstaff's statement in passage 2 is at once an insight into the symbol of corpulence, and a scoff at the canny reductiveness of medical explanation, which domesticates the dis-ease of "some other grief" so as to submit it to the cure of pneumatic or hydraulic pathology. A similar move occurs in passage 5, from *All's Well That Ends Well*. This is the old courtier Lafew's critique of the dubious knowledgeability of the doctors trying—pretentiously and without success—to diagnose the king's mysterious illness.

Lafew's comment is itself pretentious and seemingly knowledgeable. It thus fails to keep the folly he assigns to the third person plural from penetrating the show of wisdom that puffs up the first person singular. Anyone who chooses to appropriate and utter Lafew's insight, present company not excepted, is subject to the same penetration. Nevertheless, as the hapless Duke of Albany would say, does say, "that's but a trifle here," and I plan to elevate Lafew's comment to a dramaturgical principle that will make modern and familiar things supernatural and causeless.[19]

The first step in this plan is to identify *what passes show* with the rhizome and *the passing show* with the Hydra. This produces the relational pairs shown in the accompanying list. This diagram models not only the structure of the Henriad but also the general structure of Shakespearean dramaturgy.

Rhizome	**Hydra**
semiotic chains	narrative chains
latent conditions	manifest circumstances
discursive action . . . interlocutory action . . .	dramatic action
text, language . . . . a script, speech	events, bodies, performance
inward wars	stern tyrant War
grief	grievances
terrors	trifles
unknown fear	seeming knowledge
"some other" within	external manners, trappings, suits

Barry Weller remarks of Shakespeare's characters that they "frequently manifest the desire to be recognized as something other than they 'seem', that is, [the desire] to belie the visible and audible evidence of their presence onstage by suggesting that it does not and cannot adequately represent what they are."[20] I add that Shakespeare's plays manifest the same desire, and that the way they do so in the Henriad conforms to the Lafew Principle.

A *trifle* is not only something trivial but also, in one of its older senses, a false tale or lying fable told to deceive or divert. I want to explore and test a particular hypothesis about Shakespearean dramaturgy, which is that the play text represents its dramatic and theatrical circumstances as forms of defensive trifling. The hypothesis is based on a modern and familiar theory of the relations between latent and manifest content, and of the dynamic mechanisms—condensation, displacement, visualization, dramatization—that preside over their transformations.[21]

To redirect Freud's model to plays does not mean to reduce plays to dreams or jokes, since the dynamics of his model gives shape to the economy of many other representational activities. Dreamwork, jokework, and playwork are different expressions of the same general field of forces. In applying the model to Shakespeare's writing, I focus on the passage from latent psychological *conditions* or relationships to the manifest *circumstances* of narrative, dramatic, and theatrical performance.

My reason for choosing the two terms italicized in the preceding sentence is based on etymological considerations. In using *circumstance* I mean to activate not only such senses as "factors that modify a course of action" and "additional or accessory information" but also those implied in the phrases "circumstantial evidence" and "pomp and circumstance." Buried in my use of the word *condition* is the Latin verb *condere*, which means, among other things, to write or compose, to collect, to preserve, to bury, to conceal.

Earlier, I suggested that the relation between Harry's private and public wars resembles Freud's distinction between latent and manifest content. I now want to introduce a distinction between two kinds of latency: the latency of what may be called deep-structural *psychological* conditions and the latency of *textual* conditions. Textual conditions consist of the rhetorical, syntactical, and lexical play of meaning that's most fully accessible when the system of verbal signs is committed to writing and offered to readers for interpretation. The problem is that the relation between textual conditions and theatrical circumstances is polarized and conflictive.

The polarity arises from the different aims and structures of literary and theatrical interpretation. Theatrical interpretation asks for winged thought, whereas literary interpretation is "cripple tardy-gaited" thought[22] that meanders painfully about the text and leaves filthy little tracks like a snail. Or, putting it in the language of corpuscular theory, theater induces quick motions that heat up the mind, while reading induces slow motions that make it pale, cold, and melancholic.

Actors and spectators display the symptoms Falstaff attributes to the "twofold operation" of sack. On the one hand, it makes them "full of nimble, fiery, and delectable shapes . . . delivered o'er to the voice" and ear (and eye), and it makes the blood "course from the inwards to the parts' extremes" until "it illumineth the face." On the other hand, because readers are more "sober-blooded" and eschew "inflammation," they suffer from the anemia of "demure boys" who imbibe thin potations and get wenches. Or so it seems to those who insist that "the foolish and dull and crudy vapors" environing the text be burned off in accordance with the criteria of performability and who think the "learning" of armchair interpreters to be "a mere hoard of gold kept by a devil."[23]

These are relatively mundane observations, even more trifling if all they refer to is a polarity between text and performance, or between reading and playgoing. How can such empirical statements be made to converge with thematic claims about the relation of psychological or textual conditions to dramatic or theatrical circumstances? In *Imaginary Audition*, I tried to situate the polarity *within* reading and treat it as a conflict between stage-centered and text-centered reading. I then complicated the scheme by introducing a *via media* which I called the literary model of stage-centered reading and distinguished from the theatrical model.[24]

One effect of these moves is to shift the center of the representational medium from the mutual presence of theatrical performance and audience to that of text and reader. This deprives theatrical performance of pride of place as the actual medium that "imitates," communicates, and interprets a dramatic fiction. The relation between performance and reading is no longer an empirically fixed prior condition that escapes and determines interpretation. Rather, theater joins drama as one of the absent referents of the text. Its use and meaning, its relations to dramatic fiction and text, are now among the variables that are open to the reader's interpretive decisions.

From here it's only a short step to a second move, one that will allow me to state my claim in its strongest and most controversial form. Situating the text/performance dialectic within reading produces the following consequence: Whether and why reading should or should not be constrained by the structural characteristics of theatrical performance become substantive problems that affect the meaning of the dramatic fiction. This problematic is built into the Shakespeare text as a critical thesis about theater in particular and theatricality in general. The critique may be extended to the theatrical model of stage-centered reading. But it is fully accessible only to the literary model of stage-centered reading, which provides an interpretive standpoint outside the direct or indirect influence of the stage.

Shakespeare's writing defends against the reduction of latent conditions to manifest circumstances by representing the circumstances as defensive transformations of the conditions. It does so in a manner that may be elucidated by Freud's analyses and the Lafew Principle. Reading guided by the literary model postulates that both actors and performance, both characters and story, may be construed as circumstantial embodiments. They are the "nimble, fiery, and delectable shapes" that *stand around* the psychological conditions buried in the text. They are shapes that fence those conditions off and keep them just out of earshot.

In the more conventional and innocent version expressed by Theseus in *Midsummer Night's Dream*, the conditions are the "things unknown," the "airy nothing," that "imagination bodies forth" and "the poet's pen / Turns

. . . to shapes," giving them "a local habitation and a name."[25] In the Henriad the "things unknown" become Lafew's "unknown fear," and for the text-centered reader this "buried fear" vibrates in "secret whispers," in "creeping murmur and the poring [eye-straining] dark" of meanings that ramify like rhizomes through the subsoil of the text. On the Freudian model, to body them forth and visualize them is to repress them, and to repress them is to stimulate their rhizomatic growth, for they have the same properties as crabgrass or the Hydra.

For the pale hermeneutical farmer who circles tirelessly if tediously around fields of text and practices reading-intensive cultivation, these rhizomatic manifestations take a particular form. The denotative function of linguistic *reference* is given priority over the connotative play of linguistic *meanings*. The effect of binding language to referents is to control or repress other meanings.

My point is that the other meanings needn't be dismissed as irrelevant or unstageable. They may be unwanted and dangerous. Theatrical performance can impose a kind of ideological closure on the semiotic power of the text. The question for interpretation then becomes whether this closure in any instance appears motivated in terms that affect the play's meaning. Do the conditions of theater work as agents of repression, and if so, what do they repress?

8. *Falstaff, Carnival, and the Perils of Speech-Prefixity*

In chapter 1, I referred to a brilliant study published more than fifty years ago by A. P. Rossiter, and I want to return to that study here. Rossiter wrote that "the difficulty of establishing the Right in . . . an England under no rightful king, is paralleled and parodied throughout in Falstaff's 'manner of wrenching the true cause the false way.'"[1] "Parodied *in* Falstaff's manner" could mean "parodied *by* Falstaff's manner"—that is, by Falstaff—but in this sentence it doesn't. Rossiter is concerned with Falstaff's "manner" as a factor in the network of parallels and contrasts that constitute the plays' multiple plot structures. Therefore, he centers on Falstaff primarily as a symptom of defects in the social body the play represents. This focus tends to marginalize other possible relations of Falstaff's speech to its speaker. Suppose, for example, that the words assigned to Falstaff construct a speaker who presents himself representing himself and who represents himself *as* a symbol of defects in the social body?

Valerie Traub approaches the question of Falstaff in more gender-specific terms: "Falstaff represents to Hal not an alternative paternal image but rather a projected fantasy of the pre-oedipal *maternal* whose rejection is the basis upon which patriarchal subjectivity is predicated."[2] The opening construction is loose enough to let it mean that *Falstaff represents himself* to Hal as a maternal (rather than paternal) figure, but it doesn't mean that here. In her impressive and still timely study, Traub is concerned with what Harry sees in Falstaff, and she thus discusses Falstaff as the object of *Harry's* representations rather than as the subject of his own.

Traub's aim is to reposition a psychoanalytic approach to the Harry/Falstaff relation. First, she factors in the scapegoat function that the play assigns to the fantasy of the female reproductive body mapped onto Falstaff, who "is figured in female terms." Second, she explores what it shows about "both the Shakespearean and psychoanalytic dramas" that "the parent who is rejected, metaphorically killed, is figured in the iconography of the female body."[3] How would Traub's double move be affected by redirecting attention to the victim's—the metaphoric mother's—discourse of self-representation? This question about Falstaff is modeled on Traub's question about Katharine in *Henry V.* After having discussed Katharine as "the object of Henry's discourse" and shown how "Henry's subjectivity and sexuality are predicated upon his repression of Katharine's linguistic power," she asks, "What of Katharine as the subject of her own discourse?" She answers with a concise and persuasive account of the princess's limited resistance to the imperatives of the traffic in women.[4]

If Traub's question about Katharine is redirected to Falstaff—does he contribute to his victimization?—it makes contact with Jonathan Goldberg's brilliant account of his complicity in *Sodometries,* published in the same year as Traub's *Desire and Anxiety*:

> From their first scene together, Falstaff stands to be abused. It's often said that we desire Falstaff's resurgence . . . , but it is his condition throughout the play, and if we desire his repeated comebacks it is because it is on his desire that ours floats. . . . That desire is, importantly, the desire to take abuse. *If we accept his banishment, it is then because we take it up as our position, because we have been accepting it all along, and because it is part of the way in which we need never give up desiring Hal.*[5]

The "we" in this passage signals the ironic mimicry of critique; it activates the formula "*we* minus *I* equals *they.*" "We" are the critics who continue to be charmed by Harry and thus to reproduce the incipient heterosexist discourse of homophobia/misogyny visible in his "engrossing" of Hotspur and Falstaff.[6]

Let's rewrite the italicized passage in a form that brings out the mordancy lurking in the phrase, "Falstaff stands to be abused": "If Falstaff accepts his banishment, it is because he takes it up as his position, because he has been accepting it all along, and because it is part of the way in which he need never give up desiring Hal." "Stands to be abused" means "solicits, desires, offers himself to abuse, is complicit in getting himself abused." This kind of "standing to be" implicates the exhilaration of risk-taking, the search for opportunities not only to seduce and outwit the abuser but to prolong the pleasure of the desire for abuse and to defer its anticipated consequences.

How much and what kind of interpretive control can the speech prefix have over the speech that interprets it and over the interpreters who convert the speech prefix into a character? For example, how would the consequences of my revision of Goldberg's phrasing be affected by replacing the name "Falstaff" with the name "Oldcastle"? Or, as Goldberg suggests, by keeping "Falstaff" but reading the dispersed traces of the Oldcastle/Brooke affair as allusions by means of which the censored text of the play remarks "the censored name and even the agents of that censorship"?[7]

Gary Taylor argues that the play brings together "two opposing conceptions of Oldcastle current in the sixteenth century"—Oldcastle the soldier and martyr versus Oldcastle the "robber, traitor, heretic and hypocrite"—in such a way as to produce "a deliberate and brilliant caricature of the dead Oldcastle." The caricature is produced in part by conflating "the historical Oldcastle with the theatrical Vice." To assign the words that evoke this rich structure of "historicity and ambiguity" to the name "'Falstaff' fictionalizes, depoliticizes, secularizes, and in the process trivializes the play's most memorable character," thus robbing it "of that tension created by the distance between two available interpretations of one of its central figures."[8]

At this late date it would be redundant to belabor Taylor's shaky presuppositions about authorship and authority (Goldberg and many others have done that), or the simplistic opposition he draws between the historical and the fictional. My claim is only that if the words assigned to Falstaff are construed as a "caricature of the dead Oldcastle"—the portrait of "a Protestant martyr as a jolly hypocrite" whom the author "deliberately lampooned" (98, 99)—their speaker is perforce reduced to the object of the representations of others.

Taylor's construal puts Falstaff in the position of the innocent dupe or dope whose relation to author, actors, and audiences is the same as that of the native to the outside observer who is the one-supposed-to-know in the classic but long discredited mode of ethnographic narrative. But why not attribute the caricature of the historical Oldcastle to the fictional Oldcastle? Why not construe the words and behavior of the character as *his* deliberate lampoon of his namesake? There would then be two different Oldcastles, 1 and 2, the former the historical butt, the latter the fictional lampoonist. Or would there instead be a single figure, self-divided Oldcastle 1/2, who makes fun of himself?

The point is that both Oldcastle 2 and Oldcastle 1/2 would differ from Oldcastle 1—unless, of course, the historical Oldcastle is represented in the record as someone given to self-parody, which, as far as we know, he wasn't.[9] Therefore, if the representation of Oldcastle 1 were developed in the spirit of parody or self-parody, it would make sense to stabilize the difference between the performer and the performed by changing the speech prefix from Oldcastle to—for example—Falstaff. But let's explore these options a little more slowly.

A. The hilarity of seeing Falstaff as the historical butt Oldcastle 1 would be at Falstaff's expense and without his knowledge. He would be neither the subject nor the object of his discourse. He might as well be called Oldcastle—or Shakespeare.
B. The hilarity of seeing Falstaff as lampoonist Oldcastle 2 would be shared by Falstaff, but in a way that subordinates his function as character to that of the actor who presents the satiric representation of Falstaff-as-Oldcastle to a theater audience. Oldcastle, not Falstaff, would be the object of his discourse. To the extent that the lampooning of Oldcastle is exorbitant—directed at the offstage audience and not recognized by other characters in the play—the moments in which it occurs rematerialize the *platea* as a theatrical but extradramatic space, because the audience for the speaker's satire cannot be Harry or Poins or any other *dramatis persona*.

How, then, to describe Falstaff's relation to Oldcastle in a consistent manner that doesn't confuse options (A) and (B)? On this topic, Charles Whitney's compelling account of the "festive Falstaffian mimicry" shines a bright light:

> [1] Shakespeare's Oldcastle . . . burlesques the historical Oldcastle in a way not altogether different from his burlesque of King Henry IV in the great tavern scene of Act II. [2] Where the historical Oldcastle became a devout Lollard after a period of self-confessed sinfulness, Shakespeare's character lives riotously, occasionally thinks about repenting, and frequently expresses himself in religious language. . . . [3] On the whole, Shakespeare's festive character . . . embraces a laughably irresponsible, grasping, dissolute, and hypocritical version of the proto-Protestant martyr.[10]

Assertion [1] indicates that the burlesque may be intentional on Falstaff's part. Somehow he knows about Oldcastle and puts him down in satiric impersonation just as he does Harry's father. Assertion [2] is in the form of a comparison that subordinates the idea of Falstaff's intentional burlesque to an objective contrast between him and Oldcastle.

In assertion [3] it seems unlikely that Whitney means to attribute the "version" to Falstaff as *his* parodic project. Though "embraces" could mean "adopts" or "takes up," here it probably means no more than "contains." Whitney goes on to argue that whether Falstaff is depicted as Oldcastle 1 or Oldcastle 2, whether "Falstaffian mimicry" means "mimicry *by* Falstaff" or "mimicry *through* Falstaff," is of little importance when attention is focused on issues of topicality and reception. "The most obvious butt of the satire is those who accept that particular hagiographic view of Oldcastle: you revere him as a martyr but he's really a killjoy, and so are you; here he is in the play as he may have been before he got religion: the reveller you can't stand."[11]

The hilarity of seeing Falstaff as Oldcastle 1/2 would be preemptively modified by the self-dividing force of speech in which a speaker is related to his or her discourse as both its subject (the one who speaks) and its object (the one who is spoken of). Under this construal, two things could happen to Oldcastle: First, if the satire is reflexively internalized, the centrifugal force of its topical or referential energy tends to diminish. Topicality is contained and turned around. Instead of seeing Falstaff as Oldcastle, instead of looking through Falstaff to Oldcastle, you assimilate what you know about Oldcastle to the interpretation of Falstaff.

If the satire on Oldcastle the historical figure lingers on, it does so only as an added attraction. Falstaff uses puritan rhetoric and discourse to target both Harry's moral scenario and his own indulgence in it. To the extent that such passages of mimicry work as allusions to the bible-quoting proto-Protestant martyr and/or hypocrite, the figure of Oldcastle becomes less a historical person and more a personification, a caricature of the misuse of puritan discourse.

Gary Taylor's proposal—that the play brings together "two opposing conceptions of Oldcastle current in the sixteenth century"—was rejected by Kristen Poole in a strong argument similar to Goldberg's but based on a more specific historical objection:

> To annihilate the effects of Shakespeare's contemporary censors is to rewrite history in a disturbingly Orwellian fashion and to deny the text's sociopolitical setting. In addition, if, as Taylor effectively argues, Elizabethan and Jacobean audiences were well aware of Falstaff's "real" identity as Oldcastle, then part of the pleasure of this theatrical experience would have been the knowledge that one could read the clandestine identity hidden behind the name. . . . In short, rather than depoliticizing the play

or robbing it of tension, the presence of the name "Falstaff" and the knowledge of the character's "true" identity combine to heighten awareness of the political circumstances of the play.[12]

Poole goes on shift the emphasis from the portrayal of a particular historical figure to the broader context of antipuritan discourse—the Martin Marprelate controversy—in which the figure of Oldcastle works to transpose Falstaff "into a register of religious/political language familiar to his Elizabethan audience" (54). The shift is compatible with the transition to the more complex construction of Falstaff as Oldcastle 1/2 described above. Does this strategy then enable her to avoid the reduction produced by Taylor's thesis?

"In Falstaff, as in Martin Marprelate," Poole asserts, "social and discursive orders are undermined and overturned" (71). Does "*In* Falstaff" = *by* Falstaff? *Through* the figure or symbol of Falstaff? *In* the person of Falstaff? Is Falstaff as the subject of his speech the source of subversive discourse? Is he, as the object constructed by his speech, the comic embodiment of subversion in the carnival figure of the grotesque puritan?

Poole wants to have it both ways, but her polemic against critics who assume that Falstaff self-consciously mocks puritans leads her to emphasize his function as an *object* of satire. She argues that an audience attuned to "stage lampoons of Martin Marprelate" and to the history of Oldcastle "would have laughed not only *with* Falstaff but simultaneously *at* him" (68). She goes on to concede that he is also a satirist who "articulates overtly subversive sentiments, freely criticizing—even mocking—king and prince." But she is careful to restrict the scope of his satire to generalized social critique by reducing king and prince to symbols of the "social and discursive orders" that Falstaff, like Martin Marprelate, irreverently puts down (70–71).

Poole's is in fact a double restriction. If it is unlikely that Falstaff would criticize puritans, it is equally unlikely that he would criticize himself. Both exclusions are motivated by respect for the expectations the critic imputes to the theater audience. Thus she rejects the opinion that "Falstaff's tendency to speak in biblical idiom and puritan jargon . . . is intended as active mockery of the puritans" on the grounds that it would "not make much sense" to "an audience that identifies Falstaff with Oldcastle": "The parody would have to be self-reflexive, with Sir John ridiculing his own religious inclinations—those same beliefs for which the historical Oldcastle was martyred" (67). Why couldn't Falstaff himself be the target of his parody as well as Oldcastle?

The word "audience" in Poole's essay fluctuates uncertainly but strategically between two denotations: At times it seems to function as an embodiment of the cultural expectations of Shakespeare's contemporaries in "the context of Elizabethan polemical religious discourse," and at times it signifies people in theaters (53).[13] Such an attempt to reify the virtual audience constructed not by the play but by the scholarly hypothesis seems logically connected to the denial of the possibility that the character's speech may construct him as a subject capable of self-interpretation. Poole argues that what "Shakespeare's audience would most likely have recognized" is that "the person of Falstaff is in and of himself a parody of the sixteenth-century puritan." She aims "to uncover an important context that influenced the ways in which Elizabethans recognized and reacted to Falstaff as a social representation" (54, 64).

Poole clearly discerns the problem this poses. After citing a list of the labels that have been affixed to Falstaff—"Vice, Parasite, Fool," etc.—she states that he "is, in fact, all of these and yet none in particular; he both deflects and absorbs such labels," and she protests that she is "not attempting to reduce Falstaff's psychological and cultural complexity" (64). Yet to say that he *is* all these things, where "is" means "exists as a social representation of," is to reduce him to an object. It isn't "he" who deflects and absorbs these labels by performing his representation of himself as Vice, Parasite, and Fool.

Poole's point is rather that these are "the many discursive registers through which Falstaff is constructed" by others—by Shakespeare and by the culture and its embodiments in potential playgoers (67). In a passage illustrating Falstaff's recourse to puritan jargon, she notes that he "compares himself to a 'saint,'" that he "speaks of his 'vocation,'" that he mimics biblical rhetoric, "makes references to psalm-singing," and "wishes he 'were a weaver'" (66). This series implies not simply that he is or symbolizes but that he *performs* the role of the grotesque stage puritan. It provides the basis for a study of the discursive registers through which Falstaff as the agent or subject of his speech represents and interprets himself and his relation to Harry. We may then ask for whose laughter and pleasure, for whose mockery and contempt, he presents this representation.

To answer with Poole that the audience the character addresses is an audience actually or potentially in an Elizabethan theater is to bypass the ambiguity it is one of the virtues of Poole's essay to articulate.[14] Falstaff obviously performs both for Harry's pleasure and for his own. His puritan parody targets the self-righteous rationale he predicts Harry will resort to in casting off his fat misleader. But the parody may at the same time be part of a performance perversely aimed at soliciting Harry's contempt, a performance aimed at giving the prince further incentive to cast him off. It is as if Falstaff himself keeps open the possibility that he will eventually receive his just if bitter deserts. In that sense, which isn't exactly the sense Poole features, there is something deeply puritanical about Falstaff.

This calls for an account of Falstaff as object that differs from the one Poole gives. He is not merely the symbolic object of some form of iconographic analysis, nor is he merely a representation of *X* constructed by and for others. The character named Falstaff is an object constructed and interpreted by his own speech. His verbal behavior in the Coventry scene (*1 Henry IV*, 2.4) has been brilliantly illuminated by William Empson and Charles Whitney.

Here, first, is Empson:

> Falstaff has just boasted that he took bribes to accept such bad recruits ("I have misused the King's press damnably"—and the audience would not think him a coward here, but that it took a lot of nerve to be so wicked) and he boasts later that he got them killed to keep their pay . . . but this makes his reply all the more crashing, as from one murderer to another.[15]

The reply Empson mentions is Falstaff's "Tut, tut, good enough to toss; food for powder, food for powder. They'll fill a pit as well as better. Tush, man, mortal men, mortal men" (4.2.64–66). This is, he claims, "the most unbeatable of all Falstaff's retorts to Henry" (52). But to whom has Falstaff just boasted that he took bribes?

Empson's aside on what the audience would think reinforces my suspicion that he reads the retort as part of an ongoing flyting contest staged for the benefit of a collective third party offstage. Falstaff performs his wickedness in order to score another point and win another round of applause. If, in making himself a mirror of Harry's irresponsibility, his utterance conveys any note of irritable self-reproach, it is occluded by Empson's focus on performance.

Charles Whitney brilliantly elevates Empson's character-to-audience swerve to a methodological principle. His acute and compelling comments point up the reflexive implications of Falstaff's speech:

> Falstaff's treatment of his recruits and his use of the word "prodigal" may express his own feelings of apprehension about being abandoned by Hal; what Hal may do to him, he will do to the recruits. Such behavior on

> Falstaff's part parallels the "displaced abjection" of carnival violence that scapegoats those lower in the social scale rather than those who are responsible for the revellers' abjection.
>
> With his line "food for powder" Falstaff performs . . . [a] festive inversion, shifting responsibility for the recruits' fate from himself to Hal. . . . "Whose fellows are these that come after?" Hal asks. "I never did see such pitiful rascals." As Falstaff answers, the nobles' faces show consternation which grows the more they stare and the more they hear the words of reassurance meant to have an opposite, horrific effect. . . . The irony of "food for powder" is so massive that here one tends to find Falstaff sympathizing with his recruits, where just before he was cackling at them. The irony suggests that Hal, as a leading member of the elite, has some responsibility for beggars being sent into battle; Sir John here contrives to become the wry spokesman for the very lower orders he is fond of exploiting.[16]

Though this is a standard perception about the displacement of responsibility, it has seldom been applied to Falstaff's performance here, and it invites closer attention to Falstaff as the auditor to whom "the wry spokesman" addresses his ironies and evasions.

His sympathizing with those he exploits, for example, may comment on his own as well as on Harry's displacement of responsibility. He isn't merely Being Bad. He is showing himself up. There is anger in his words, but it is not aimed solely at the prince. The soliloquy solicits self-reproach.

Whitney doesn't read the passage this way, and he turns away from that possibility in his next words:

> One may say here that Falstaff is simply demonstrating his ability to avoid responsibility for his actions. But a kind of representation typical of festivity—mimicry—seems to fit him well here. The character has a marvelous self-awareness about his impersonations, one that has sometimes been hailed as a sign that he is truly a rounded and coherent character, but is actually a sign that, as Dryden said, he is really a "miscellany of humors or images, drawn from so many several men"—a miscellany played . . . by an actor exploring comic roles.

As Whitney sees it, the "festive multiplicity emphasized by this latter reading" helps explain how Falstaff "manages to be both exploiter and spokesman for the exploited." At this point, Whitney appeals to Bakhtin: Falstaff's "lines exhibit a double-voicing or doubly-oriented speech that suggests the speech's unhinging from individual persons."[17]

Not merely *like* an actor, but *as* an actor, Whitney's Falstaff materializes the *platea* and regales the theater audience with witty cynicisms that reflect and appeal to its baser instincts:

> Falstaff's joy is evident in his main speech (11–48), . . . [which] directly addresses the playgoers as if all were cronies in a tavern chuckling over Falstaff's particularly clever ruse. That ruse turns out to embody the subversion of fellowship . . . . Falstaff smirkingly confesses that he is ashamed of his soldiers, but his pleasure in what he has done is evident, and contagious—perhaps to our horror, we are clearly supposed to laugh with him. . . .
>
> . . . In the Coventry scene holiday cheer supports victimization: the audience is put in the position of someone like a tavern crony to whom Falstaff conspiratorially boasts of how he is making a bundle off the war. The scene shows festival appropriated by exploitative groups.[18]

Whitney emphasizes the carnivalesque features of the Coventry scene and depicts Falstaff working his theater audience with the presentational awareness of a standup comic:

> Carnivalesque play includes the playgoers and encourages the diversity of response that already seems to have been a common feature of playgoing. Shakespearean theater is in a process of evolution from a semi-professional drama enacted during holidays, in which playgoers were interactive participants, to a commercial, representational drama staged daily. Carnivalesque forms in this theater often still encourage participation of the playgoers, allowing for interpretive authority to be dispersed among them. (413)

The claim to find carnivalesque and participatory elements in this scene is incontrovertible. Yet if it would be ridiculous to reject outright the theater-centered premise of direct address associated with the claim, it can't be accepted without serious modification.

Whitney insists that his advocacy of "an audience-centered politics of mirth [that] would consider the mingling and mangling of diverse topical responses . . . need not entail scrapping one's sense of a play as a whole" (415). This reassurance is misplaced because the aesthetic integrity of a play "as a whole" is no longer something many of us lose much sleep over. I, at any rate, lose more sleep over the way Whitney's extradramatic focus tends to diminish my sense of Falstaff as an auditor for whose benefit or bane he performs his self-representations and impersonations. And my response to

Falstaff's performance depends less on my general sense "of a play as a whole" than on the concrete effect of a series of scenes that comment both on each other and on the performances of their major speakers.

Whitney's orientation toward the theater audience threatens to diminish our sense of continuity and conflict. For him, the cash value of John Dryden's view of Falstaff as "a miscellany of humors or images, drawn from so many several men" lies in its claim that carnivalesque play allows "interpretive authority to be dispersed among" Elizabethan playgoers who represent diverse social and political interests. This centrifugal thesis depends on a problematic strategy of reading: Whitney produces the effect of carnival by taking the scene out of its narrative/dramatic/textual context.

He treats the scene as an isolated moment embedded in an imaginary theater he populates with "diverse playgoing groups"—pro-war supporters of the Essex faction, plebeians, burghers—each of which gives the scene's topical allusions a different interpretive skew (448). Falstaff, whom Whitney imagines as directly addressing these groups, becomes their Rorschach test. The problem this poses for me is how to retain Whitney's insights into carnival while replacing his centrifugal reading with one that fastens on Falstaff as the self-testing subject of his own speech.

9. *Interlude*

The Clown as Dog

To imagine Falstaff as subject is to imagine the speaker on the model of the actor. He performs *like* the actor, but not *as* an actor. He *presents* his representation of himself, and he continuously audits and monitors this performance. It stands to reason that the speech of only some, perhaps relatively few, speakers lends itself to such "thick" interpretation.

Of course, I may be overstating the problem: We're not in danger of being swamped these days by an outpouring of thick and close interpretation. In our post–New Critical age, the opposite is more likely to be the case. There is a danger of reductive reading in which the relation of major speakers to their language is characterized in terms of the analysis of minor speaking parts. To illustrate this problem I turn to Robert Weimann's attempt, in his study of *Two Gentlemen of Verona*, to define a comic position that gives the character more parity with the actor—the position of characters the audience laughs *with* as opposed to those it laughs *at*.[1]

Weimann's example is Proteus's servant, the clown Launce. He distinguishes Launce from another clown, Speed, who is Valentine's servant. Whereas Speed's asides provoke laughter at others, Launce "and his family experience are the objects of his own mirth." Just as if he were the actor making fun of the character he plays, Launce joins the audience in laughing at himself. He is the "free and willing subject" of his mirth: "Much like Falstaff," he is "not merely witty in himself but the reason that others have and enjoy their own wit."[2]

Weimann's point is that in the traditional situation the audience laughs with the actor at the comic figure the actor plays but that the character who laughs with the audience at himself assimilates the perspective and position of the actor. "The real performance of the actor and the imaginative role of . . . [Launce] interact. . . . Within this unity the character's relations to the play world begin to dominate, but the comic ease and flexibility of these relations are still enriched by some traditional connection between the clowning actor and the laughing spectator." Because this connection increases the character's "insight into and criticism of the action of the play," it brings together actor, audience, and character in the utopian "laughter of solidarity."[3]

This is a rich and powerful insight, but Weimann's coupling of Launce with Falstaff as critical "countervoices" is too easy, He fails to distinguish between different intensities of self-representation. Suppose that we find in the language of both speakers "implicit insight into and criticism of the action" of their respective plays.[4] Do we also find that the insight and criticism are equally attributable to both Falstaff and Launce?

Because Weimann's reading practice is disciplined to follow the track of his social history of theater, particular passages of analysis are often narrowly constrained by their function as examples of his theme, and his treatment of Launce is no exception. Weimann uses him to illustrate Shakespeare's contribution to the changing structure of relations between theatrical and fictional "worlds." Launce is like the actor who shares with his audience the genial laughter occasioned by (his performance of) Launce the character.

Meredith Skura takes Weimann to be arguing that Launce's "ridiculousness within the play's world—his shame and isolation—is mitigated by the actor [Will] Kempe's connection" to the spectators: They "laugh at Launce but identify with Kempe."[5] Skura distorts Weimann's claim, which is that spectators identify with Launce, or Kempe-in-Launce. But her distortion accurately registers the fact that his argument for the integration of actor with character sometimes denies the character the richness or complexity Weimann clearly wants to confer on it.

Skura's critique of Weimann is based on a darker interpretation of Launce's soliloquies. Her reading is reinforced by a study of the Elizabethan actor's subculture that differs from Weimann's in two ways. She pays greater attention to the effects on the actor of his problematic social position, and she analyzes the interplay of those effects with greater subtlety.

Skura compares Launce's speech in act 3, scene 2—in which he complains about his "cruel hearted cur," Crab (he "has no more pity in him than a dog")—to the "introductory monologue" of the "typical Elizabethan clown." Launce is "a kind of comic Aeneas, stepping forth to tell his sad tale to the only Dido he has: to us, the spectators in the audience. In soliciting our response, Launce's soliloquy foregrounds his ambiguous relation to the audience, who both are and are not there; he calls attention to the precariousness of the actor's position and to the audience's multiple roles in validating it."[6]

This precariousness is comically intensified by the uncertainties—behavioral as well as ontological—connected with the presence on stage of a real dog representing Launce's dog Crab (but not presenting itself as representing Crab).[7] Skura goes on to observe that although Weimann "also finds Launce an epitome of theatrical precariousness," he avoids the "dystopian implications of clowning," and of its social cost to the performer, by confining his comments to this speech, which is the first and lighter of Launce's two monologues about Crab.[8] Weimann, who never mentions the dog, doesn't deal with the more humiliating moment in act 4, scene 4, when Launce "literally takes on the dog's identity—at least takes on his sins"—and makes the audience laugh at his "self-abasement . . . like a player 'playing the fool', as Thomas Nashe sneered, to earn a few pennies—and our laughter."[9]

As a clownish servant, Launce is a boundary figure: He dramatizes the paradoxes inherent in the theater's edgy negotiations with illusion and reality. The audience he conjures up by extradramatic address is invited to laugh not only at him but also at the serious knots and plots of the main action: at the deceptions, desires, self-delusion, and self-abasement, inscribed in the language-games of romance and friendship.[10] *Two Gentleman* continually indexes the conventionality of these games by the conspicuousness of its citational play.[11] This makes Launce more important as a source of irony directed reflexively by the play at itself than he is as the subject of his own speech.

Skura nevertheless ably succeeds in depicting him as a complex version of the clown figure by identifying the theatrical pressures his monologue exhibits with the clown/actor's occupational vulnerability. In a remarkable discussion, she focuses on the social dependency, the ethical self-abasement, and the psychic cost, attendant on "the use the clown makes of himself in order to secure unity with society." She notes that such "self-deprecating humor" as Launce displays when he "takes on the role of 'dog'" may elicit from the audience laughter that is "tinged with sadism even in its solidarity."[12] This amounts to an acerb revision of the bland and blinkered praise Weimann bestows on Launce because, "much like Falstaff, [he] is not merely witty in himself but the reason that others have and enjoy their own wit."[13]

Skura is careful not to lump Falstaff together with Launce. She devotes a chapter to the former, six pages to the latter. Nevertheless, she focuses on something they have in common: their canine connection. A transition from Launce to Falstaff is easy to make in terms of her analysis by noting that the evocation of "laughter tinged with sadism" may reflect the tinge of masochism in a character who both suffers—even enjoys—his haplessness and wants to be put down for it. Thinking of Launce, Falstaff, and Crab, I'm tempted by a fortuitous analogy to confuse small things with great, and comedy with pathos, by mentioning the last words of Joseph K. as he watches (not feels) "the final act" in the putative ending of *The Trial*: "'Like a dog!' he said; it was as if he meant the shame of it to outlive him."

10. *The King's Names*

Only one of the three versions of the protagonist's name adequately designates the consistency of his self-representation throughout the tetralogy. It may be that some purely irrational prejudice makes it easier for me to sympathize with a Harry than with a Henry, but I find the heartiness of "Hal" generally repelling. The cultivation of sympathy is not unimportant in an approach oriented toward reading "with suspicion," yet there are more substantive reasons behind this preference.

One is to help counteract a tendency to emphasize discontinuity between *1 Henry IV* and *Henry V*—as, for example, in William Babula's statement that "E. M. W. Tillyard is right in his assertion that Shakespeare in *Henry V* was 'jettisoning the character he had created' in the Henry IV plays. The Hal that developed out of those earlier histories is not present at the opening of *Henry V*."[1] This accords with the notion that Harry's "I would have all such offenders so cut off" (3.6.111) includes Hal among the offenders: Henry = Harry – Hal. "Hal" signifies the figure that condenses within it the interaction between Harry and Falstaff while "Henry" signifies the antithetical figure produced by rejecting "Hal" and Falstaff.

Whether the amputation of Hal—which, in this view, is the price of kingship—is judged essential or too costly, the difference between Hal and Henry often gets attributed to the demands imposed on Shakespeare by his adherence to chronicle history. Since it's assumed that the change from madcap prince to heroic warrior king was dictated by Shakespeare's sources, it becomes possible to confine interpretation of the consequences to *Henry V* and deal with the problem of King Henry in isolation from the other plays.

There's nevertheless an important insight in the premise that Hal has been "jettisoned," but it is distorted by attributing it solely to Shakespeare. Why bypass Harry? Why not credit him with the discontinuity produced by his reformation? Whatever the reason, it's clear that the strong tonal contrast between the two names, "Hal" and "Henry," makes it easier to view their bearers as two different characters and thus to view the plays in which they appear as discontinuous.

We can restore continuity by insisting that it is Harry who plans to appear before the world as Hal first and Henry after. It's he who jettisons Hal but continues to enjoy the relatively informal appellative style of "Harry." It's Harry who values his flexibility, values his ability to move upward or downward on the scale of social being between Hal and Henry, and who plays the Prince of Wales or conqueror of France with as much élan as he plays the Corinthian prince of good fellows.

Most interpreters of *Henry V* refer to the king as Henry, no doubt because he is the titular hero. Apart from the aid and comfort this gives to interpretive isolationism, it is misleading at the simplest factual level: From the time he is first mentioned in *Richard II* everyone calls Harry Harry (or Hal, or the Prince) and no one calls him Henry until the final scene of *Henry V*, where he is responsible for the two exceptions in the tetralogy:

(1) While wooing Katharine, he offers her—in exchange for the voluntary self-submission that will mitigate what is otherwise one article in the conqueror's schedule of demands—not only England, Ireland, and France, but also "Henry Plantagenet" (5.2.249–53). Plantagenet is the family name of the line of English kings descended from Geoffrey of Anjou. Here it connotes the French origin of the dynasty embodied in the fifth Henry, who is now taking steps to perpetuate it.

(2) Shortly after this, Exeter cites the article in which Harry demands to be addressed in official documents as "filz Henry, Roy d'Angleterre, Héritier de France" (repeated in Latin; 5.2.357–60). Both the dynastic name and the formal title are functions in the game of genealogical politics. Harry reserves the formality and severity of "Henry" for such ritual instruments of conquest as the promissory foreplay of courtship and the ceremonial rubric by which, refathering himself, he legitimizes his claim to French lands, displaces the Dauphin, and negotiates his liberation from his first father's tainted inheritance: "No king of England, if not king of France" (2.2.193); "Now beshrew my father's ambition! he was thinking of civil wars when he got me" (5.2.236–37).

A few lines later he names himself not Harry but Henry, and not Monmouth nor Lancaster nor even England but Plantagenet (5.2.253). By this move he distances his identity from recent fissures and inserts it in the more venerable, more inclusive, house of the Anglo-Gallic Angevins. Even as he aspires to be the formidable Henry of chronicle fame, he resists the loss and incorporation of Harry into that figure. Political legitimacy is not quite enough.

That the courtship is gratuitous from the standpoint of alliance and that it evokes comedic conventions of fulfilled desire and mutual consent indicate a need on Harry's part not so much for approval or acceptance as for Katharine's voluntary assent to his persuasion. This will make her a partner, give her a share in the responsibility for her own conquest and thus limit his ethical liability. Although he dramatizes his advantage in the scene, as when he insists that she speak in broken English although he knows French, he seeks moral and personal legitimacy by making her a coequal accomplice in what would otherwise be a kind of rape.

Taken by itself, *Henry V* solicits an objective response to its protagonist: either praise or something else for this mirror of all Christian kings. It allows you to wonder a little about the reasons behind his notorious disclaimers of responsibility, and if you do you're at liberty to rationalize, condemn, or ignore them. But it doesn't ask you to worry too much about what Harry might think of himself. His fear of attaint, his continual search for self-exculpation, his desire to avoid "the imputation of wickedness"—these become the main issue only when you situate the play in the tetralogical echo chamber. What does the Prince know, and when did he learn it?

Tetralogically speaking, the most important thing Harry inherits and appropriates from his predecessors is the discourse of a wounded and self-wounding conscience. This discourse is represented as operating on two interrelated levels. The first is his fear of being tainted by the fault his father made, and his desire to distance and decontaminate himself from the guilt of usurpation and regicide. The second is the bad-faith scenario through which he actualizes this desire: the scenario announced in his "I know you all" soliloquy early in *1 Henry IV.* There he played the Prodigal Son, blamed his wild oats on his "misleaders" as if they had been responsible, and exultantly castigated the world for believing what he encouraged the world to believe.

Harry's deep and protracted investment in this scenario can be gauged by comparing two passages. The first is from the soliloquy I just mentioned.

> So when this loose behavior I throw off,
> And pay the debt I never promised,
> By how much better than my word I am,

> By so much shall I falsify men's hopes;
> ....
> I'll so offend, to make offence a skill,
> Redeeming time when men least think I will. (*1 Henry IV,* 1.2.203–12)

The second passage is from the announcement that precedes his denunciation of Falstaff at the end of *2 Henry IV*:

> Presume not that I am the thing I was;
> For God doth know, so shall the world perceive,
> That I have turn'd away my former self;
> So will I those that kept my company. (*2 Henry IV,* 5.5.56–59)

Since these two passages represent a promise and its fulfillment, they dramatize the singleness, the integrity, of the speaker's purpose over time. Therefore, they contradict the assertion that he is not the thing he was. He knows that he never was but only played the prodigal, that he was and therefore remains the misleader of his misleaders and the falsifier of the hopes he falsely planted in others.

He knows this in part because Falstaff never stops reminding him of the possibility that he (Harry) may be more sinning than sinned against. Critics often follow Harry's lead in treating Falstaff as a kind of Lampwick figure who corrupts young "Hal"—as young Harry likes to be called—in the stews of Pleasure Island. But it's time to start thinking of Falstaff as Harry's oversized Jiminy Cricket.

From the moment of Harry's interview with his dying father late in *2 Henry IV* to the end of *Henry V,* his language betrays the dominance of one motive: the concern for moral solvency. This is suggested by the rhetorical intensity with which he "scours [the] faults" of others while persisting in his famous disclaimers of responsibility. When he asks the Archbishop of Canterbury whether he can claim the French throne "with right and conscience," he's told that he can do it because he's the direct heir and surrogate of his "mighty ancestors," and especially of Edward the Black Prince and his father, Edward III, whose claim to French territories Harry in effect inherits.

In exhorting him to emulate "the former lions of your blood," the peers articulate his desire to cross Bolingbroke and Richard off the lineage chart and to refather himself in order to avoid being tainted by "the fault / his father made." For Harry to go to France will be magically to go back in time and to reverse recent history—in Freud's terms, to make it unhappened. "No king of England, if not King of France" (2.2.193) is more than a boast. It precisely expresses the need he feels to disown his paternal inheritance, make himself his grandfather's direct heir, and thereby purge England and himself of the moral taint of usurpation and regicide.

This is the tetralogically grounded cause of his claim to France, and it's the justification the peers make for his pursuing the French throne with right and conscience. It's what he asks his soldiers to risk their lives for, in his stirring St. Crispin's day aria and elsewhere. And it's in bad faith. It has nothing to do with the national interest.[2] For this essentially private war, the king's press will produce food for powder, and with it, all the disruptions of common life the soldier, Michael Williams, itemizes with his moving comments on why soldiers don't die well (4.1.135–49). Blood will be shed, people will be asked to risk their lives and leave their affairs in disorder, but not for England and Saint George. They will die for Harry "solus" and "egregious," and Williams insists that "if the cause be not good, the king himself hath a heavy reckoning to make" when the body parts of slain soldiers gather together "at the latter day" (4.1.135–36, 138–39).

Harry doesn't respond immediately, but shows himself troubled by this at the end of the scene when, praying to God, he worries that his public acts of penance for his father's usurpation and regicide come too late (4.1.298–311). But the prayer only brings out the true orientation of a war that has little or nothing to do with the safety or well-being of England, and everything to do with dynastic guilt and bad conscience. And this, as the language of act 4 repeatedly suggests, is a source of profound danger to a king who cherishes his self-respect, a king whose language betrays the desire to overbear any attaint to which his political decisions expose him.

By act 4, the Chorus has a harder time subduing his language to its political task of organizing a nation of Harry-watchers into a cheering and marching section. Now that he has to help the beloved royal warrior "overbear attaint," some of those dark touches irrupt in his own encomiastic rhetoric. Sounding the "dreadful note of preparation," guttering his description with infernal flickers, his imagery fuses military with spiritual danger, and sets the historical drama within the cosmic field of the drama of salvation and damnation.

If it's been established that the sentiments of the Chorus are those the king would like himself and the world to believe, then by the same logic shouldn't the Chorus's dark touches register the buried fear that motivates Harry's intense need for justification? This need becomes more critical as he moves from play to play, from Shrewsbury to Westminster to Agincourt, and as he approaches the moment when he will ask his "ruin'd band" to sacrifice themselves for a cause that touches the royal captain more nearly than it does England. ("God for Harry, England and St. George." Harry comes first.)

The need for justification is nevertheless made to rely on an inadequate objective correlative, the medium of stage warfare, and can only find satisfaction in that melodramatic form of closure. The Chorus describes the scene of battle as a form of flight that mocks the historical event it refers to, and he concludes with another appeal for our help:

> And so our scene must to the battle fly;
> Where, O for pity! we shall much disgrace
> With four or five most vile and ragged foils,
> Right ill-dispos'd in brawl ridiculous,
> The name of Agincourt. Yet sit and see;
> Minding true things by what their mock'ries be. (48–53)

Against the nocturnal background of the preceding lines, this apology points in two different directions. On the one hand, it does its conventional choric work by asking us to help the play transcend the limits of theater so that Harry's famous victory may receive the imaginative and political justification it deserves. But on the other hand, the exhortation only extends the limits of theater to the history it represents. It marks historical theater and theatrical history as merely different levels of "smooth comforts false." Both the stage battle and its referent in chronicle history are displacements of Harry's and England's inward wars. Both are mockeries of "true things" and "true wrongs" that can't be adequately represented on the stage.

As I said before, "No king of England, if not King of France" states the method by which Harry plans to purge England and himself of the taint of usurpation and regicide. And only in this context can we account for the entertaining but weird portrayal of the French. The main question to be asked about the French is why they are such total Losers. C. L. Barber long ago noted that Shakespeare makes the French "comically contemptible," and what Gary Taylor says about Pistol applies equally well to the French—his "whole style holds out the promise of a crushing deflation."[3]

Several critics have noted that the Dauphin, whom Harry eventually replaces as heir to the French throne, is a pathetic bungler. Peter Erickson points out that Harry himself casts the Dauphin in "the role of the undependable bad son who deserves to be beaten."[4] Since that's a role Harry earlier had pretended to play, the Dauphin serves—among other things—as a site of exorcism and displacement. In his effeminacy and hippophilia he also stands as a parody of Hotspur, who waged a strenuous campaign in *1 Henry IV* against contamination by anything connected with the frailty named Woman. The French are represented as magnificently incompetent, a chivalry of braggart soldiers worried about what the women they jokingly equate with horses will think of them.

Although the Dauphin and his father may by themselves serve the scapegoat function specific to Harry and his inward wars, they're also members of a collective French scapegoat constructed by allusions to the prior history of those wars in the Henriad. *Henry V* exports from England to France the parodic representation of an impotent political community. This community asks for trouble and tends toward self-subversion.

"The king," says Corporal Nym, "hath run bad humors on the knight" (2.1.121), meaning Falstaff. After Harry runs bad humors on the three traitors (2.3.166–81), he leads the English army to France. In the light of Corporal Nym's science of physiology, the English campaign is Harry's way of evacuating the "bad humors" of the Henriad kings, his way of enabling Englishmen "swoln with some other grief" to transfer their inward wars to a legitimate target, an alien nation.

The French war displaces, condenses, represents, and legitimizes—because it exports—the apprehensions that threaten the English throughout the Henriad: apprehensions about one's moral being or manhood, anxiety about diminishing self-esteem, the fear and desire of self-evasion and self-undoing that attach to the dialectics of the quest for honor, autonomy, power, and good conscience. I want to emphasize the generalized character of this displacement. Not much is to be gained by concentrating blame on Harry for his tendency to pass bad humors on others since the same tendency is evident in the play as a whole: *Henry V* passes bad humors from England to France.

The source of this tendency is not the "psyche" of Harry nor of any other single character. Its source is the text. But which text, that of *Henry V* or that of the Henriad? In the isolated play, the treatment of the French produces the effect of nationalism. But in the tetralogical echo chamber of the Henriad, it produces the effect of surrealism. (The Olivier production beautifully conveys this effect by moving from the "unworthy scaffold" to the "vasty fields" of a France visually represented as a fairyland, half pastoral and half illuminated miniature.)

Harry's war and his famous one-sided victory are surreal because in a variety of ways the French are portrayed as desiring, as asking for, the punishment the English underdog inflicts on them. In effect they extend Harry the same invitation Richard II had, more mischievously, extended to Harry's father: "Here, cousin, seize the crown." Their complicity is implied, for example, by the simile the French king uses when he notes that "England his approaches makes as fierce / As waters to the sucking of a gulf." The figure betrays the complicity of the French gulf in attracting England's "heady currance."

This mutual attraction is dramatized by the juxtaposition of Harry's "once more unto the breach" aria in act 3, scene 3 to the English language lesson in act 3, scene 4. First, Harry tries to scare the French by loudly inviting his soldiers to commit gang rape on the women of Harfleur. Then in the next scene we see Katharine learning to enumerate her body parts in English, as if she already anticipates having to do so and is preparing to offer her body as the prize or victim of armed conflict.

Thus the desire that had pervaded the England of *2 Henry IV*—the desire to "be had" (or "get had"), to get oneself punished, to invite violation and judgment—is transferred to the French. The anxiety about manhood and fear of woman featured in Hotspur's discourse of honor, and sustained in the ferocious parodies of *2 Henry IV,* is first exported to France on the slow boat of the Archbishop of Canterbury's speech about the Salic law (1.2.35–95). He demonstrates in ear-deadening detail how the French imposition and breaches of that law testify to their failed attempt to eliminate the power of women in dynastic politics. The Archbishop makes it clear that when they apply the law to invalidate Harry's claim, they also invalidate that of all "the kings of France" from Carolingian rulers "unto this day" (1.2.90). This preliminary hint of their penchant for self-undoing introduces the more active campaign served up by the Dauphin's insult to Harry.

In all these ways, France, the French, and the French war provide the conspicuously inadequate objective correlative of the Henriad's inward wars. When T. S. Eliot introduced the concept of the objective correlative, he criticized its deficiency in *Hamlet,* which, he complained, "is full of some stuff that the writer could not drag to light, [or] contemplate."[5] In my view, the French in *Henry V* are full of some tetralogical and Lancastrian stuff that the English couldn't or didn't want to drag to light. For example: Richard's war on himself and on his usurper's conscience, which leads to the war the usurper, Henry IV, wages on himself via his conflicts with the Percy faction and with his son Harry, which in turn leads to the threat of inward war Harry deflects from himself by running bad humors on Hotspur, Henry, Falstaff, and other factors or scapegoats at home and abroad.

I conclude with a comment on the way Shakespearean strategies of conclusion dramatize the intimate relation between their textual inadequacy and their theatrical effectiveness. In the Henriad, the complex "inward wars" of Richard, Henry, and Harry—the wars of discourse that divide each against himself and all against each other—are precipitated out and discharged in civic and foreign quarrels. Moving from text to stage they are, in a word, detextualized. In what may be called terminal detextualization, the staging of battles and other external forms of conflict resolution appears as unsatisfactory because it is the reductive displacement of inner self-division to outward circumstances.

These scenes produce resistance or dissatisfaction in spectators and readers because they have the effect of policing unruly passages and stubborn textual overtones that vibrate out of tune with the music at the close. "I understand a fury in your words, / But not the words": When the fury is channeled outward in physical violence, the perplexity continues to vibrate. Shakespeare's final Exeunts order us out of the theater because the unfinished business it leaves us with can't be transacted there.

It is as if, after all the buildup, physical battle tests nothing more significant than skill in fencing and counterfeiting; as if the historical victories and theatrical closures punctuated by athletic swordplay and the other conventions that provide this traveling music are—again in Rumor's words—"smooth comforts false." For that isn't where Shakespeare's protagonists kill and die. They kill and die in their language, and we have to follow the lethal traces down into its burrows and rhizomes. What stage death offers the hero is an escape from this verbal dying into the rest that is silence. What it offers the audience is something like a critique of this commitment to stageable closure. When the hero is on the verge of escaping from his bondage to words, woman, civil life, and perhaps life itself, his drive toward transcendence may be betrayed, diminished, by the very convention of theatrical closure to which he has committed himself.

Henry V shows how both theater and the history it represents—Harry's French campaign—can be used to make trifles of terrors: They turn English terrors into French trifles. Placed under textual perusal, the forms of action congenial to staged narrative, the performances that make for good theater and effective politics, are represented as opportunities for strategic displacements of responsibility and culpability.

Shakespearean texts thus offer a moral critique of the performance that is their fate, a preemptive critique of theater in particular and theatricality in general. However much the conspicuous theatricality of *Richard II* differs from that of *Henry V*, it works in both plays to raise moral questions about the projects of Richard and Harry—about the motives informing their practices of self-representation, self-justification, self-doubt, and self-evasion. Although the texts of the history plays proclaim their ability to do justice to theater, they question the ability of theater to do justice to them. This questioning thematically informs the behavior of royal actors who, in staging themselves, simultaneously delight in their performances and fail to be fully persuaded by them.

11. *Rabbits, Ducks, Lions, Foxes*

A Henrician Bestiary

Once more into the fray may be one time too many. Still, the vaunted generosity of the Shakespeare text seems both to seduce and to justify the interpreter into whose flanks the "more, more" of Blake's madman digs its spurs. The battle between celebratory and cynical responses to Harry continues to rage despite irenic attempts to clear it up.

Norman Rabkin argued in 1976 that we see *Henry V* sometimes as a duck and sometimes as a rabbit, but never both at the same time. He attributed the incompatibility of rival interpretations to the "rival gestalts" of the play itself.[1] A few years later, Gary Taylor converted Rabkin's duck/rabbit interpretation into a distributive thesis about media differences. "It is," he writes, "as though spectators consistently saw a rabbit, where readers consistently saw a duck."[2] The figure implies that plays scamper swiftly on stage but waddle awkwardly when confined to the page.

A lion/fox would better represent this dilemma than a rabbit/duck, since, according to Taylor, playgoing produces the leonine "mirror of all Christian kings" while reading produces a vulpine "Machiavellian militarist."[3] If rabbits run, lions ramp, and if ducks waddle, foxes slink. The transformation retains Taylor's values, for the lion's heraldic ramping suits the theater of *Henry V* while the fox finds refuge among the rhizomes of the text.

Taylor's thesis was anticipated by A. R. Humphreys in a passage elaborating on D. A. Traversi's remark that *Henry V* has been "most generally popular when imperfectly understood." Humphreys insists that imperfect understanding is appropriate to the play's theatrical mode:

> The play raises fewer questions in the theater than in the study—impetus carries one over obstacles, whereas deliberation makes them seem larger than they are. It raises interestingly the problem of criticizing a dramatic

> action . . . : how much analytical going back and forth over the evidence is admissible when the very nature of dramatic art is to carry the narrative vigorously onwards? . . . The play's dynamism as it passes on the stage allows little time for thought, and the Chorus, as presenter of events, delivers us over, unreflecting, to those heroic assumptions which are its creed. *And, basically, this is right*: the play's aim is to celebrate heroic actions under a heroic king.[4]

Taylor articulates this basic position much more fully and aggressively than Humphreys. He makes five points:

(1) A superior interpretation of the play obeys the principle of economy by putting forth "the simplest hypothesis which explains the data."

(2) In the shift from seeing to reading, the benign comic and heroic emphases that dominate performance diminish while theme- and analogue-hunting produces hypotheses too complex to be grasped in the moment-by-moment flow of theatrical presentation.

(3) When critics take advantage of their leisure to develop an analogy—between Harry and Hotspur, Harry and Pistol, and so on—they tend to stress "an abstracted similarity in conceptual content" and to disregard "dissimilarity of detail." This produces patterns different from those grasped by audiences who lack leisure and attend to the detail of the theatrical moment.

(4) Since these unbalanced analogies are invidious and ironic, they go against the grain of the heroism featured by performance, so that

(5) in a single blow, critical reading violates the integrity of the play, the heroic lion, and the playgoer's response.[5]

For Taylor, then, the very structure and opportunities of reading are liabilities because they encourage antitheatrical reactions. These reactions coalesce in an unfavorable view of Harry. A more adequate account of the play would suppress the characteristic operations of reading in order to approximate or imitate those of performance and playgoing.

Even if we were to grant Taylor's first premise for the sake of argument, there are still several weak links in his position. Premise (2) suggests that the shift from seeing to reading is more determinate than it actually is. Reading per se may diminish the benign emphases by distancing the power of performance, but readers are not slaves to the limits of their medium. They are perfectly capable of imagining any kind of performance they want, including the kind Taylor describes and prefers.

Premise (3) is absurd. The implied charge that critics in general ignore the differences in their analogies is bizarre enough to require more documentation than Taylor supplies. And it is belied by many studies in which authors try to avoid the lion/fox alternatives, studies that register the complexity of Shakespeare's conception of Harry by striking a balance between critical and sympathetic reactions. The obvious purpose of this premise is to make the point contained in premise (4) and to nail down the case against reading in premise (5). Taylor's argument, then, defends the double claim (a) that opposing assessments of the play and/or its protagonist line up with the differences between media, and (b) that the playgoer's positive view of Harry the lion is superior to the negative view of Harry the fox that reading encourages and literary critics actualize.

Buried in this argument is the seed of a valuable insight into the politics of theater and the tensions of stage-centered reading—the tensions produced by the conflicting emphases of the theatrical and literary models. But the seed won't sprout unless it gets transplanted from Taylor's reductive theatrical model to the soil of a literary model that encourages a policy of equal time for opposing viewpoints—a model that allows both for the theatrical critique of armchair interpretation and for the literary critique of theater.

These two critiques carry different historical orientations: The critique of armchair interpretation is restricted to contemporary controversies, whereas the critique of theater makes contact with Elizabethan concerns. On the one hand, there doesn't seem to have been much need for Elizabethan playwrights to criticize armchair interpretation, though the modern critic may easily find and apply the odd phrase that describes this target ("sicklied o'er with the pale cast of thought," "thinking too precisely on th'event"). On the other hand, there is evidence not only of Elizabethan writers' dissatisfaction with theater but also of their textual representation of its defects and constraints.

If we strip Taylor's argument of its invidious asymmetry, the buried insight begins to emerge: The Shakespeare text demands its readers to shuttle back and forth between two incompatible perspectives on Harry. One is produced by reading the play slowly. The other is produced by imagining it staged at performance tempo.

In order to transplant this shuttle insight from Taylor's argument to mine, two obstacles, one minor and one major, have to be cleared away. The minor obstacle consists of a limitation in the rabbit/duck analogy: It belongs to the class of visual conundrums that prevent the simultaneous apprehension of differing or opposed interpretations. No visual object in this class can provide an adequate model for the complex interplay of discourses that ambiguates the text.

Taylor notes this limitation and criticizes Rabkin's use of the analogy.[6] He claims that the figure will not work for *Henry V* because it suggests a more complex response than is possible for either playgoers or readers. But even as he discounts the figure, he deploys it to drive home his distinction between the playgoer's rabbit or lion and the reader's duck or fox. He thus activates the notion he criticizes. His use of the analogy differs from Rabkin's only in assigning one interpretation to playgoers and the other to readers. In doing this he flirts with the danger that weakens Rabkin's solution to the problem of "rival gestalts": the danger of assuming that it is more important for readers and viewers to reach a simple verdict about Harry than it is to explore his language for signs that the lion/fox dilemma may pose a serious problem *for him*.

The major obstacle to Taylor's insight is the tendency for theatrical reductionism to bleed into political reductionism. There are two versions of this tendency. The first is promoted by approaches (like Taylor's) that discredit negative assessments of Harry as critical mistakes produced by overzealous and antitheatrical reading. If we can show—as Rabkin has convincingly shown—that such "mistakes" are supported by textual evidence, then ruling the evidence inadmissible discourages the effort to take the negative view of Harry seriously enough to try to modify or counter it. It discourages the propensity for a close reading and sympathetic "hearing" of Harry's language—a reading that explores his anxious desire for moral legitimacy. The second version of the reductive tendency derives from what is in effect a critique of the kind of political endorsement implicit in the celebratory view defended by Taylor and others. I'll say more about this than about the first version because the example I've chosen illustrates some of the strengths and weaknesses of strategies we've come to associate with New Historicism.

Taylor's view of *Henry V* appears to better advantage in his introductory essay to the Oxford edition of the play than it does in *Moment by Moment*. The former takes more account of the trouble with Harry, and therefore the attempt to domesticate the trouble stands out more clearly. It may be indebted to the war-is-hell defense of Harry that A. R. Humphreys makes in the New Penguin edition.

Humphreys takes the position that *Henry V* relates "real heroism to the real grimness of war and the real conditions of life." Shakespeare depicts Harry as aware that "war is a nightmare as well as an adventure," and, far from glorifying war, he brilliantly conveys what it "requires from leaders and followers in times of desperate danger." Nevertheless, he accepts "without question the popular case for the war, the popular zest that went with it, and the popular sense of triumph that resulted from it."[7]

In similar fashion, Taylor doesn't blink away the cold-bloodedness evinced by Harry's rejection of Falstaff, his ultimatum at Harfleur, and his killing of the French prisoners. Nor does he ignore the doubts the play initially raises about the motives behind Henry's claim to the French throne. But he asserts that all these episodes induce a single pattern of reactions: "Shakespeare first makes us suspicious of or repelled by an action, and only afterwards justifies, emotionally at least, Henry's behavior."[8]

Taylor argues persuasively that "the Dauphin's insult convinces an audience that the French deserve what Harry has decided to give them; at Harfleur 'Use mercy to them all' and the discovery that Harry was bluffing transform our responses to his vicious ultimatum; at Agincourt the senseless French atrocity of the killing of the boys emotionally justifies, retrospectively, Harry's necessary atrocity in killing the prisoners." The atrocity is necessary "to save his small army, which cannot afford to guard the prisoners while at the same time resisting a second French attack." Taylor notes that Shakespeare's juxtaposition of this act "with the equally cold, equally disturbing rejection of Falstaff is entirely his own. The inference could hardly be clearer: only a man capable of the one could have been capable of the other, and only a man capable of both could have become the hero-king of Agincourt."[9]

In this penetrating commentary, Taylor's focus is restricted to the larger dramatic action. For him the subject of *Henry V* is Harry's military campaign and triumph, which we should judge by the same criteria we use to judge actual or historical events. He doesn't entertain the possibility that the play may be as much about "theater" as it is about "history"—the possibility that it may be *about* the meaning of the relationship between the dramatic event and its theatrical representation.

The effect of Taylor's narrow focus is to reduce his statement about the play to a political statement, and such statements are inherently controversial. As a defense of the war, of the hero-king, and of Tudor ideology, his reading is vulnerable to all the familiar arguments opposed to this position.

And since it rules certain kinds of interpretive evidence inadmissible, it deprives itself of textual resources that could have strengthened his defense of the hero's moral legitimacy. This exposes Harry to the kind of ideological critique mounted under the banner of "cultural materialism" or New Historicism.

Stephen Greenblatt's trenchant version of this critique in "Invisible Bullets" resembles Taylor's in exploring the play's arousal and containment of negative reactions to Harry. In my opinion, Greenblatt's is the greatest essay ever written about Shakespeare's history plays. He both explicates and questions the celebratory view of containment taken for granted by Taylor, Humphreys, and others.[10] He gives his account of the containment pattern a different slant from Taylor's, and there are two reasons for the difference. First, he considers *Henry V* in tetralogical context and develops an ingenious hypothesis about the pattern of political change the Henriad displays. Second, he isolates a particular mechanism that enables him to demonstrate the moral dubiety inscribed in the politics of containment. These two moves are dialectically related: The sequence is depicted as enacting a particular form of the disenchantment pattern, while the mechanism paradoxically counters and secures that pattern by a strategy of reenchantment.

As to the first, Greenblatt argues that the questionable qualities and strategies monopolized by Harry in *1 Henry IV* radiate in the next play into "the 'larger order' of the Lancastrian state." In *2 Henry IV* not only "the self-fashioning of the modern prince" but also "the founding of the modern state . . . is shown to be based upon acts of calculation, intimidation, and deceit." The "moral authority" of England's "monarchical power" rather than Harry alone gives rise to "a hypocrisy so deep that the hypocrites themselves believe it."[11]

Greenblatt claims that *Henry V* extends to the theater audience the task of falsification and self-deceit, the need to invest in "the illusion of magnificence" necessary to overcome "the subversive doubts the play continually awakens."[12] In the larger context of the tetralogy this reenchantment is delegated to the fourth play. But it is reproduced *in parvo* throughout the last two plays by "an anticipatory subversion of each of the play's central claims."[13] Greenblatt brilliantly observes that the ideology articulated in Henry's insomnia soliloquy in *2 Henry IV*, 3.1, was expressed by Falstaff in the preceding scene, but expressed "as humbug *before* it makes its appearance as official truth."[14]

The effect of this "proleptic" parody "is not (as with straightforward parodies) to ridicule the claims of high seriousness." It is "rather to mark them as slightly suspect and to encourage guarded skepticism." Greenblatt treats this as a variation of Marx's famous *Eighteenth Brumaire* formula: "The great events and speeches all occur twice: the first time as fraud, the second as truth"—and the "truth" is therefore hollowed out by "intimations of bad faith."[15]

Greenblatt's view of containment and reenchantment has often been misrepresented as benign, but he himself centers on its subversive character. Thus his deployment of the hypothesis and mechanism mentioned above casts dark shadows over his explanation of the politics of reenchantment in *Henry V.* Confronted with "subversive doubts" and a consequent "gap between real and ideal" featured in the representation of Harry and the monarchy, "the spectators are induced to make up the difference" and "to be dazzled by their own imaginary identification with the conqueror. The ideal king must be in large part the invention of the audience" in the theater as it is in the Elizabethan theater-state.[16]

To understand this, "we need in effect a poetics of Elizabethan power . . . inseparable . . . from a poetics of theater." Greenblatt's effort to put such a dual perspective into play leads him to extract from the play's politics of audience co-optation the general message that "all kings are 'decked' out by the imaginary forces of the spectators, and a sense of the limitations of king or theater only excites a more compelling exercise of these forces." *Co-optation* is my term rather than Greenblatt's, but it reflects his tougher-minded version of the containment pattern Gary Taylor picks out, and it also reflects his insistence that the play "is remarkably self-conscious about this dependence upon the audience's power of invention."[17]

Greenblatt's powerful analysis suggests to me that Humphreys and Taylor have been co-opted. Viewed in terms of the mechanisms he describes, their enthusiastic support of Harry's war and the grounds on which they defend its validity indicate a heavy investment in "the illusion of magnificence." Their investment is narrowly aestheticized and centered on "a poetics of the theater" that is hermetically sealed off from serious attention (and skeptical reaction) to "a poetics of Elizabethan power."

Humphreys, for example, insists that the play requires us to be "willingly naive rather than innocent. It would be innocent to rise from it feeling idealistic about policy or war," since "the underside of such things is sufficiently revealed, though at times in an oddly incidental, or accidental manner." For the play to work, one needs to cultivate naïveté, to "give one's skepticism a day off and let one's gusto serve instead, though it will at times prove a disturbing gusto, as at others exhilarating." If one goes along "with the play's fine confidence about what it is doing" and "yields to its convictions, the result will be a slight anaesthetizing of the intellect but a marked exhilaration in the pulse, a stirring pleasure in eloquence."[18] Gary Taylor's view, as we saw, is similar except for the narrative shape he gives to the pattern of containment. Any "necessary atrocity" along the way is smoothed out by the war-is-hell theory, by the subsequent justification of Harry's behavior, and by the carnival release of the play's romantico-comico-heroical ending.

If this benign reading appears to be subverted by Greenblatt's account, the subversion is contained by a move that brings the account back into line with the Taylor-Humphreys approach in one important respect. Greenblatt states that "the intimations of bad faith" which the play gives off are "deferred"—deferred "even today, for in the wake of full-scale ironic readings . . . it is not at all clear that *Henry V* can be successfully performed as subversive."[19] That, however, is his only reference to "readings." Everywhere else he refers to spectators, audience, theater, and stage. This is symptomatic of a problem in his interpretation.

Greenblatt's analysis far surpasses those of Rabkin, Humphreys, Taylor, and others who try to explain or explain away the play's ambivalence. He shows how both critical and uncritical responses to *Henry V* are effects of the play's representational strategies. This makes it possible for him to redirect critique away from Shakespeare on the one hand and from wide-eyed playgoers and slit-eyed armchair readers on the other. But it isn't enough to aim the critique at the "discursive practices" Greenblatt so brilliantly exhibits at work *outside* the theater when he exposes the "ideological strategies" inscribed in the culture's social and political texts.[20] That still leaves it unclear whether the tetralogy merely imitates and reproduces those strategies or whether it represents their moral cost. It also remains unclear whether the tetralogy solicits responses that can remain sympathetic even while registering the corrosive signs of disenchantment and the bad faith of reenchantment.

Greenblatt's approach delivers and encourages such complex responses. The problem is that the approach doesn't fully meet the condition required to bring them off, though his essay suggests what that condition is in its one reference to the opposition between "full-scale ironic readings" and performance. The condition is willingness to ride the stage/page shuttle both ways, and the only line the shuttle runs on is the one managed in accordance with the principles of the literary model of stage-centered reading.

The particular form of negotiation and circulation "Invisible Bullets" examines in the history plays ("acquisition of charisma through subversion of charisma") does not require a two-way run on the shuttle.[21] It calls for a stage-centered approach to the Henriad that is more theatrical than literary. Greenblatt's interest in linking the poetics of power to the poetics of theater is thus open to the dangers of theatrical and political reductionism.

It would be possible to use Greenblatt's account as the basis of a study that shows how the anxiety in Harry's language may be motivated by the dialectic of disenchantment and reenchantment. His reading, however, is dominated by an institutional and structural perspective. Its focus is on the representation of "monarchical power," "state betrayals," "official strategy," and "a system of beliefs."[22] It centers on *positional* discourses, that is, on the discursive practices sedimented in the roles, relations, and ideological strategies of the Tudor state.

One effect of this approach is to marginalize the interplay of *ethical* discourses. This in turn blocks access to textual evidence that could support a more complex and sympathetic reading of Harry, at whom Greenblatt directs a salvo of unflattering epithets: "a 'juggler', a conniving hypocrite"; "the prince and principle of falsification"; "an anti-Midas: everything he touches turns to dross"; "self-fashioning . . . based upon acts of calculation, intimidation, and deceit"; "the genial master of illusory subversion and redemptive betrayal."[23]

What I call a "sympathetic" reading is not one that refuses to acknowledge these charges. Rather it's one that interrogates Harry's language for signs that he would not wish to be guilty of them but can't fully persuade himself that he isn't. A sympathetic reading recognizes the danger that the subversiveness of containment might pose for *him*. This perspective can be put into play by shifting emphasis from the morality of politics to the politics of morality, from state betrayals to the fear of self-betrayal, from official strategy and a public system of beliefs to the private strategies involved in the inner-directed production of beliefs, and from political bills of grievance to "some other grief."

The closer we get to the language of the plays, the less we feel that what mystifies the Henriad kings is the fraudulent basis of monarchical power, and the less we feel that the flat epithet "hypocrite" adequately describes any of them. Rather, what haunts them is the question—the knowledge or suspicion or fear—of fraudulence in themselves. Greenblatt's powerful and compelling argument may be tellingly employed against both the reductive ironic reading of Harry the fox and the equally simplistic reading of Harry the lion. But its penetrating analysis of the politics of audience co-optation can be made even more compelling by coupling it to an analysis of the discursive strategies of *self*-co-optation.

By bringing these strategies into view through decelerated reading, we can reconceive the conflicting assessments *of* Harry as a problem *for* Harry. It's the problem of self-representation posed by the divergent claims of his private and public wars—by his desire for moral as well as political legitimacy. There's no reason why we have to restrict ourselves to one or the other perspective rather than continue to ride the shuttle both ways, alternately cultivating and questioning, challenging and recuperating, "imaginary identification with the conqueror."

The effort to achieve such identification is especially important for those who (like myself) are seduced by the possibilities of "full-scale ironic readings." It makes a difference whether ironic reading is directed only toward the representation of the protagonist or also toward the representation of the theatrical medium. Decelerated reading still reveals a protagonist who seems genuinely to want "right and conscience" on his side. It reveals a protagonist whose language seems haunted by the sinner's fear of "attaint" and by "the imputation of . . . wickedness." It reveals a protagonist who deals with this fear by occasionally desperate forays into the defenses provided by the discourses of the donor, the hero, the saint, the judge, and the victim/revenger. When reacceleration restores the broader, simpler planes of political theater and theatrical politics, it discloses the pressure exerted on that ethical warfare by the dangerous if unavoidable demands—"royal hypocrisy, ruthlessness, and bad faith"—Greenblatt attributes to the "poetics of Elizabethan power."

Whether we like or dislike the portrait of Harry that emerges from the interpretive shuttle is less important than our ability to understand how that pressure afflicts *him*. His problem is aptly described in Barry Weller's comment that "much of the argument in Shakespearean drama" could be viewed "as a struggle not so much for self-awareness, as for self-representation." Harry is among those "characters in quest of self-representation" who "seek not only to occupy the space of the stage but to impress a certain vision of themselves upon the world."[24]

Such characters may also struggle to escape a vision of themselves imposed by others. To carry through the logic of Weller's reflections, the decelerated analysis of the discourses suggests that Harry is among those who seek ultimately to impress a vision of themselves upon themselves. It suggests that if, as Weller brilliantly observes, the protagonist tries to enforce the vision "upon the other characters and to receive it back, as a truth not of his own creation," the hope motivating his effort is that what begins as a self-created fiction of identity may be authorized by the validating audience as his reality.

The obstacles in the way of this project are dramatized in many plays, most notably *Othello*, *Coriolanus*, *Antony and Cleopatra*, *Julius Caesar*, *Troilus and Cressida*, and *Hamlet*. It may be because the problems can best be represented in terms of the contradictions in the hero's discourse of honor that so many of these are classical plays or plays whose protagonist is a warrior. For honor is in the gift of the other and

> no man is the lord of anything,
> Though in and of him there be much consisting,
> Till he communicate his parts to others;
> Nor doth he of himself know them for aught,
> Till he behold them form'd in the applause
> Where they're extended. (*Troilus and Cressida*, 3.3.115–20)

This is part of an exchange (between Ulysses and Achilles) the language of which vibrates with uneasy suggestions of intercourse, warfare, and debts. It picks out the anxiety not only of the honor-seeker but also of the evaluators at whom he *aims* his virtues. The autonomous manhood the hero seeks and prizes is placed in question by the very terms of the discourse of honor. This accounts for the frequent intertwining of this ethical discourse with the symbolism and sexual politics inherent in the positional discourse of gender.

Self-representation and its problems are also intimately linked with the discourse of theater. Cleopatra knows what can stale her infinite variety: "I shall see / Some squeaking Cleopatra boy my greatness," a prophecy whose pathos increases if you imagine it to be piped by some squeaking Cleopatra-boy. Coriolanus's passion for self-creation is only the logical consequence of the impotence that the player and hero may feel before the tyranny of the audience in a performance-centered community—a community in which the hero "Cannot make boast to have that which he hath, / Nor feels not what he owes, but by reflection" (*Troilus and Cressida*, 3.3.98–99).

Characters like those in *Troilus*, as I argued long ago,[25] always seem to want to escape from their corrosive stage visibility into the fastness of the epic book. In that medium their sometimes mean-minded struggles over the prizes and honors the Greeks called *timē* could be glossed over, distanced, justified, and eventually mystified by the ultimate glory of the epic report. The bard confers *kleos* on them in his effort to win it for himself.

Hamlet's desire to "have that within which passes show" is foiled partly by his dependence on a validating audience he can't respect and partly by his inability to persuade or deceive the most demanding auditor his performances address: himself. He knows, therefore, that he must absent himself and die, like all aspiring authors, in order to safeguard "the illusion of magnificence" from his own oppressive gaze. And yet when Horatio begins to execute his last instruction, it is clear that—to borrow Troilus's words—a self "so fathomless" is on the verge of being buckled in "with spans and inches so diminutive" as the "fears and reasons" Horatio delivers.[26]

Against the tendency of critics to emphasize the differences between Hamlet and Harry, Peter Erickson, in the best discussion of *Henry V* I know, stresses their common concern for self-representation:

> A sharp contrast between Henry V as a man of action and Hamlet as a man of thought is misleading because both are primarily men of long speeches. In each case, the long speech symbolizes a continual search for a justifiable identity. The urgency of self-definition is intensified by a conscience based on atonement with the father. . . . Hal as Henry V is a player king who unsuccessfully attempts to stage situations that will give his identity complete credibility. . . . It is as though he keeps redoing the image he projects in the speeches in an effort to make it come out right.[27]

Whether Harry can find and respect the validating audience he seeks, whether he can persuade or deceive himself—all this remains to be seen.

12. *Harrying the Stage*

Henry V as Tetralogical Echo Chamber

1

And we understand him well,
How he comes o'er us with our wilder days,
Not measuring what use we made of them.
....
But tell the Dauphin I will keep my state,
Be like a king and show my sail of greatness
When I do rouse me in my throne of France:
For that I have laid by my majesty
And plodded like a man for working-days,
But I will rise there with so full a glory
That I will dazzle all the eyes of France,
Yea, strike the Dauphin blind to look on us.
....
But this lies all within the will of God,
To whom I do appeal; and in whose name
Tell you the Dauphin I am coming on,
To venge me as I may and to put forth
My rightful hand in a well-hallow'd cause. (*King Henry V*, 1.2.266–93)

Harry's enthusiastic recourse to the scenario revealed in his "I know you all" soliloquy, and the obvious echoes of that soliloquy, provide a point of entry into the topic of this chapter. I'll try to show that the drama of his transactions with himself, with Falstaff, with his father, and with the rest of the world unfolds coherently from the second scene in *1 Henry IV* through the tetralogy. In the preceding chapter I restricted attention to *Henry V*, and my aim was to demonstrate that in certain respects it is relatively self-contained. Once you distinguish Harry's cause from his claim to the throne, once you acknowledge the necessity of looking to prior plays for explanations of that cause, *Henry V* by itself offers much evidence that the king's language continually defends against, but never overcomes, anxiety about the justice of his cause.

This evidence of discursive conflict is one major source of the play's peculiar power. But it is reinforced by another source that is diffusely located in the Henriad as a whole: the dappled and reverberating field of echoes, reprises, and shadows from the other plays. Ghostly voices that haunt the language of *Henry V* fill it with a rich and strange resonance that smokes the edges of its speakers so that even if we imagine them as embodied characters, they seem at moments to be surreally transformed, invested and troubled by spirit voices.

The return of the dead is a theme the play alludes to several times:

> Though we seemed dead, we did but sleep. (3.6.124–25)

> The organs, though defunct and dead before,
> Break up their drowsy grave, and newly move
> With casted slough and fresh legerity. (4.1.21–23)

> Mark then abounding valor in our English,
> That being dead, like to the bullet's crasing,
> Break out into a second course of mischief,
> Killing in relapse of mortality. (4.3.104–7)

Even the "wounded steeds," as if fearing the continued mastery of the dead, "Yerk out their armed heels at their dead masters, / Killing them twice" (4.7.80–83). And perhaps the same fear motivates Harry's re-interment of Richard (4.1.301).

Because *Henry V* unfolds in a kind of tetralogical echo chamber, it suffers when it is performed as an independent play rather than as the last in a series. The continuity of the sequence adds richness and specificity to the protagonist's motivation. Should this continuity get bracketed out in the interest of theatrical self-sufficiency, those involved in the production and performance of *Henry V* would have to pretend that factors intrinsic to its motivational drama either don't exist or are relatively trivial. Respect for the play's *relative* self-sufficiency has to share the stage with attention to the textual affiliations that bind it to the other plays. Turning now to follow some of those affiliations back through the Henriad, I begin with the echo-chamber effect in passages from act 1, scenes 1 and 2 of *Henry V*.

2

Before delivering his "merry message" to the Dauphin, Harry tells the French ambassadors that his passion "is as subject" to his grace "as is our wretches fetter'd in our prisons" (1.2.242–43). This image makes us suspect that Harry's passion (which is to say, Harry) desires, like Mowbray in *Richard II*, to "cast off his chains of bondage, and embrace / His golden uncontrolled enfranchisement" so that the hero's "dancing soul" can "celebrate / This feast of battle with mine adversary" (*Richard II*, 1.3.89–92).

Such sentiments belong to the rhetoric of the discourse of honor, which is cultivated by Hotspur, who cedes or spreads it to Harry. It lies dormant during *2 Henry IV* but gets reactivated in the appeals the bishops and nobles make to Harry during the second scene of *Henry V*. The Dauphin's taunt offers him a chance to put this discourse into play and describe his "coming on" as a riposte to a personal affront—a trial by battle, with God as judge.

The violence of Harry's threatened vengeance may have a merely tactical function—"to make the sender blush" (1.2.299). But the passion unfettered in his rhetoric indicates a danger that motivates "a Christian king" (241) to shore up his "grace" with new appeals to God. Thanks to God and the Archbishop, Harry's cause has become "well-hallowed" enough to justify collecting "our proportions for these wars" and urging "every man" to "task his thought / That this fair action may on foot be brought" (1.2.304–5, 309–10).

The conflict between Harry's "passion" and his "grace" produces a sense of uneasiness that passes beyond his language into that of his subjects and interlocutors. We encounter it early in the first scene, in the rhetoric of Canterbury's praise:

The breath no sooner left his father's body,
But that his wildness, mortified in him,
Seem'd to die too; yea, at that very moment,
Consideration like an angel came,
And whipp'd th' offending Adam out of him,
Leaving his body as a Paradise,
T'envelop and contain celestial spirits.
Never was such a sudden scholar made;
Never came reformation in a flood,
With such a heady currance, scouring faults;

Nor never Hydra-headed wilfulness
So soon did lose his seat—and all at once—
As in this king. (1.1.25–37)

J. H. Walter remarks that "the linking of significant words 'consideration', 'angel', 'paradise', 'celestial spirits', indicates that Shakespeare was . . . thinking of repentance and conversion in the religious sense."[1] But forget Shakespeare: What is Canterbury "thinking of"?

He thinks primarily of a fearful violence, and the slippage of his imagery from soul-purging to stable-purging registers his uneasy reaction to what he imagines. The violence of Harry's grace scares Canterbury no less than the violence of his passion. The containment Canterbury mentions at 1.1.31 reminds me of Stephen Greenblatt's powerful thesis of the subversive production and containment of subversion: "The subversive doubts the play continually awakens originate paradoxically in an effort to intensify the power of the king and his war."[2] But even as Canterbury undertakes this effort, his words betray his worry: The qualities that will make Harry useful and friendly to the church also make him seem dangerous and alien.

In Canterbury's estimation it took the expulsive force of an angelic flagellant, the repressive force of a Hercules (himself a figure of wildness), to tame Harry's former wildness. To listen closely to this language is to hear something Canterbury has heard in Harry's speech, some reverberation that makes him recoil. Thus although the following lines cling fast to one kind of *wonder*, admiration, their rhetoric is breached by another kind as it responds in doubt and perplexity to a violence that modulates into furtiveness:

Hear him but reason in divinity,
And, all-admiring, with an inward wish
You would desire the king were made a prelate:
Hear him debate of commonwealth affairs,
You would say it hath been all in all his study:
List his discourse of war, and you shall hear
A fearful battle render'd you in music:
Turn him to any cause of policy,
The Gordian knot of it he will unloose,
Familiar as his garter; that, when he speaks,
The air, a charter'd libertine, is still,
And the mute wonder lurketh in men's ears,
To steal his sweet and honey'd sentences. (1.1.38–50)

It is, continues Canterbury, "a wonder how his grace" should manage all this, considering that

> his addiction was to courses vain;
> His companies unletter'd, rude, and shallow;
> His hours filled up with riots, banquets, sports;
> And never noted in him any study,
> Any retirement, any sequestration
> From open haunts and popularity. (1.1.54–59)

Canterbury's initial expression of the wish that Harry might be one of them soon translates into a perception that he already is one of them. A consummate politician, he is to be envied and feared not only for his mastery of the discursive instruments of power but also for his command of the seductive rhetoric by which it is legitimized. The skill with which Harry hid his acquisition of these arts is cause for misgiving as much as for admiration.

The misgiving is registered in the progress of Canterbury's sentiments. He charts the outward surge of Harry's violence from spiritual self-flagellation through the musical discourse of fearful battle to the Gordian knot metaphor, which is the first occurrence of the Alexander analogy. In the New Penguin edition, A. R. Humphreys takes the figure to imply that "Henry outdoes Alexander by untying" rather than cutting the knot.[3] Yet since "unloose'" may just as well mean that he cut it with a sword, the figure diffuses the violence of angelic "consideration" into his discourse of policy.

"The air, a charter'd libertine": Samuel Johnson found this phrase "exquisitely beautiful," but I find it hard to pin down.[4] Why *should* the air be called a "charter'd libertine"? What kind of "wonder" is denoted? Why is it "mute"? Why does it "steal"?

For me these words have the resonance of displacements. The lines speak cautiously, apprehensively, of something in Harry's discourse that can't fully be trusted. The "sweet honey lord" who both licensed and hid behind the thievery of dissolute companions continues to charter the air as the medium of his verbal seduction, and he makes others do the same. In their bid for royal protection the church politicians are compelled to "steal" his honeyed sentences, that is, to secure his advocacy.

Even now, Canterbury's honeyed words reverberate both the furtive violence they fend off and the perplexity they try to mute. The same wonder steals into Ely's response:

The strawberry grows underneath the nettle,
And wholesome berries thrive and ripen best
Neighbour'd by fruit of baser quality:
And so the prince obscur'd his contemplation
Under the veil of wildness; which, no doubt,
Grew like the summer grass, fastest by night,
Unseen, yet crescive in his faculty. (1.1.60–66)

The Arden and New Penguin editions supply two horticultural glosses on Ely's berries: T. Hill's observation that "Strawberye . . . aptly groweth in shadowie places, and rather ioyeth under the shadow of other herbes, than by growing alone," and Montaigne's report that gardeners say "Roses and Violets are ever the sweeter & more odoriferous that grow neere under Garlike and Onions, for so much as they suck and draw all the ill-savours of the ground unto them."[5] Gary Taylor ignores the Montaigne passage in his Oxford edition and adds a more positive gloss: The strawberry "often appeared in religious illustrations as 'the symbol of perfect righteousness'" because (according to St. Francis de Sales) "although it creeps along the ground, and is continually crushed by serpents, lizards, and other venomous reptiles, yet it does not imbibe the slightest impression of poison, or the smallest malignant quality."[6] Ely's strawberry, however, more closely resembles Montaigne's plants because their adaptive strategy illustrates an effective method for becoming a symbol of perfect righteousness. It is the very strategy articulated by Corporal Nym when he comments on Harry's rejection of Falstaff: "The king hath run bad humours on the knight" (2.1.121).

Ely's "contemplation," like Canterbury's "consideration," once again displays uneasiness: It conspicuously obscures suspected "shadowie places" in Harry under a veil of pietistic rhetoric. Robert Ornstein sees this as a sign of tactfulness: "They will neither impugn the King's motives nor examine too closely their own reasons for supporting his intended campaign."[7] But the language is more troubled than that, and it is *because* they are tactful and worldly speakers that we're struck by the show of muffled fear or doubt.

We sense trouble, for example, when "veil of wildness" steps forward to claim the relative clause intended to modify "contemplation" so that whatever *Ely* means to say, *his language* says that Harry's veil of wildness grew unseen along with contemplation. This seconds the idea that escapes from Canterbury's "heady currance" speech: Harry's wildness may simply have been transferred from the forces of riot to those of reformation.

As Canterbury presents it, that reformation is itself a libertinism chartered by piety. The "no doubt" that Ely interjects in trying to compare contemplation to summer grass (1.1.64) is a puzzled effort to suppress the doubt "crescive" in his syntax. His bewilderment is echoed in Canterbury's reluctant concession:

> It must be so; for miracles are ceas'd;
> And therefore we must needs admit the means
> How things are perfected. (1.1.67–69)

3

My aim in the preceding discussion was to see if I could detect differences between the statements the clergymen seem intent on making about Harry and the more disquieting reactions embedded in their language. I would not know what to do with the results of this inquiry were I to confine myself to the audience-response criteria promoted by theater-centered criticism. Most likely, those results would have to be abandoned as inflations of a local excrescence, an unusable surplus, produced by the reader's violation of the kind of interpretive perception possible in the moment-by-moment flow and tempo of performance.

Yet if I ignore those performative criteria, Canterbury's language is anything but anomalous. It echoes and responds to several prior utterances. Compare, for example, the first words of his praise in *Henry V* with two passages from *2 Henry IV*, Harry's protestation to his father and his pronouncement to his brothers:

> The breath no sooner left his father's body,
> But that *his* wildness, mortified in *him*,
> Seem'd to die too. (*Henry V*, 1.1.25–27, my emphasis)

> If I do feign,
> O, let me in my present wildness die,
> And never live to show th'incredulous world
> The noble change that I have purposed! (*2 Henry IV*, 4.5.151–54)

> My father is gone wild into his grave,
> For in his tomb lie my affections;

And with his spirits sadly I survive
To mock the expectation of the world,
To frustrate prophecies, and to raze out
Rotten opinion, who hath writ me down
After my seeming. (*2 Henry IV*, 5.2.123–29)

In Canterbury's lines the momentarily indefinite personal pronouns shadow an argument latent in Harry's language: that his wildness is attributable to his father and may be purged by running its "bad humors" into the soil of Henry IV's achievement. To go even farther back: In Harry's words, in Nym's scapegoating formula (2.1.121), in Ely's strawberry logic, and in Canterbury's puzzled incredulity, we recognize the outlines and predicted effect of the scenario that Harry first elaborated in *1 Henry IV* in his "I know you all" soliloquy (1.2.190–212). There he planned to "thrive and ripen best" by running bad humors on "the base contagious clouds." He planned eventually to cast them off or whip them out as his misleaders so that "like bright metal on a sullen ground, / My reformation, glitt'ring o'er my fault, / Shall show more goodly" (1.2.193, 207–9).

In the third of the passages quoted above, the underlying aggressiveness of his scenario surges up to a crest of rhetorical violence which Harry immediately tempers in lines that anticipate Canterbury's account of the flood of reformation:

The tide of blood in me
Hath proudly flow'd in vanity till now.
Now doth it turn, and ebb back to the sea,
Where it shall mingle with the state of floods,
And flow henceforth in formal majesty. (*2 Henry IV*, 5.2.129–33)

The figure impressionistically evokes the image of the tide flowing in from the Channel toward London and then flowing back—an image that assimilates the "little body with a mighty heart" of England to that of the king. The Hydra-headed tide of blood is bad when it flows inland and its vanity invades the center of the King's Two Bodies. But it is good when it flows outward and assumes legitimacy by mingling with the "state of floods"—that is, the floods of state that will soon wash over France.

In the lines following that passage the confluence of the tide of blood with the stately flood of formal majesty makes it as difficult to distinguish the interests of the body politic from those of the king as it is difficult for the king to distinguish war from peace:

Now call we our high court of parliament,
And let us choose such limbs of noble counsel
That the great body of our state may go
In equal rank with the best-govern'd nation;
That war, or peace, or both at once, may be
As things acquainted and familiar with us;
In which you, father, shall have foremost hand.
Our coronation done, we will accite,
As I before remember'd, all our state:
And, God consigning to my good intents,
No prince nor peer shall have just cause to say,
God shorten Harry's happy life one day! (*2 Henry IV*, 5.2.134–45)

Accite does not manage to stay within the intended formal bounds of a legal summons. Here it gets infiltrated by the headier currance of its more willful senses: *incite*, *excite*, *agitate*. Harry may be preparing to run his watery and fiery humors on the French in accordance with his father's advice "to busy giddy minds" and "waste the memory of the former days" of civil war (*2 Henry IV*, 4.5.213–15). But it's uncomfortably obvious that this preparation has a darker purpose. He is determined to mock the expectation of the world and frustrate its prophecies so that he can "raze out" the very same "rotten opinion" that he himself solicited and encouraged by his former days of riot.

4

When I review the preceding section from the standpoint of theater-centered criticism, one thing seems clear. In the space of a few pages I not only committed the two major crimes of which that criticism accuses the armchair reader. I also combined them in a way that seems to bear out the thesis that they mutually implicate each other: (1) I collected parallels and echoes from widely separated regions of text, a procedure that Gary Taylor calls "anachronistic" reading and one that constitutes the disease of Fluellenism in Richard Levin's nosology;[8] (2) I dished up an increasingly negative profile of Henry V.

A fairly straightforward argument can be made in defense of the first crime. If we find echo-relationships between Harry's earlier and later utterances, and between his speech and Canterbury's, what should we do with them? Should we look into them or should we ignore them? If we don't ignore them, how do we interpret them?

For one thing, they give Canterbury's and Ely's language much more resonance. Their echoes of Harry's speech tell us what they hear in that masterful utterance. They hear something dangerously aggressive and seductive: An abiding wildness lurks "crescive" in the considerations of a careful conscience. Their words convey this whether or not they show themselves aware or desirous of hearing it, whether or not Harry shows himself aware of conveying it.

Though Canterbury and Ely are too interested to be called choric vehicles bearing "the play's" message, they aren't important enough to be characterized by the conveyance I just mentioned. They serve as auditory reflectors that register Harry's effect on his interlocutors. But let's assume that we adhere to theater-centered principles, and that this effect has to be disallowed because it is the product of operations that lie well beyond the perceptual and interpretive capacity of playgoers. Then, as I note above, we're left with an unusable reader's surplus.

If we suppose that playgoers who focus on Canterbury's praise of Harry are made uneasy by this surplus, should we conclude that they would discard it as a local anomaly or ignore it as incomprehensible noise? And should this response provide the standard in terms of which to judge the limits of interpretation? To me, the Canterbury scene makes far more sense and is far more interesting if the surplus is figured in, and it is eviscerated if the surplus is ignored. Therefore, I think any interpretive criterion that favors evisceration needs to be justified by a stronger argument than Gary Taylor's, especially since I find it easy to imagine playgoers in the Age of Reading who come to a performance of *Henry V* familiar with the text of *1* and *2 Henry IV*.

This still leaves the second crime to be accounted for. Does my reading replace Harry the lion, mirror of all Christian kings, with the Machiavellian fox? Here a more elaborate defense is required. I suggested earlier that the lion/fox alternative can be avoided by redirecting attention from our assessment of Harry to his assessment of himself. The suggestion may be developed by slowing down one of the moments in which Harry's stated intentions would seem to render him most vulnerable to the charge of Machiavellian scheming.

13. *Harry's Question*

"May I with right and conscience make this claim?" That is the question. It is the question Harry puts to the Archbishop of Canterbury in the second scene of *King Henry V* (1.2.96) after the Archbishop has explained the legal basis of the king's claim to the French throne. The first two scenes of the play connect the justice of his "cause" to the legality or validity of "this claim" to the French throne. As Harry had suggested before the explanation, his question may be of vital importance to him, but it will be even more important to those who answer it:

> For God doth know how many now in health
> Shall drop their blood in approbation
> Of what your reverence shall incite us to. (1.2.18–20)

The disclaimer of responsibility is the classic move of the victim's discourse: "It's not my fault. If terrible things happen, the blame will be yours. You put me up to it." This testifies to Harry's uneasiness about what he is about to do.

In these scenes whatever psychological effects we attribute to previous events in the tetralogy are glimpsed only in the process of being transformed into Harry's decision to stake his claim to the throne. That transformation is obscured by the tendency to identify Harry's cause—what he is fighting for—with his claim. I don't think the language of the scenes supports the identification, and I'll try to show why it doesn't.

When we survey the sequence of disclosures that reveal Harry's French project, we see that his claim to the throne is not the prior cause but the posterior justification of that project:

1. Henry IV's advice to busy giddy minds with foreign quarrels (*2 Henry IV*, 4.5.213–14).

2. The rumor of an impending French campaign announced by Prince John in the concluding speech of *2 Henry IV.*

3. The *Henry V* Prologue's generalized iconic depiction of "the warlike Harry," at whose heels "famine, sword, and fire / Crouch for employment."

4. The Archbishop's report to the Bishop of Ely of his effort to secure Harry's advocacy by the double offer of money for the French war and genealogical proof of his claim to the French throne, a proof Harry was prevented from hearing by the arrival of the French ambassador (*Henry V,* 1.1.85–97).

5. Canterbury's teasing remark, at the end of act 1, scene 1, that he can guess what the ambassador's message would be, though we don't hear what it is until late in the next scene, when we also learn for the first time that

6. at some point before the discussion in act 1, scene 1, Harry, "lately sending into France, / Did claim some certain dukedoms, in the right / Of your great predecessor, King Edward the Third" (1.2.246–48). Herbert Coursen compactly exposes the plan:

> This is the claim Canterbury knows will be rejected by the French ambassador. The claim has been made . . . before the king has heard a full exposition of its validity. The final decision to invade, then, waits only on a formal rejection of Henry's claim.[1]

The scenario that gradually emerges through this sequence is that after Harry decided (for whatever reason) to bear "civil swords and native fire / As far as France" (*2 Henry IV,* 5.5.106–7), he put forth a claim whose rejection he anticipated. That is, he put it forth so that it would be rejected. This would allow him to hold France responsible for the consequences.

After the Archbishop verifies not only the original claim but also the title to the throne of France, after Harry's interlocutors exhort him to lead his "loyal subjects" to France "with blood and sword and fire to win your right," after he prompts them to satisfy him that the backdoor danger of Scottish invasion can be contained, but before he hears the ambassador's response, Harry states his decision: "Now are we well resolved" to rule "in large and ample empery / O'er France and all her almost kingly dukedoms" (1.2.222, 226–27). Thus he prepares to give France what she deserves and to vindicate his rightful claim.

It was the Archbishop who volunteered—not Harry who demanded—the exposition on the Salic law. Canterbury offered to reveal "the severals and unhidden passages" (1.1.86) of Harry's titles not merely to the dukedoms already claimed but also the throne of France. He didn't expect to get the chance to do this before Harry's audience with the ambassador, but Harry defers the audience until he can hear the Archbishop "justly and religiously unfold / Why the law Salic that they have in France / Or should, or should not, bar us in our claim" (1.2.10–12).

Since, as the Archbishop presents it, that law pertains primarily to the throne, we can assume that Harry comes into the scene anticipating rejection of his claim to the dukedoms. He is prepared to escalate his demands. But he is also eager to give his claims moral validity—or at least to avoid contamination by any possibly questionable motives behind the offer.

For Harry to say he will believe the Archbishop speaks only what "is in your conscience wash'd / As pure as sin with baptism" (31–32) is to allow for the lingering impurity of original sin in the speaker while keeping his own paradisal body clear of Canterbury's "offending Adam" (1.1.29–30). He can then proceed in good faith to argue that—in A. R. Humphreys's words—his "claim is lawful and French resistance to it unlawful, so that by contumacy France provokes an 'impious war' not only against her rightful sovereign but against God, the source of royal authority."[2]

Humphreys is aware of all the "teasing questions" in the episode, including the modern objection to the idea that "the French are the aggressors for standing their ground." He himself finds the play's emphasis on patriotism "uncritical" and at times "disagreeable." Yet he insists that such problems are unintended by-products of Shakespeare's "zest of composition."[3]

In taking this line, Humphreys ignores or dismisses the sequence of disclosures that show that Harry had been provoking the war well before the question of his rightful sovereignty was raised by Canterbury. What was the cause of that provocation? Whatever it was, it was not the claim to the throne that Harry decides to make as a punitive response to the rejection of the earlier more modest claim. The legality of the grander claim is another pretext brought in to validate the original provocation and its cause.

That cause is complex and obscure, but some aspects of it glimmer through Canterbury's exposition and the exchanges that follow it. Warned by Harry not to risk bloodguilt by falsifying the claim, the Archbishop puts on his best and most precise Holinshed to persuade the king that the only legal bar to his title, the Salic law that prohibits succession through a woman, is a canard. He claims that the French wrongly apply it to France rather than to Saxony, for which it was instituted some four centuries after the mythical date they assign (1.2.40–64). He also points out that the French kings themselves consistently violated the law (1.2.65–90).

In view of the importance the Henriad accords to the uses of gender symbolism—the uses, that is, of woman—the double standard attributed to the French has pronounced thematic resonance. On the one hand, the law was established because the French settlers in Saxony held "in disdain the German women / For some dishonest manners of their life" (1.2.48–49)—the women are untrustworthy and lecherous and will foul up lineal successions with bastards (see 3.5.5–31). On the other hand, French contempt and distrust of women is balanced by their dependence on women's legal and biological instrumentality. Women are as necessary as they are dangerous, and they are both because, in modern jargon, they are "bearers of the phallus."

This thematic resonance is sharpened by the Archbishop's three major examples of violations of the law (1.2.64–85): Succession through a woman is used to legitimize usurpation; one violation offsets another. Pepin and Hugh Capet deploy that genealogical device to legitimize their seizures of the throne. Capet resorts to a factitious lineal claim ("Conveyed himself as heir to the Lady Lingare," who was descended from Charlemagne, 1.2.74–77). Lewis, the "sole heir to the usurper Capet, / Could not keep quiet in his conscience, / Wearing the crown of France," until he satisfied himself that his grandmother, Queen Isabel, was also descended from Charlemagne (1.2.77–85).

Under its explicit argument the speech suggests to the sole heir of the usurper Bolingbroke that he has the same right as the kings of France: the right to legitimize usurpation by finding or inventing a link to a well-connected woman. If he still has any scruples about wearing the crown of England, he can quiet them by becoming king of France: "No king of England, if not king of France" (2.2.193). And by the end of the play he will in effect have displaced or deposed the Dauphin, won his sister, greeted the French king and queen (another Isabel) as his siblings, and proclaimed himself the son and heir of that king.

But there is more than this to the Archbishop's innuendo. In Holinshed the Archbishop first declared that Harry was "the lawfull and onelie heir of . . . the whole realme of France, as heire to his great grandfather king Edward the third." He then twice inveighed "against the surmised and false fained law Salike" under color of which the French would "barre the kings and princes of this realme of England of their right and lawfull inheritance."[4]

Shakespeare's Archbishop concludes his speech with the more pointed accusation that the French are actively practicing on Harry himself:

> Howbeit they would hold up this Salic law
> To bar your highness claiming from the female;
> And rather choose to hide them in a net
> Than amply to imbar their crooked titles
> Usurp'd from you and your progenitors. (1.2.91–95)

He goes on to urge him to "stand for your own" and

> Look back into your mighty ancestors:
> Go, my dread lord, to your great-grandsire's tomb,
> From whom you claim; invoke his war-like spirit,
> And your great-uncle's, Edward the Black Prince,
> Making defeat on the full power of France;
> Whiles his most mighty father on a hill
> Stood smiling to behold his lion's whelp
> Forage in blood of French nobility. (1.2.101–10)

Here, as in Holinshed, it is not mentioned but obviously understood that the French invoked the Salic law because Edward III's claim formally derived from his mother, Isabella, the daughter of Philip the Fair. Thus Harry has to "look back" very far—to his great-great-grandmother—to find the genealogical pretext behind the act of usurpation that deprived him of his "own."

The Archbishop's language makes it appear that the duplicity practiced by the French on Edward III, Harry's great-grandfather, is at the same time aimed personally at "your highness." Yet up to now the French have had no specific occasion to address his claim to the throne, since he hasn't asserted it. As the Archbishop depicts them, the French, like Harry's father, are usurpers. They have stolen his property (just as Richard had stolen his father's Lancastrian inheritance). By standing for his own, he can deal with several threats to his conscience and honor in a single course of action.

The compression of Edward III with Harry may be one reason why A. R. Humphreys finds that although Shakespeare "means his clerics to argue truly," the "Salic law" speech

> falls as far short of proving their bona fides as it does of achieving poetic charm. . . . Exeter is later to assure us that Henry's right is not based on pettifogging legalism:

> 'Tis no sinister nor no awkward claim
> Picked from the worm-holes of long-vanished days,
> Nor from the dust of old oblivion raked. . . . (II.4.85–87)
>
> But since, by following Holinshed too closely, this is just what Shakespeare made the claim sound like in the Archbishop's mouth, he unintentionally cast into doubt what is not meant to be in doubt at all . . . —the legality of Henry's claim.[5]

Gary Taylor disagrees with this verdict. He argues that the tediousness for which the speech has chiefly been acclaimed is functional in producing the effect of legality.[6] According to Taylor, "Our [positive] judgment of the justice of Henry's claim to the throne, and so of the war on which he embarks," derives from the Archbishop's "discussion of the Salic law."[7]

Harry's response to the discussion suggests to me that both Humphreys and Taylor are wrong: "May I with right and conscience make this claim?" implies, first, that he may still harbor a doubt, and second, that the justice of the war does not automatically follow from the justice of the claim. The legality of the claim isn't by itself enough to justify his acting on it. Why should English blood be spilled in defense of a claim "from the dust of old oblivion raked"? (2.4.87).

This question is both raised (for us) and answered (for Harry) by a tactic of conspicuous compression that simultaneously betrays a "pettifogging" strain and provides the rhetoric to overcome it. The Archbishop, and after him the other speakers, seek to appease Harry's concern for right and conscience by addressing him as the direct heir and surrogate of his "mighty ancestors." Appealing to his blood and honor, they urge him to emulation:

> ELY.
> Awake remembrance of these valiant dead,
> And with your puissant arm renew their feats:
> You are their heir, you sit upon their throne,
> The blood and courage that renowned them
> Runs in your veins; and my thrice-puissant liege
> Is in the very May-morn of his youth,
> Ripe for exploits and mighty enterprises.
>
> EXE.
> Your brother kings and monarchs of the earth
> Do all expect that you should rouse yourself,
> As did the former lions of your blood. (1.2.115–24)

To my knowledge, Peter Erickson was the first to argue that "a tension between two versions of paternal inheritance" is initially presented in this scene and recurs throughout the play. The "heroic call . . . sidesteps the guilt associated with Henry IV and recovers an earlier father, Edward III," offering Harry the role of his heroic son, but Harry "cannot completely disregard the more problematic . . . image . . . of his own father."[8] Erickson thinks the play at first "skirts this difficulty" (49), but I think his insight applies equally well to the first two scenes and that the tension takes a specific and more aggressive form in the above passage.

The covert theme that rides on the point of Canterbury's injunction to "Look back," on Ely's repeated instances of "their," and on Exeter's "former lions," is that Harry should elide Bolingbroke and Richard out of the lineal picture. They urge him to reinsert himself in, and revive, the heroic golden age his immediate predecessors destroyed. They define the cause for which he is to assert his claim not in terms of national interest but in terms of dynastic, personal, and chivalric justification, that is, mystification.

Yet even as Canterbury's harking back to Harry's "mighty ancestors" suggests a bypass of the figures and actions in the middle distance, the terms with which he leads the rhetorical charge evoke them: "Gracious lord, / Stand for your own" (1.2.100–101) echoes the crucial interchange in which Richard denies Bolingbroke a fallback position and solicits usurpation: "My gracious lord, I come but for mine own. / Your own is yours, and I am yours, and all" (*Richard II,* 3.3.196–97). Richard's response to Henry will be duplicated and writ large in the overall French response to Harry. The ethical warfare waged by Richard against Henry—the seductiveness and power inherent in the discourses of the victim/revenger and the donor—will be renewed by the French against Harry.

Since father and son face in opposite directions, Henry toward England and Harry toward France, the analogy suggests an equation: France and the French are to Harry what England and Richard were to Henry. The Henry and England Harry escapes from will materialize in the French throne and kingdom he seeks. This gives a subversive—because tautological—turn to "No king of England, if not king of France."

The tension described by Erickson becomes even sharper if we hear the echo of another encounter in Canterbury's reference to the "mighty father" smiling down on his son's conquests at Crécy. This is the single encounter with Hotspur that Harry envisaged as his moment of glory and proposed at Shrewsbury "before my father's majesty" in order "to save the blood on either side"—the encounter his father managed to forestall. Canterbury's image offers Harry the prospect of a replay before the majesty of a better father and in the service of a better cause.

By finding in France the battle glory Henry IV thwarted at Shrewsbury, he will refather himself. The behest to invoke Edward's "warlike spirit, / And your great-uncle's, Edward the Black Prince," is an invitation to undo—in Freud's term, "to make unhappened" (*ungeschehenmachen*)—recent history, in effect to replace Richard and bypass Bolingbroke. For Harry to go to France will be magically to go back in time. For him to make war on the French will be to make war against the war his father and Richard made in England, to whip those offending fathers out and thereby purge England and himself of the moral taint of disordered rule, usurpation, and regicide. Given this network of suggestions, the faint aroma of an appeal to mental (i.e., imaginary) usurpation lurks in Ely's "You are their heir, you sit upon their throne."

Exeter's appeal to Harry to "rouse" himself (1.2.122–24) implies that the brotherhood of rulers may have been mildly appalled by the goings-on of some of its recent English members. This leads Westmoreland and Canterbury to chime in that Harry needn't worry about letting the brotherhood down:

> [N]ever king of England
> Had nobles richer, and more loyal subjects,
> Whose hearts have left their bodies here in England
> And lie pavilioned in the fields of France.
> CANT. O, let their bodies follow, my dear liege,
> With blood and sword and fire to win your right. (1.2.126–31)

This stirring call to battle, dressed in the nobility of the word "pavilioned," is also a periphrase that prefigures glorious death: the bodies abandoned by prone pavilioned hearts and "dying" to rejoin them, the prospective rush of loyal subjects bearing those bodies toward the fate of a more profound repose, and all "to win your right."

Caught up in the euphoria of the war whoop, Canterbury drives home his appeal with the offer of "such a mighty sum / As never did the clergy at one time / Bring in to any of your ancestors" (133–35), and Harry's reply—his first utterance since his "right and conscience" question—is interestingly indirect:

> We must not only arm t'invade the French,
> But lay down our proportions to defend
> Against the Scot, who will make road upon us
> With all advantages. (1.2.136–39)

This is either a conditional statement or a recommendation: either "if we arm to invade France, we must also defend against the Scot" or "when we arm to invade France, etc." Either, that is, Harry is still showing himself uncertain, still testing his interlocutors—wondering aloud, for example, whether the church can afford to foot the Scottish as well as the French bill. Or else, while he continues to test them, he lets them know he has made his decision, has been persuaded, and is ready to plan his campaign.

If it is an announcement, its force is muffled partly by the uncertain modality of the statement and partly by the diversionary introduction of the Scottish problem. The latter encourages the peers to continue their persuasions but to redirect them from Harry's own cause and claim to the welfare of the kingdom. It is as if Harry prudently digresses in defensive reaction both to their focus on his welfare and to the Archbishop's perhaps too blatant offer of money in that cause. He reminds them, in effect, that he hasn't been swept away by Hotspurian seductions—by appeals to redeem his banished lineal honors, to redress the wrongs perpetrated by the French (and others closer to home), and to restore the Plantagenet dynasty into "the good thoughts of the world again." He won't ignore the possible harm the pursuit of his rightful claim may inflict on his kingdom and subjects.

In Holinshed and Hall, Westmoreland had voiced this concern. By shifting it to Harry, Shakespeare intensifies the sensitivity his responses display to the moral and political touchiness of his situation. Assuming his role as sovereign protector of his people, Harry points out the danger of the Scots' pouring into the breach and "galling the gleaned land with hot assays" as they had done during Edward III's campaign (146–54), and—as Herbert Coursen smartly observes—doing to "unfurnish'd" England what Harry will propose to do when he "exports" disorder to France.[9]

Coursen argues that since Harry has already decided to invade France and is already convinced that the Scots can be contained, his strategy is, in the first case, to promote the appearance "that the decision is made for him during the scene," and, in the second, to allow his interlocutors "to convince themselves."[10] Harry makes his prelates and peers share responsibility by persuading them to persuade him that the war will be morally justifiable and practically feasible. If it is in their interest for him to risk shedding the blood of loyal subjects, let them participate in the discourse of justification. Let them commit themselves to the cause. Let it have their approval and imprimatur. Let it be their war as well as his.

If the commons and the peerage stand to gain by stripping the church of its property (1.1.7–9), let peer and prelate, the Duke of Exeter and the Archbishop of Canterbury, agree that "government, though high and low and lower, / Put into parts, doth keep in one consent." Let them agree that "many things, having full reference / To one consent, may work contrariously," yet "end in one purpose" (1.2.180–81, 205–6, 212). This benign image of harmony doesn't account for the peers' response in the discussion about France. Even if they join Canterbury in taking the sin upon their heads, the effect of their exhortation is to throw the war back to Harry by representing it to him as his personal cause.

In the discussion about Scotland, they don't seem to need much convincing. The one brief prudential objection (1.2.166–73) is easily disposed of by Exeter and by Canterbury's windy blather about bees. It is Harry who sees problems in the plan. He wants to make them guarantee that if he follows their advice to go south and play Edward and the Black Prince, he will not be responsible for creating a vacuum that sucks a parallel disorder into England from the north, as it did in Edward's time.

If we endorse Exeter's and Canterbury's opinion that the Scottish danger is negligible, the scruple Harry airs about the Scots assumes moral rather than practical weight, for he could then be supposed to use that "danger" to make the point—with their help—that any threat to England caused by a French invasion would come from outside the kingdom. It would come from the "giddy neighbor" to the north (1.2.145) rather than from the potentially "giddy minds" within England, who would be distracted and pacified by "foreign quarrels" in the service of a rightful claim. In making this point, Harry reverts bookishly ("For you shall read," 146) to the glorious past of Edward III when England was still united under the former lions of his blood. No doubt he knows that the learned Archbishop would be able to reassure him from the same book.

The Archbishop also has other books of reassurance at his command: tracts on the hierarchic "state of man" and polity, collections of edifying similes from ancient poets, and manuals on the production of copia, or elegant variation, or, in a word, redundancy—the redundancy so often useful in overcoming unwanted and unsettling "noise" in interlocutory communication. His texts are from the same library consulted in the last century by E. M. W. Tillyard when he discovered or invented the Elizabethan world picture.[11] Exeter mentions the Tillyard topos of political music primarily to allay Harry's concern over Scotland, but it also has a secondary function in domesticating the image it follows:

> While that the armed hand doth fight abroad
> Th' advised head defends itself at home:
> For government, though high and low and lower,
> Put into parts, doth keep in one consent,
> Congreeing in a full and natural close,
> Like music. (1.2.178–83)

Just for a moment the armed hand and advised head compose into a single gigantic figure. If this foreshadows Hobbes's awesome image of the body politic as a leviathan, it also reminds me of Gloucester's horrific description of Harry at the beginning of *1 Henry VI* (1.1.8–16). The language of Harry's interlocutors betrays a sense of something alien and fearful in the king whose reformation came with Herculean violence in such "a flood, / With such a heady currance, scouring faults" (*Henry V,* 1.1.33–34). Since in Exeter's shift from the bodily to the musical analogy "high and low and lower" doesn't quite square with the head/hand figure or Harry's relation to it, there is an effect of conspicuous blandness in the explanation, an attempt to domesticate that frightening figure.

Apart from this, Exeter's message to Harry is concise and clear: The system of government is perfectly capable of taking care of itself and England in his absence. He can go off and exercise his armed hand and "puissant arm" without giving national security a second thought. It isn't certain whether Exeter was rounding to "a full and natural close" on this point or was going to say more, because Canterbury interrupts him by completing his final verse line:

> Congreeing in a full and natural close,
> Like music.
> CANT. Therefore doth heaven divide
> The state of man in divers functions,
> Setting endeavor in continual motion;
> To which is fixed, as an aim or butt,
> Obedience: for so work the honey-bees,
> Creatures that by a rule in nature teach
> The act of order to a peopled kingdom. (1.2.182–89)

Like a swelling organ tone, his portentous "Therefore" modulates to a heavenly key, digresses from the Scottish question, and takes Exeter's conclusion away from him. But the dilation of Exeter's "high and low and lower" from human government to the cosmic diapason of God, humans, and bees would have been smoother without the passing discord of "as an aim or butt." The allusion to archery garbles the transition implied by "for so work the honey-bees": Their work seldom requires them to use bows and arrows.

This would not be worth mentioning if Canterbury didn't return to the figure after finishing with his bees: "As many arrows, loosed several ways, / Come to one mark" (1.2.207–8). The direction of arrows in the initial figure is a little unclear because "fixed to" might suggest that the obedience affixed to the endeavor of the subjects is held up to the king as a target. The suggestion is not totally outlandish. When Canterbury obediently says, "The sin upon my head, dread sovereign" (1.2.97), he offers a butt at which the king may aim—that is, displace—darts of responsibility. My point about this is that it isn't only the critics who notice Harry's habit of running bad humors on others. It worries the language of some of the dread sovereign's interlocutors and introduces such small disturbances as the one mentioned in the preceding paragraph.

Of course, the sensible way to read the archery figure is to take obedience as the target at which subjects shoot. Obedience is the object of their competitive and warlike skill. That produces a more agreeable idea: To strive in all one's endeavors to aim at obedience to Harry, and to compete with others in this effort, is to prepare for war.

Though the aggressive lines of force in the image are centripetal, and the center is the king's symbolic place, the Archbishop obviously doesn't mean to install Harry as the target and expose him to the fate of Saint Sebastian. Nevertheless, the image provides a fair description of what has been going on in this scene. The interlocutors aim their obedience at Harry. The true blank of his conscience, his desire for moral legitimacy and honor, is the target toward which the other speakers nervously bend their rhetorical efforts, "congreeing" however "contrariously" to meet the challenge of justification. They ply their skill to motivate him through direct and indirect appeals aimed at what they perceive to be his overriding investment in the "heady currance" of his "reformation."

The contribution of the bee analogy to this project may best be gauged by noting the effects of its omission:

> [To which is fixed, as an aim or butt,
> Obedience. So, many things, referred]
> To one consent, may work contrariously;
> As many arrows, loosed several ways,
> Come to one mark; as many ways meet in one town;
> As many fresh streams meet in one salt sea;
> As many lines close in the dial's centre;
> So may a thousand actions, once afoot,
> End in one purpose, and be all well borne
> Without defeat. Therefore to France, my liege. (1.2.206–13)

The series suggests the transformation or displacement of centripetal vectors from one mark to another, from Harry to France. This is one way to secure the obedience of "contrarious" forces set in motion by heaven. But the justification is weak. It echoes Henry IV's advice in *2 Henry IV* (4.5.213–15) about the usefulness of foreign quarrels, especially when their motion is "continual."

According to Henry's logic, the order that channels those forces outward in foreign war would be a defensive strategy by the king, and the "one purpose" it serves would be his alone. The Prologue's "into a thousand parts divide one man" would then be echoed with invidious effect: Since division here equals multiplication, the thousand actions and agents would be extensions of the hero's body and instruments of his purpose. They would be more the servants than the beneficiaries of his cause.

The redundancy of the series of "as many" clauses rhetorically mimes the thesis that many things can have full reference to one consent. This redundancy registers Canterbury's anxiety to defeat the contrarious or refractory implications of his argument. It registers his anxiety to reverse the unfortunate emphasis of the opening inference on the phrase "may work contrariously" so as to produce the more satisfying closure of "End in one purpose . . . / Without defeat."

The Archbishop's bee simile counteracts these effects in several ways. First, by comparing great things to small, like an epic poet, the learned prelate not only ensconces Harry in the heroic panoply this context provides. He also defuses the uneasy image of obedience by reconceiving it in the time-honored pastoral reduction of human effort to an instinctive "rule in nature" (1.2.88).

Second, he minimizes the sources of internal disorder. The apian magistrates who "correct at home" (191) are instanced by the "sad-eyed justice, with his surly hum" who delivers "o'er to executors pale / The lazy yawning drone" (203–4). The puns and caricature accentuate the disparagement of homebred danger.

Third, warfare is conceived as one of nature's acts of order and given "the flavor of a church picnic."[12] More important, the economic and social functions of church picnics are extended to the warrior bees, so that their ventures abroad resemble those of merchants:

> Others, like merchants, venture trade abroad,
> Others, like soldiers, armed in their stings,
> Make boot upon the summer's velvet buds;
> Which pillage they with merry march bring home
> To the tent-royal of their emperor:
> Who, busied in his majesty, surveys
> The singing masons building roofs of gold,
> The civil citizens lading up the honey,[13]
> The poor mechanic porters crowding in
> Their heavy burdens at his narrow gate. (1.2.192–201)

"Make boot upon the summer's velvet buds": The Archbishop's attempt at conspicuous prettification is obvious, especially if we recall Harry's "Galling the gleaned land with hot assays" (1.2.151). But the prettification is structural as well as imagistic. The soldiers' "pillage" supplies the raw materials that enable "the singing masons" to build "roofs of gold," a project to which the whole community contributes and from which it profits. The emperor's military and architectural campaigns blend into one.

This benign order gives a more positive meaning to the Archbishop's subsequent inference that "many things . . . may work contrariously." The phrase now signifies the cooperative division of labor and thus suggests a reading of the redundant series that differs from the one I gave above. Without the apian pastoral the redundancy signifies the anxiety to control the message, to get it right and drive it home. With the pastoral, the series builds through an anaphoristic crescendo of "as many's" that delays and so increases the triumphant effect of the concluding "So may a thousand. . . ." Without the pastoral, the Archbishop's argument tends to collapse the English body politic into Harry's heroic body natural. With it, the two bodies are kept distinct, and the fulfillment of the king is justified by that of the community. Yet to the extent that the church picnic effect is conspicuous, so is the effort at rhetorical blandishment—the effort, that is, to damp down fears that "work contrariously" against the common project of validating Harry's cause and packing him off to France with a clear conscience.

Canterbury digressed from the Scottish problem to the bee kingdom in order to demonstrate how heaven divides "the state of man in divers functions." He now returns with a proposal Harry won't be able to refuse, since it offers him the chance to imitate heaven by dividing the state of England:

> Divide your happy England into four;
> Whereof take you one quarter into France,
> And you withal shall make all Gallia shake.
> If we, with thrice such powers left at home,
> Cannot defend our own doors from the dog,
> Let us be worried and our nation lose
> The name of hardiness and policy. (1.2.214–20)

On hearing this, Harry declares himself "well resolv'd" and indeed shows himself so well resolved that the rafters if not all Gallia begin to shake:

> Now are we well resolv'd; and by God's help,
> And yours, the noble sinews of our power,
> France being ours, we'll bend it to our awe
> Or break it all to pieces: or there we'll sit,
> Ruling in large and ample empery
> O'er France and all her almost kingly dukedoms,
> Or lay these bones in an unworthy urn,
> Tombless, with no remembrance over them:
> Either our history shall with full mouth
> Speak freely of our acts, or else our grave,
> Like Turkish mute, shall have a tongueless mouth,
> Not worshipp'd with a waxen epitaph. (1.2.222–33)

The royal plural of the king body politic only briefly contains the singularity of the hero seeking enlargement, and the gigantic figure whose noble sinews connect the advised head to the armed hand is further magnified by the contrastive echo of the bee king's little empery: Harry will "sit" in France as in a "tent-royal" (1.2.196).

Now that he has been satisfied that his claim is just—is not illegal—and that he can leave the homeland securely in others' hands, his language relishes in the violent release of a carnival moment, a pleasurably punitive fantasy of all or nothing. More than a mere fit of Tamburlaine, this is righteous anger at the wicked enemy. Harry sharpens the threat by staking his all on the outcome to show how much it means to him.

He fancies this wager enough to repeat it and dwell on the violent and shameful impotence, the silent humiliation, of the fate he proposes to embrace as the only alternative to victory. But the repetition increases the transparency of the royal plural that veils the singular hero. To construe oblivion in terms of the double impotence symbolized by the tongueless eunuch is to shift the register of concern from the monarch's responsibility and legitimacy to the quest of the honor-seeking hero's triple crown: manhood, power, and enduring fame.

For Harry to deny himself this crown is the costliest sacrifice and the worst punishment he can imagine. In that shift of register we recognize both the resurgence of the Hotspurian spirit and his commitment to the scenario sketched out in the "I know you all" soliloquy: the plan to prepare the sullen ground that will enable him to falsify hopes, to "mock the expectation of the world," to stage his glittering reformation, and to redeem his banished honors from—among other things—the fault his father made.

Harry's surge of rhetorical violence thus reveals the message he receives from his interlocutors. The legality of his claim, which he perfunctorily acknowledges ("France being ours"), gives him permission to take up in more expansive terms their invitation to make the French war a personal chivalric exploit: "My thrice-puissant liege / Is in the very May-morn of his youth, / Ripe for exploits and mighty enterprises" (2.1.119–21). They appeal to his desire to be—in Pistol's words—"solus" and "egregious" (2.1.45).

Canterbury urges him to let his subjects' "bodies follow . . . to win your right." But when he shifts the emphasis from Harry's right to his fame, he fails to mention that their bodies will be staked along with his in a chivalric fantasy centered on the hero's pursuit of glory. If, as I suggested earlier, Harry's interlocutors in effect offer him a second chance to realize the dream his father foiled at Shrewsbury, there is the obvious difference: At Shrewsbury Harry proposed a single encounter that would "save the blood on either side"; here, he has already signaled his awareness that a project conceived in the same chivalric terms would have the opposite effect:

For God doth know how many now in health
Shall drop their blood in approbation
Of what your reverence shall incite us to.
Therefore take heed how you impawn our person,
How you awake our sleeping sword of war:
We charge you, in the name of God, take heed;
For never two such kingdoms did contend
Without much fall of blood; whose guiltless drops
Are every one a woe, a sore complaint
'Gainst him whose wrongs gives edge unto the swords
That makes such waste in brief mortality. (1.2.18–28)

Granted that he is only trying to put moral pressure on the Archbishop, what counts for my purposes is Harry's apparent assumption that this argument indeed constitutes moral pressure. Nothing in his language or rhetorical strategy indicates that he is free of the compunction he tries to arouse in Canterbury. If others are to die, it had better be for a good cause. But having been persuaded that the claim makes the cause good, Harry succumbs to the "contrarious" appeal of singular "exploits and mighty enterprises." When the appeal is conveniently intensified by the Dauphin's insult, the veil of the royal plural drops away for twenty-one lines (1.2.273–93, in which twelve of the thirteen reflexive pronouns are singular) as Harry reaffirms the project of personal justification and revenge first expressed in the "I know you all" soliloquy.

I conclude from this reading of the second scene that whatever the remote causes of Harry's war may be, the proximate cause is the appeal to dynastic and chivalric self-interest. The opening scenes confirm him in his quest of a personal victory and in the vindication of his lineal rights. War against France will continue Harry's war against Henry and Richard.

A transitional moment in this process is marked by an interesting detail of the treason scene, act 2, scene 2, a scene that has always provided a field day for Harry-haters. For me, what gives the scene its power in the discursive economy of the Henriad is the hint of déjà vu implicit in the names of the traitors suborned by the "treacherous crowns" of France: Richard (Scroop), Henry (Lord Scroop), and Thomas (Grey) of Northumberland, with Henry receiving the brunt of the king's exhilarated invective. As he prepares to sail for France, the French obligingly make it possible for him to transfer the "inward wars" and "other grief" of the recent past to "the stern tyrant War" abroad.

The bracing effect of act 1, scene 2 is most conspicuous in the first of Harry's two military actions in the play, the siege of Harfleur. Approaching the audience, the Chorus of act 3, "like a . . . whiffler, 'fore the king / Seems to prepare his way" (5.Ch.12–13), and urges all males between pubescence and dotage not only to imagine Harry's expedition but also to join it. He reports the failure of the French king's latest attempt at negotiation and describes the firing of "the devilish cannon," the ordnance "with fatal mouths gaping on girded Harfleur" (26–34). Behind this panoply of sennet and Alarum, Harry's fatal mouth discharges his "once more unto the breach" aria with enough confidence to urge his men either to scale the wall or close it up "with our English dead" (3.1.1–2). He exhorts them not only to act like tigers but also to make the eye glare like a cannon and the body stretch like a bow (6–17). Their interchangeability with weapons is accented by the Chorus's figure of cannons with "mouths gaping," and by his subsequent pun, "show us here / The mettle of your pasture" (26–27).

When he compares them to "greyhounds in the slips, / Straining upon the start" (31–32), we recall the Prologue's heraldic image of "the warlike Harry" at whose "heels, / Leash'd in like hounds, should famine, sword, and fire / Crouch for employment" (5–8). And when he enjoins them to "follow your spirit" (33), the Arden editor notes the echo of Canterbury's "O, let their bodies follow, my dear liege, / With blood and sword and fire to win your right." In Harry's final exhortation, "Cry, 'God for Harry, England, and Saint George!'" (34), the sequence may be read as a graded list of incentives. This is why I prefer Taylor's shrewd emendation of this line to "God for Harry! England and Saint George!," which he justifies on the grounds that "God . . . for Saint George" makes no sense; the emendation allows England and Saint George to be placed in apposition to God, so that all three are for Harry.

Only at one point in this aria is there any hint of Harry's vaunted anxiety. It occurs during his plea to the soldiers to respond to "the blast of war" by looking fierce in order to make themselves feel fierce:

> Then lend the eye a terrible aspect;
> Let it pry through the portage of the head
> Like the brass cannon; let the brow o'erwhelm it
> As fearfully as doth a galled rock
> O'erhang and jutty his confounded base,
> Swill'd with the wild and wasteful ocean. (3.1.9–14)

In their brilliant comment on this passage, C. L. Barber and Richard Wheeler focus on the "phallic imagery, deliberately ruthless," that is not only fearful in the sense of inspiring fear but is also "inspired by fear," since "the base of the rock [is] confounded," and "galled" means "'made sore,' exasperated," as well as "washed away."[14] To amplify this reading, the figure could connote psychic precariousness, a state of being vexed and eaten away by "inward wars," fretted by passions or anxiety, frightened by the prospect of imminent collapse or self-destruction. The eye/cannon would then function like a basilisk venting its poison outward, discharging its gall into Gallia.

Such a figuration is confirmed in the play's final scene when the Queen of France uses the same imagery in greeting Harry. She is relieved to see that

> Your eyes, which hitherto hath borne in them,
> Against the French, that met them in their bent,
> The fatal balls of murdering basilisks;
> The venom of such looks, we fairly hope,
> Have lost their quality, and that this day
> Shall change all griefs and quarrels unto love. (5.2.15–20)

But in the greeting that follows, Burgundy indicates that Harry's passion has already been unfettered and that the venomous humors have passed from England to France.[15] Though Harry's injunction seems intended only as a piece of state-of-the-art war psychology, the language articulates his basic recipe for dealing with interior anxiety and aggressivity by redirecting them outward.

As Alfred Harbage implies, Harry's "when the blast of war blows in our ears" (3.1.5) is a misdirection, since he "is not the attacked [as the phrase suggests] but the attacker."[16] The battle cry and tallyho of the aria supply the blast of war. Though Harry challenges his nobles and yeomen to prove their "blood" and "breeding," respectively, his assimilating them to weapons and predatory animals revives the implicit argument of act 1, scene 2. Under the aspect of leashed hounds and artillery, as also of "the armed hand," "the noble sinews of our power," and the "blood and sword and fire," the English army is reduced to an extension of Harry's "puissant arm."

By act 4, the confidence with which this position is asserted has markedly diminished. Even at the high point of inspirational utterance in act 4, scene 3, Harry doesn't make any wholesale proposals about closing up walls with native corpses. His more bizarre ideas on the subject are directed at French ears (4.3.95–108). In the scenes that anticipate the big battle, the question of why the subjects whose "obedience to the king" compels them to risk their lives should do so becomes urgent.

Equally urgent, from Harry's first speech in act 4, scene 1 on, is the emphasis on the religious character of the war. It is God's war rather than Harry's, and it is waged against what Elizabethans would view as the Catholic enemy of "the country's peace"—the references to the Essex campaign and the Holy Roman Emperor in the Chorus of act 5 bear this out. The language of the fourth act is densely populated by the imagery of salvation and damnation, suggesting that the stakes are those of spiritual conflict. When, in the predawn debate to which I now turn, the soldiers question Harry's cause in those very terms, their resistance makes his rhetoric sing like an overloaded electric wire.

The debate in act 4, scene 1 has sometimes been interpreted as the result of a visit Harry pays his dejected soldiers before the day of the battle of Agincourt. Since that visit backfires, some have assumed that an ironic Shakespeare was turning the tables on such idealized or romanticized versions of the disguised leader motif as those found in Tacitus or in recent dramatic precedents. Against this view, Gary Taylor argues that there is no evidence in the quarto or folio text of the play to support the reading that Harry seeks out his soldiers: The only explanation offered for his disguise is "the desire for solitude"; his encounters are initiated by the other parties.[17] I think this is an important difference, and Taylor is right to insist on it, given the terms in which Harry states the desire: "I and my bosom must debate awhile, / And then I would no other company" (4.1.31–32). He wants not only to be alone but also to confer with himself, which to me implies an alternative scenario foiled by what subsequently happens. A speculative formulation of that scenario and its relation to the debate with the soldiers will bring out the significance of Taylor's point.

Suppose that Harry had succeeded in secluding himself. Then the "debate" would probably have emerged as a soliloquy, but surely not the one we hear later in his diatribe against ceremony and his ungrateful subjects. Its likely topic might have been a meditation on the theme variously expressed earlier in such statements as "'Tis good for men to love their present pains / Upon example; so the spirit is eased" (4.1.18–19), and in the lines with which he opens the scene:

> Gloucester, 'tis true that we are in great danger;
> The greater therefore should our courage be.
> Good morrow, brother Bedford. God Almighty!
> There is some soul of goodness in things evil,
> Would men observingly distil it out;
> For our bad neighbor makes us early stirrers,
> Which is both healthful and good husbandry:
> Besides, they are our outward consciences,
> And preachers to us all; admonishing
> That we should dress us fairly for our end.
> Thus may we gather honey from the weed,
> And make a moral of the devil himself. (4.1.1–12)

Given the dark prospect painted by the Chorus of act 4, Harry has reason to worry. Maybe if he had been left alone he would have confronted his own uncertainty or fear and studied how to "dress himself fairly" so as to ease his army's spirit with an example of courage that might have quickened their minds (4.1.20).

Some clues as to how that imaginary debate might proceed are offered when the disguised Harry, in response to questions by Williams and Bates, tells them that he serves under Sir Thomas Erpingham (as he is now under his cloak), and that although Erpingham views their prospects with little hope—"as men wracked upon a sand, that look to be washed off the next tide" (4.1.97–98)—he hasn't betrayed his fears to the king,

> nor is it meet that he should. For, though I speak it to you, I think the king is but a man, as I am: the violet smells to him as it doth to me; the element shows to him as it doth to me; all his senses have but human conditions: his ceremonies laid by, in his nakedness he appears but a man; and though his affections are higher mounted than ours, yet when they stoop, they stoop with like wing. Therefore when he sees reason of fears, as we do, his fears, out of doubt, be of the same relish as ours are: yet, in reason, no man should possess him with any appearance of fear, lest he, by showing it, should dishearten his army. (4.1.100–113)

Whatever else goes on in this speech, it is important to note the speaker's pleasure in the kind of auditory voyeurism Richard II had resorted to when playing with the same topos: "I live with bread like you, feel want, / Taste grief, need friends" (*Richard II*, 3.2.175–76). The varied repetitions of the king's resemblance to the speaker signify enjoyment both in the play of double senses and in the superiority this gives him over interlocutors who remain in the dark. That superiority cuts across and qualifies his assertion of equality.

Erpingham had not said what the king reported him as saying (see 4.1.16–33). Harry's sentiment is closer to his own references to "great danger" and "present pains." From this I assume that he is covertly expressing his own fears under the guise of communicating those of his betters. At the same time he is testing his soldiers with disheartening news.

This leads to another assumption, which is that in using Erpingham's discretion as a model, Harry aims to show his soldiers how to help the king set the example of courage that will ease all their spirits. Thus, as if "I and my bosom" are continuing to debate aloud, Harry takes the opportunity offered by the soldiers' interruption to practice his debate agenda. Staging the ideal subject, the loyal commoner, for their instruction ("Upon example"), he seeks to solicit sympathy and moral assistance for the king by profiling an idealized view of the bond between ruler and ruled. The king is linked to his subjects in the brotherhood of their common humanity yet securely ensconced above them by "ceremonies" and by affections that "are higher mounted."

This idealized relation is about to explode, but it is already edged with tension in two segments of the speech. The first is the falconry image in lines 106–8: As the Arden editor notes, "stoop" describes "a hawk plunging down on its prey"; if "the like wing" implies that the king's subjects are lower-flying birds, doesn't it also imply that they are prey of the predatory hawk? They will be, in a few moments. The second site of tension is the final sentence. A positive reading is that his subjects have to help the king help them overcome fear. But the negative reading is more characteristic: Once again, Harry is ready to hold others responsible for frightening the king with a show of fear that might ricochet from him to the army.

So far, the externalized debate reveals that Harry seems to focus his attention on a tactical approach to the problem of army morale. And maybe this would have been the subject of the inner debate that didn't transpire. But the language of act 4 suggests that the tactical approach would be reductive or evasive. The problem has a religious or spiritual dimension, and one that touches Harry with "attaint."

The terms of the proposed interior debate change when Harry is forced to conduct it on the more unfavorable ground established by the soldiers

Bates and Williams. Their concerns shift the focus to the justice of his cause and his moral responsibility for his soldiers' fate. Gary Taylor remarks that in the discussion with Bates and Williams Harry "does not deny the king's responsibility for the justice of his cause, nor does he deny that some (or even many) of his soldiers will die. But he does deny responsibility for the state of their individual souls."[18]

This slides over the first issue in the same way Harry does when he takes advantage of a diversion by Williams. Significantly, it is Harry who broaches the question, and does so in a phrase that has an odd syntactic wobble: "Methinks I could not die any where so contented as in the king's company, his cause being just and his quarrel honorable" (127–29). The force of the ablative absolute construction may be either conditional ("if his cause be . . .") or causal ("since his cause is . . ."). The clause is shoved aside in a way that suggests that conditionality is being acknowledged and then suppressed in the facticity of something taken for granted.

Paul Jorgensen's profound insights cut to the heart of the issue:

> This easy attitude only brings to the surface the major source of his soldiers' resentment. "That's more than we know," Williams replies. Bates, however, refuses to get into the controversy about the justness of the cause: "Ay, or more than we should seek after; for we know enough if we know we are the King's subjects. If his cause be wrong, our obedience to the King wipes the crime of it out of us." Bates's attitude was discreet. The subject was a dangerous one in Shakespeare's day. . . . But there was more than discretion in Bates's disinclination to know more. In rejecting responsibility, he had a valid reason for moderate peace of mind. . . . John Norden advised soldiers in 1597 not to be concerned over whether the authority is right or wrong: "As touching the justice and lawfulnes of the cause present, it sufficeth us to know it is to preserve our state, the superiour Magistrate commandeth it, and we are to obey it in a treble dutie, to God, our Soveraigne and commonweale."[19]

These comments admirably bring out the richness of the situation. Bates's is a good Tudor sentiment, and one that John of Gaunt had sought shelter behind in the second scene of *Richard II*. But in absolving himself by shifting responsibility to the king, Bates is playing Harry's game, and this gives us valid reason to wonder how the move affects the king's peace of mind.

Williams seems at first to support Bates's opinion—"if the cause be not good, the king himself hath a heavy reckoning to make." But he goes on to redirect attention to the fact that the demands of battle give few men the leisure to put their affairs in order and die in good spiritual condition. So, he continues, if they face the Day of Judgment in a state of sin, "it will be a black matter for the king that led them" (4.1.133–48).

This is the proposition Harry chooses to spend forty-two lines refuting. He sidesteps the question of what it is the men are to risk their lives for. Is his cause right or wrong, just or unjust? Gary Taylor's answer, which I here transpose to Harry, is similarly evasive: "I do not deny my responsibility for the justice of my cause, and I don't deny that some or many of you will die, but I do disclaim responsibility for the state of your individual souls."[20] The first clause leaves the moral question unanswered, and its coordinate relation to the second clause has disjunctive force. It places the possibility of death outside the area of moral responsibility even though "every subject's duty is the king's" (182–83). In short, theirs is not to reason why. Since Harry insists that "every subject's soul is his own," the argument absolves the king of everything, moots the question raised by Bates, and places that subject in double jeopardy, legal and moral.

Gary Taylor accepts this reasoning. He assumes that "what critics sometimes describe as 'Henry's war' is instead a conflict between two peoples, two nations," and he seems not to be troubled by the logical and rhetorical overkill of Harry's long response to Williams (4.1.150–92).[21] But even a cursory examination of that speech shows that Harry himself treats the war "as 'Henry's war.'" His moral justification is both defensive and accusatory. He cares for right and conscience and wants above all to persuade himself and others of his moral legitimacy.

Harry begins with a triple analogy: If a son sent by his father "about merchandise do sinfully miscarry upon the sea," the father is not to be blamed for "his wickedness"; if a servant commanded by his master to transport "a sum of money" is robbed and dies "in many irreconciled iniquities," the "servant's damnation" is not to be imputed to his master; if a king orders his army to war, he "is not bound to answer the particular endings of his soldiers." Since father, master, and king "purpose not their death when they purpose their services," they cannot be held accountable for the spiritual state in which son, servant, and soldiers die (4.1.150–63). This is a monstrous inflation of the disclaimer of responsibility. Because the king's soldiers are like wicked sons and sinful servants, it isn't the father's or master's fault if sons "sinfully miscarry" or servants die "in many irreconciled iniquities." The emphasis on the wickedness of son and servant rubs off on the soldiers.

The distortions in the analogies are conspicuous. Death by drowning or robbery is (however likely) accidental to the purposes and services of the first two examples, but death in battle is a danger inherent in the military service commanded by the king, who cannot therefore be said not to "purpose" his soldiers' deaths. Of these comparisons, the paternal analogy is the most interesting. Harry's self-defense admits into its recesses a latent defense of Henry that counters his own subsequent imputation of his father's wickedness and responsibility: "the fault / My father made in compassing the crown" (4.1.299–300; "compassing" is an impressively devious euphemism). Henry's ghost infiltrates and possesses Harry's language, as it does later when the speech on ceremony touches off echoes both of Richard's discoronation ritual and of Henry's insomnia soliloquy (4.1.265–70 and 273–90).

Harry goes on to remark that no king, however "spotless" his cause, can count on waging war "with all unspotted soldiers," and he lists three kinds of spots—categories of peacetime criminal activity—that blacken what seem to be more than a few of the soldiers he "calls . . . brothers, friends and countrymen" (4.0.34). "Some, peradventure," are guilty of "premeditated and contrived murder," some "of beguiling virgins with the broken seals of perjury," and some of "making the wars their bulwark, that have before gored the gentle bosom of peace with pillage and robbery" (4.1.166–71). As he enumerates his "some's" and continues, "peradventure" loses the cautious restraint of a speculative "perhaps" and gives way to a more positive emphasis—"probably," "indeed," "no doubt." This is because the listed items get more familiar, and the third opens up a breach for the warriors from Eastcheap to pour into memory even as the whole phrase bears a resonance similar to "busy giddy minds with foreign quarrels."

The catalogue also looks back to the fantasy of violence and violation with which, in act 3, scene 3, Harry tried successfully to frighten the French at Harfleur into quick submission and spare the disease-afflicted English force an untimely battle. There, in a purely imaginary scenario, he depicts his rabid army doing to the French in war what here the many "some's" do to their fellow citizens in peace. And there as here, he shifts accountability from himself even though the utterance is a mere scare tactic uttered with counterfactual intent. First, he blames the French in advance for provoking the rampage ("What is't to me, when you yourselves are cause," 19), and then he blames the soldiers whose "licentious wickedness" (22) he will not be able to control ("bootless [to] spend our vain command / Upon th' enraged soldiers in their spoil," 24–25). Thus in both act 3, scene 3, and in act 4, scene 1, he is as ready to slander or scapegoat his "happy few" as elsewhere he is ready to praise them.

The slander in act 3, scene 3 is justified by its positive military purpose: He paints spots on his soldiers—"filthy and contagious clouds / Of heady murder, spoil, and villainy" (31–32)—for their own health and safety. But we can hardly overlook the enthusiasm with which Harry out-Herods Herod. He blasts away as if the tactical function and counterfactual intent of the speech give him permission to unleash his rabid rhetoric and to savor in the image an outrage he would never allow.

In act 4, scene 1 the echoing slander has a different function: not to protect his army but to protect himself from their "imputation of his wickedness" by belaboring *their* wickedness. On the one hand, Harry's basic point is unarguable: "Every subject's soul is his own" (183–84). But by the time he reaches his conclusion he has managed to insinuate that every subject's soul is a mess and that, if every soldier prepares himself, spiritual "death is to him advantage" (186–87)—death in Harry's war, that is. On the other hand, and this is his most startling claim, he maintains that if spotted soldiers "die unprovided," far from having their damnation on his conscience, he will have served God by providing God with a war that will do the divine office of "beadle" and "vengeance" (171–82).

On this reasoning Harry will have earned spiritual points whether those who die for him are thereby saved or damned. This argument, with its key premise, "be his cause never so spotless," doesn't so much evade Bates's "if his cause be wrong" as rule it irrelevant. Harry neither denies nor affirms responsibility directly. What he does is to shift the criterion of justice from prior motives to consequences, and to claim that regardless of whether his cause is wrong or right the war will be instrumental in assuring that his soldiers will receive their just rewards.

Once again, as in act 3, scene 3, Harry's rhetoric strikes the ear with greatest resonance when he fulminates against the wickedness of others. His behavior dramatizes a meaning different from the one intended by the Chorus in his laudatory description of the way Harry "overbears attaint" (4.0.39). One of the senses of "attaint" (etymologically related to touch, as in "a little touch of Harry") is "an imputation or touch of dishonor." Harry overbears his soldiers' imputation with a sermon on divine vengeance that rises to a pitch of prophetic exhilaration as he decontaminates himself and takes shelter under God's arm.

Here again, I find Paul Jorgensen's analysis illuminating and worth quoting at length:

> The truth of the matter . . . is that the King has explained away only a fraction of what is troubling Williams. The soldier . . . has a real point. "But if the cause be not good," is his premise. The King in his argument makes no mention of a bad cause; the entire premise of his argument is a good cause. The parable of the father depends for its meaning upon a blameless venture and a blameworthy son. Williams, on the contrary, was talking about a blameworthy venture and a blameless soldier. At least he was so talking during the first part of his speech—the longest and most effective part. There he expresses the plight of mutilated bodies at the "latter day," the destitute wives and children, the debts unpaid. What if these victims of war were virtuous men damned because they fought in a bad cause? The King does not answer this question.[22]

Instead, Jorgensen continues, he focuses on only the last segment of the speech, in which Williams shifts from the difficulty of dying well "in an unjust battle" to the impossibility of dying piously in any battle. "It is easy for Henry to interpret this as an attempted defense of wicked soldiers in war" who would blame the king "for their own transgressions."[23] The question is whether he remains troubled by what he doesn't deal with, and I think the language of the soliloquy that ends the scene supplies evidence that he does.

By this time we may well wonder about the fate of Harry's plan to withdraw and debate with himself. If "we are in great danger" militarily and "should dress us fairly for our end," and if he wanted to seclude himself to confront his own uncertainty and prepare to set the example that would make his men "love their present pains," he discovers how hard that task would be, given the men's skepticism. He also discovers how much the problem exceeds merely tactical considerations, how much it implicates fundamental questions of right and conscience. If he began the discussion with an idealized picture of the common humanity shared by king and subjects, he is jolted into a diatribe that implies that to be "but a man" and "have but human conditions" is, for many of his soldiers, to be spotted with sin. The problem is how a king who is pondering the means to inspire his army can do so when at the same time he assigns himself the job of God's justicer in the domain of spiritual warfare.

The soliloquy on ceremony (4.1.236–90) acknowledges the bite of Bates's "if his cause be wrong" and Williams's "if the cause be not good" by continuing to worry the assignment of responsibility for souls and sins as well as for lives, debts, and families. Ceremony was on Harry's mind, or in his mouth, at the beginning of the episode ("his ceremonies laid by"). He reverts to it now from the embittered perspective of the unappreciated royal donor and sacrificial scapegoat: "We must bear all. O hard condition!" (239).

Harry continues to argue against Bates and Williams by mingling self-pity with demeaning epithets that reduce his subjects to a nation of fools, beggars, slaves, lackeys, wretches, and peasants. They don't appreciate and little deserve the "mortal griefs" he suffers on their behalf. The idea that they have no right to question his cause is reinforced by his closing misdirection: the slave enjoying his country's peace "in gross brain little wots / What watch the king keeps to maintain the peace, / Whose hours the peasant best advantages" (288–90).

The contemptuous contrast that jingles in "little wots / What watch" rubs off on the lackey-like peasant (275–83), who gets more out of the king's peace than the king does. This may be why, we're reminded a moment later, the king is currently maintaining the war, not the peace. It may also be why he voices anxiety about the courage of subjects conscripted for a cause that—as the soldiers have just implied—better "advantages" their king than them:

> O God of battles! steel my soldiers' hearts;
> Possess them not with fear; take from them now
> The sense of reckoning if the opposed numbers
> Pluck their hearts from them. (4.1.295–98)

"The sense of reckoning" evokes a thought of Williams's: "If the cause be not good, the king himself hath a heavy reckoning to make" (4.1.135–36). But why should God possess them with fear? The reason Harry gives himself is that despite all he has done in the way of "imploring pardon!' (311), his cause may not be good:

> Not to-day, O Lord!
> O not to-day, think not upon the fault
> My father made in compassing the crown! (4.1.298–300)

Were God to possess the army with fear and make the battle miscarry, it would mean that God visited upon the son the sins of the father who sent him overseas to busy giddy minds with foreign quarrels. Yet the moral logic of this scenario was contradicted earlier in Harry's argument with the soldiers, when he compared the king to a father and the soldiers to his son.

The pressures of self-division that afflict Harry's prayer cast mordant shadows over the ingenuous fervor of his desire to be free of paternal contamination, so that we have to wonder about the force and direction of

> Though all I can do is nothing worth,
> Since that my penitence comes after all,
> Imploring pardon. (4.1.309–11)

Investing in religious insurance, Harry has ordered priests to sing for Richard's soul (4.1.307–8) but not for Henry's. If he is arguing that pardon is not in his own gift, that only God can grant it, wouldn't one who sympathizes with the speaker of these words wish that he could confront his own need for pardon and come to atonement with his father by saying, as Henry had once said to Aumerle, "I pardon him, as God shall pardon me"?[24]

To ask this question is no doubt to judge him and risk falling into ethical reductionism. But it is also to observe and register and respond to the persistent self-wounding of a speaker who wants above all to persuade himself—not merely the world—that right and conscience are on his side. His overtures to God reflect more than a desire for religious legitimation of the war. They also reflect a concern for his own spiritual welfare.

In Harry's next appearance, the appeal to the saint's discourse of religion is shored up by a return to Hotspurian ground and the hero's discourse of honor. But the famous Saint Crispin aria in act 4, scene 3 vibrates with odd overtones because it echoes themes touched on in the conversation with the soldiers:

> If we are marked to die, we are enow
> To do our country loss; and if to live,
> The fewer men, the greater share of honor.
> God's will! I pray thee, wish not one man more. (4.3.20–23)

> We would not die in that man's company
> That fears his fellowship to die with us. (38–39)

> We few, we happy few, we band of brothers;
> For he to-day that sheds his blood with me
> Shall be my brother; be he ne'er so vile
> This day shall gentle his condition. (4.3.60–63)

These sentiments remember and invert Bates's "I would he were here alone; so should . . . many poor men's lives [be] saved," and Harry's retort: "I dare say you love him not so ill to wish him here alone . . . methinks I could not die any where so contented as in the king's company, his cause being just and his quarrel honorable" (4.1.122–29). The underside of the hero's desire to be "solus" and "egregious" may be a concern to minimize the casualties he will be responsible for "if the cause be not good."

A few lines after the aria, Montjoy, the French herald, alludes to this responsibility, restating it in religious terms prefaced by an image that conflates military with spiritual danger:

> For certainly thou art so near the gulf
> Thou needs must be englutted. Besides, in mercy,
> The constable desires thee thou wilt mind
> Thy followers of repentance; that their souls
> May make a peaceful and a sweet retire
> From off these fields, where, wretches, their poor bodies
> Must lie and fester. (4.3.82–88)

The constable's taunt revives the issue raised by Williams: "If these men do not die well, it will be a black matter for the king that led them to it."

Harry's reply is at first defensively and lamely hopeful—"A many of our bodies shall no doubt / Find native graves" (95–96)—and then bizarrely threatening: Those who die "like men . . . shall be famed" both because the sun will "draw their honors reeking up to heaven" and because the smell of their rotting bodies "shall breed a plague in France" (4.3.99–103). This crackling catachresis seems meant primarily to put the constable down—a Retort Functional that outlines the complete art of effective dying. Here, in contrast to Harry's sermon on damnation in act 4, scene 1, it is the French, not the sinful English, who will be the victims of a war that is God's "beadle" and "vengeance." To displace God's punishment from the English to the French is figuratively to export the war and close up the English ranks threatened by strife in the predawn debate. But if Harry's violent sport with the figure of festering bodies amounts to an interlocutory triumph, it measures his evasion of the issue encoded in the constable's warning about "thy followers."

The issue appears more sharply when we supply the thematic context of the French herald's message:

> Once more I come to know of thee, King Harry,
> If for thy ransom thou wilt now compound,
> Before thy most assured overthrow:
> For certainly thou art so near the gulf
> Thou needs must be englutted. (79–83)

From act 3, scene 5 through act 4, scene 7 the question of the king's ransom comes up for discussion in five scenes, and is parodied in another. It is introduced by the Constable, who connects it to the sad state of the English army:

> Sorry am I his numbers are so few,
> His soldiers sick and famished in their march,
> For I am sure when he shall see our army
> He'll drop his heart into the sink of fear,
> And for achievement offer us his ransom. (3.5.56–60)

The Constable predicts that Harry will pay to keep his army and himself from certain defeat. The French king commands that this message be sent to Harry through Montjoy, who warns Harry, first, to "consider of his ransom," second, that "his pettiness would bow under" the reparation he would have to make for "our losses," and third, that "he hath betrayed his followers, whose condemnation is pronounced" (3.6.131–41). After Harry confesses that he doesn't seek battle now because "my people are with sickness much enfeebled, / My numbers lessen'd" (151–52), he gives his answer: "My ransom is this frail and worthless trunk, / My army but a weak and sickly guard." Nevertheless, "tell him we will come on" (160–62).

In this response it's notable that "my ransom" and "my army" are in echoic relation and that while the epithet Harry applies to himself is courtly, coy, and topped off with a pun, the epithet he applies to the army is merely descriptive. He doesn't really think his trunk is frail and worthless, but he does think his army is weak and sickly. The parallelism of the two clauses betrays the speaker's attention to the individual hero as underdog whose army is a shadow or extension of himself and is therefore part of what he may have to "pay" (i.e., sacrifice) as the price of the "coming on" that will redeem his honor.

This is a standard move in the discourse of honor. But in Harry's case it is jarred by the vibrations of the other discourses implicated in his position of responsibility and his concern for his cause. If at this point the discourses of sinner, victim, and judge are dormant in his language, they become active in act 4, scene 1.

When Bates wishes the king "were here alone" so that he will "be sure to be ransomed, and many poor men's lives saved" (4.1.122–24), Harry doesn't respond immediately, but shows that he has this in mind by returning unbidden to the subject after his diatribe: "I myself heard the king say he would not be ransomed" (4.1.197–98). Williams retorts cynically that the king said it only "to make us fight cheerfully; but when our throats are cut, he may be ransomed, and we ne'er the wiser" (199–201). This introduces the new idea that after other men get killed the king can save his life by paying ransom. The idea goes to the heart of the question of the king's cause. It darkens the shadow cast by the Constable's taunt at 4.3.84–88: The king is urged to save himself by paying ransom and to admonish the followers who will die for him to dress themselves fairly for their end.

The theme of ransom threaded through these scenes has a deep instability woven into it. As a form of redemption, ransom involves payment and sacrifice. When the religious dimension is activated, it cuts across the economic and military dimensions. In the Chorus of act 4, this intersection produces disquieting resonances. The initial scene setting is melodramatically ominous:

> Now entertain conjecture of a time
> When creeping murmur and the poring dark
> Fills the wide vessel of the universe.
> From camp to camp through the foul womb of night
> The hum of either army stilly sounds,
> That the fix'd sentinels almost receive
> The secret whispers of each other's watch:
> Fire answers fire, and through their paly flames
> Each battle sees the other's umber'd face;
> Steed threatens steed, in high and boastful neighs
> Piercing the night's dull ear; and from the tents
> The armorers, accomplishing the knights,
> With busy hammers closing rivets up,
> Give dreadful note of preparation. (4.0.1–14)

Though the aim is to arouse sympathy and concern for the plight of the English, the two "battles" are here united in hushed foreboding of what their common enemy, the ancient scapegoat, Mother Night, will give birth to. The busy hammers on both sides ensconce the knights as if to drown out—and protect them from—the creeping murmur and the poring dark. When they have been "accomplished," they will strain "upon the start" (3.1.32), yearning for release from the foul mother of apprehension and for escape to the mutual embrace, the "golden uncontrolled enfranchisement," of "battle with mine adversary" (*Richard II,* 1.3.90–92).

The passage moves from an unknown fear to the seeming knowledge produced by military conflict and decision. Following this implication out, the night that surrounds and touches the armies hums stilly within them; its secret whispers flittering through the womb give umbrage more insidious than battle fear or anger. So, if there is a touch of Harry in the night, that circumstantial image of the inspiring leader surrounds a touch of the night in Harry.

Having united the armies against the night, the Chorus proceeds to disequalize them. The "high and boastful neighs" come to symbolize the overconfidence of the French. Their hippophiliac blather in the previous scene registered an uneasiness about their manhood that now reappears in their chiding of Mother Night:

> The country cocks do crow, the clocks do toll,
> And the third hour of drowsy morning name.
> Proud of their numbers, and secure in soul,
> The confident and over-lusty French
> Do the low-rated English play at dice;
> And chide the cripple tardy-gaited night
> Who, like a foul and ugly witch, doth limp
> So tediously away. (15–22)

Cock-crowing momentarily diverts attention from the "dreadful note of preparation." Or does it? If I strain at the association of cock-crowing with dice-playing, I almost receive some secret whispers of another dreadful preparation: the denial of Peter, the soldiers casting lots at the cross.

Though at first glance this is a long stretch, the allusion seems to be reinforced by subsequent passages that sustain the cosmic opening of the Chorus and give it an apocalyptic edge. I think not only of phrases in Harry's first speech—"There is some soul of goodness in things evil," "we should dress us fairly for our end," "make a moral of the devil himself"—but also of the image lurking in his statement that

when the mind is quickened, out of doubt,
The organs, though defunct and dead before,
Break up their drowsy grave, and newly move
With casted slough and fresh legerity. (4.1.20–23)

This is a vision that is foiled by the transformation of the resurrected organs into serpents and that will shortly be recalled by Williams's image of "the latter day" (4.1.135–48). These references to the crucifixion, the raising of the dead, and the Day of Judgment cohere about a paradigm of ransom that stands in contrast to the one discussed in the play. The English king is to be redeemed by money from the royal (or national) fisc, or by the sacrifice of his subjects; Christ sacrifices himself to redeem sinful humans.

To return to the Chorus, I don't imagine any such contrast to be part of his message, since I read him unironically as the king's representative and whiffler. If the allusion to Christ is felt in his language, the enemies are obviously the French, while Harry is his chief candidate for the role of sacrificial victim and heroic savior: the "royal captain" whose fighting talk will redeem his "ruin'd band," whose eye gives "largess universal like the sun," who thaws "cold fear" and comforts "every wretch, pining and pale before" (29, 41–45). Yet we may still wonder about the strangely infernal cast of the Chorus's imagery:

The poor condemned English,
Like sacrifices, by their watchful fires
Sit patiently, and inly ruminate
The morning's danger, and their gesture sad
Investing lank-lean cheeks and war-worn coats
Presenteth them unto the gazing moon
So many horrid ghosts. O, now, who will behold
The royal captain of this ruin'd band
Walking from watch to watch, from tent to tent,
Let him cry, "Praise and glory on his head!" (4.Chorus.22–31)

The ghosts are proleptic images of those who might die in battle and come back to haunt. The question the play insistently asks, the question I have been exploring in this chapter, is, for whose cause are they being sacrificed if not their royal captain's? "Condemned" glances back through the opinion of the dicing French to the herald's charge that Harry "hath betrayed his followers, whose condemnation is pronounced." But they are also condemned by their royal captain's insistence that "we will come on" though "weak and sickly."

One editor's comment on "poor condemned English" is that "Shakespeare has somewhat exaggerated the wretchedness of the English in order to exalt the courage of his hero."[25] Leaving Shakespeare out of it, let's grant that the claim to be an underdog is standard equipment in the hero's discourse of honor and that Harry and the Chorus make the most of it. Does the Chorus exaggerate the wretchedness? It's hard to agree that he does, since it is repeatedly attested to by Harry, by the French, and even by a stage direction in act 3, scene 6 ("Enter King Henry . . . and his poor soldiers").

Regardless of the outcome, and regardless of the playgoer's or reader's foreknowledge of it, Harry's sense of the army's wretchedness and the "great danger" they are in is verified by other evidence and can be taken as both genuine and justified. The underdog claim may be legitimate. But the underdog includes the army as well as the individual hero who is the usual subject of the discourse of honor. That discourse is thus traversed by other discourses that focus on the issue of responsibility and on the justice of the cause.

The plight of the English army is the subject of a wonderfully weird set of comments by William Empson during his long meditation on Falstaff and Dover Wilson.[26] Empson has been worrying over Wilson's remark that the death of Falstaff resembles that of Socrates, and though here as elsewhere his rhetoric sends Wilson up in the same way Falstaff sends up the Establishment, he grudgingly admits that the idea that Falstaff was (like Socrates) "a good tutor somehow was a quite public part of the play." He then goes on to observe that Wilson

> has a similar eerie flash of imagination about a stage direction in *Henry V*, where the heroes of Agincourt are described as "poor troops." He rightly complains that modern editions omit the epithet, an important guide to the producer; the story would be mere boasting if it did not emphasize that their victory was a hairbreadth escape after being gruelled. But then he goes on: "Did the 'scarecrows' that Falstaff led to Shrewsbury return to the stage?" It seems rather likely, for the convenience of a repertory company, that they did; but what can it mean, if we suppose it to mean anything? What is recalled is the most unbearable of all Falstaff's retorts to Henry—"they'll fit a pit as well as better; tush, man, mortal men, mortal men."[27]

Falstaff, Empson reminds us, "has just boasted that he took bribes to accept such bad recruits . . . and he boasts later that he got them killed to keep their pay . . . but this makes his reply all the more crashing, as from one murderer to another: 'that is all you Norman lords want, in your squabbles between cousins over your loot, which you make an excuse to murder the English people.'" Empson concludes that although this "very strong joke" fits Henry IV "as part of a vague protest against civil war . . . to recall it over Henry's hereditary claim to France would surely be reckless; besides, the mere return of those stage figures could not carry so much weight."[28]

They might, however, carry more weight for a practitioner of imaginary audition who allows himself every so often to relax into the sin or disease Richard Levin calls Fluellenism.[29] Like Fluellen, Falstaff has the military rank of captain. Jorgensen explains that because of the Elizabethan captain's "immense influence in recruiting men, leading them into battle, and dispensing royal funds, [he] was an officer of literally frightful importance."[30] I don't want to push too hard, in this context, on the Chorus's phrase, "The royal captain of this ruin'd band" of "poor condemned English," but I can't resist mentioning it. What can it mean, if we suppose it to mean anything? Clearly Falstaff is the worst of captains and Harry the best. But captains are captains, war is war, and the foreign war is haunted by ghostly displacements of the civil war. The "pitiful rascals" paraded on the stage and in the text of *Henry V* would fill a pit as well as better, even if—as it happily turns out—most of them don't.

If Falstaff's recruitment procedures in *Henry IV* Part 2 (3.2.85–182) satirize typical abuses, it isn't surprising to find the royal captain saddled with a "ruin'd band." That only makes his victory and inspiring leadership more noteworthy—but noteworthy in a slightly suspect way. In Empson's view, the tutor Falstaff should get much of the credit for Harry's leadership skills because he weaned him on good "Machiavellian" principles: "A young man is better for 'sowing his wild oats', especially if he is being trained to 'handle men'. The sort of ruler you can trust, you being one of the ruled, the sort that can understand his people and lead them to glory, is one who has learned the world by experience, especially rather low experience; he knows the tricks." Empson thus explains why Falstaff's rejection "could be presented as somehow tragic. . . . After rejecting Falstaff Henry continues to show the popular touch and so forth that Falstaff taught him; indeed, *Henry V* limits itself rather rigidly to describing the good effects of this training, for example in his treatment of the troops and of the Princess."[31]

Empson's styptic prose, especially the tart piece of etceteration, encourages readers to eye with guarded skepticism the values he appears to recommend. I don't think he would mind my filling in the "and so forth" with the arguments developed in the previous pages. Nor would he mind my emending his last clause to "Harry and the Chorus limit themselves rather rigidly," with a rigidity the text of the play marks as slightly suspect.

These reflections lead me back to the Chorus with renewed appreciation of the odd pressure his imagery puts on the lines describing Harry's reassuring visit among "his host," whom he calls "brothers, friends, and countrymen": "Upon his royal face there is no note / How dread an army hath enrounded him" (32–36). Which army? And does "dread" mean "dreadful" or "terrified"? And what about "enrounded"? Though it is usually glossed as "surrounded," why can't it also mean "amplified" or "enlarged"? Then too, there is the ambiguity of "overbears attaint" (39) that I mentioned earlier.

Everything the Chorus says—or tries to say—by way of praise is qualified by little touches of attaint, touches of the night in Harry, touches that surround the glittering choric fantasy of the heroic underdog with the shadowy edges of a fantasy of damnation. In this, the Chorus of act 4 departs from his previous performances. His speech itself sounds the "dreadful note of preparation." It figures the battle of Agincourt as a foetus in the womb—the flooded vessel—of universal night, and it gutters his description with infernal flickers.

The imagery unites military with spiritual danger in a way that sets the historical drama within the cosmic field of the drama of salvation and damnation. It sends the secret whispers of the sinner's discourse slithering through the rhizomes of act 4 where they may be glimpsed in direct references, slant allusions, or merely casual usages. If the sentiments of the Chorus are those that the king would like himself and the world to believe, then by the same logic shouldn't the Chorus's dark troping register the buried fear that motivates the intense need for justification? This need becomes more critical as Harry moves from Shrewsbury to Westminster to Agincourt. It becomes more critical as he approaches the moment when he will ask his "ruin'd band" to sacrifice themselves for a cause that touches the royal captain more nearly than it touches England and St. George.

The need is nevertheless assimilated to the chivalric fetishism of trial by battle and can find satisfaction only in that melodramatic form of closure. Thus it is as if to escape from the sullen ground of the sinner's discourse to the golden enfranchisement of the hero's discourse that the Chorus concludes with another appeal for our help:

> And so our scene must to the battle fly;
> Where, O for pity! we shall much disgrace
> With four or five most vile and ragged foils,
> Right ill-dispos'd in brawl ridiculous,
> The name of Agincourt. Yet sit and see;
> Minding true things by what their mock'ries be. (48–53)

Against the nocturnal background of the preceding lines, this apology points in two different directions. On the one hand, it does its conventional choric work by asking us to help the play transcend the limits of theater so that Harry's famous victory will get the imaginative and political justification it deserves. But on the other hand, the exhortation only extends the limits of theater to the circumstances it represents. It marks historical theater and its theatrical history as merely different degrees, less and more perfect, of the "smooth comforts false" delivered by "rumor's tongues": "smooth comforts false, worse than true wrongs."[32] Both the stage battle and the real battle are displacements that aspire to the "seeming knowledge" their resolution will produce. Both "make trifles of terrors." Both are mockeries of "true things" and "true wrongs" that cannot be adequately represented, much less resolved, by the golden fire that frets the majestic roof of theater or palace.

I assume that Harry can't know what we know: The English underdog will win a surprisingly easy victory at Agincourt. I'm encouraged from early in the play to have doubts about the battle skill of the French. The difference between what I think I know and what I think Harry knows enables me to take his concerns seriously and view them sympathetically. Shakespeare's play encourages me to do this without blinking away the uneasiness induced by the symptoms of bad conscience inscribed in Harry's language. By the same token, because I know about the happy ending, the importance of the foreign war diminishes, and the inward war of discourses advances to the foreground. *Henry V* brings to a climax the various forms of the Henriad's central activity, harrying. This concludes Shakespeare's and my accounts of the different ways in which each of the Henriad's kings—Richard II, Henry IV, and Henry V—is a self-harrier.

Notes

1. Misanthropology in Richard III

This is a slightly modified version of an essay titled "Conscience and Complicity in *Richard III*," published in *Richard III,* ed. Thomas Cartelli, A Norton Critical Edition (New York: W. W. Norton, 2009), 400–417.

1. All citations from the play follow the Norton Critical Edition of *Richard III* (2009).

2. A. P. Rossiter, *Angel with Horns and other Shakespeare Lectures*, ed. Graham Story (London: Longmans, Green, 1961), 20–22.

3. Nicholas Brooke, *Shakespeare's Early Tragedies* (London: Methuen, 1968), 78–79.

4. Patricia Parker, *Shakespeare from the Margins: Language, Culture, Context* (Chicago: University of Chicago Press, 1996), 37. See also Parker's classic essay "Preposterous Events," *Shakespeare Quarterly* 43 (1992): 186–213.

5. Linda Charnes, *Notorious Identity: Materializing the Subject in Shakespeare* (Cambridge: Harvard University Press, 1993), 62–63. The whole chapter on *Richard III* is outstanding, and I'm deeply indebted to it; see 20–69.

6. Jean Howard and Phyllis Rackin, *Engendering a Nation: A Feminist Account of Shakespeare's English Histories* (New York: Routledge, 1997), 109.

7. John Jowett, ed., *The Tragedy of King Richard III* (Oxford: Oxford University Press, 2000), 41.

8. Marguerite Waller, "Usurpation, Seduction, and the Problematics of the Proper: A 'Deconstructive', 'Feminist' Rereading of the Seductions of Richard and Anne in Shakespeare's *Richard III*," in *Rewriting the Renaissance: The Discourses of Sexual Difference in Early Modern Europe*, ed. Margaret W. Ferguson, Maureen Quilligan, and Nancy J. Vickers (Chicago: University of Chicago Press, 1986),170–71.

9. Ibid., 172.

10. Jowett, *Tragedy of King Richard III*, 43.

11. Waller, "Usurpation, Seduction," 170.

12. John N. King, *Tudor Royal Iconography* (Princeton: Princeton University Press, 1989), 32.

13. Anne Righter (Barton), *Shakespeare and the Idea of the Play* (London: Chatto & Windus, 1962), 98, 99.

14. Ibid., 99.

15. E. A. J. Honigmann, ed., *King Richard the Third* (London: Penguin Books, 1995), 31, 35.

16. See G. R. Hibbard's sensitive reading of their dialogue and its shift into verse in *The Making of Shakespeare's Dramatic Poetry* (Toronto: University of Toronto Press, 1981), 83–85.

17. George T. Wright, "An Almost Oral Art: Shakespeare's Language on Stage and Page," *Shakespeare Quarterly* 43, no.2 (1992): 165.

18. For the most astute reading of this episode, see Marjorie Garber, *Shakespeare's Ghost Writers: Literature as Uncanny Causality* (New York: Routledge, 1987), 38. Garber observes that the Scrivener displays "both moral and professional" indignation because "his task . . . had begun before the incident that was to occasion it, and ended too late to authorize—although it will retrospectively 'legitimize'—the death of Hastings."

19. Robert Weimann, *Shakespeare and the Popular Tradition in the Theater: Studies in the Social Dimension of Dramatic Form and Function*, ed. Robert Schwartz (Baltimore: Johns Hopkins University Press, 1978), 159.

20. Honigmann, *King Richard the Third*, 31.

21. Thomas More, *The History of Richard III*, ed. R. S. Sylvester, *The Complete Works of St. Thomas More*, vol. 2 (New Haven: Yale University Press, 1963), 80.

22. Ibid., 81.

23. David Bevington, *The Complete Works of Shakespeare,* 4th ed. (New York: Harper Collins, 1992), 629–30; Brooke, *Shakespeare's Early Tragedies*, 72.

24. Hibbard, *Making of Shakespeare's Dramatic Poetry*, 86–87.

25. Ibid., 86.

26. John Dover Wilson, ed., *Richard III* (1968; Cambridge: Cambridge University Press, 1974), xliv.

27. Sigurd Burckhardt, *Shakespearean Meanings* (Princeton: Princeton University Press, 1968), 166.

28. Barbara Hodgdon, *The End Crowns All: Closure and Contradiction in Shakespeare's History* (Princeton: Princeton University Press, 1991), 115, 122, 123.

29. Ibid., 122–23.

30. Charnes, *Notorious Identity*, 63.

31. Stanley Cavell, *Disowning Knowledge in Seven Plays of Shakespeare* (Cambridge: Cambridge University Press, 2003), 129.

32. William Shakespeare, *Othello, the Moor of Venice*, ed. Michael Neill (Oxford: Oxford University Press, 2006).

2. "Here, Cousin, Seize the Crown": The Triumphant Fall of Richard, the Self-Harrier

1. For details see Geoffrey Bullough, *Narrative and Dramatic Sources of Shakespeare*, vol. 2 (1960; New York: Columbia University Press, 1975), 9–15.

2. Annabel Patterson, *Reading Holinshed's Chronicles* (Chicago: University of Chicago Press, 1994 1995), 15. As Peter Saccio notes, one of the important motives visible in these Tudor-sponsored accounts was "the necessity to justify the Tudor acquisition of the throne." Saccio, *Shakespeare's English Kings: History, Chronicle, and Drama* (New York: Oxford University Press, 1977), 14.

3. Patterson's important reinterpretation of the 1587 *Chronicles* questions its general commitment to the Tudor ideology so long assumed by readers of Shakespeare's histories and others. Nevertheless, her emphasis on the "multivocality" (*Reading Holinshed's Chronicles,* 7) and anti-absolutist tenor of the edition doesn't rule out periodic reversions to the providentialist ideology as one of the several master narratives to be found in it. I think it is important to recognize that this ideology is isolated in the history plays as the dominant explanation motivating the organization and detail of the history represented in the chronicles. It is important because that explanation is itself represented in Shakespeare's histories as a target of critique.

4. *Holinshed's Chronicles of England, Scotland, and Ireland* (1587; London: J. Johnson et al., 1808), III, 24. Again, summarizing Henry IV's reign, the author attributes the unquiet years of rebellion to the people's support for Henry's "deposing of their rightfull and naturall prince king Richard" (III, 58).

5. Phyllis Rackin, "The Role of the Audience in Shakespeare's *Richard II,*" *Shakespeare Quarterly* 36, no. 3 (1985): 262–81 See also Rackin's *Stages of History: Shakespeare's English Chronicles* (Ithaca, N.Y.: Cornell University Press, 1990), 117–30. For a similar account of this change focused more intensely on the way it is manifested by changing patterns of syntax, see Stephen Booth's adroit, witty, and often hilarious "Syntax as Rhetoric in *Richard II,*" *Mosaic* 10, no. 3 (1977): 87–103.

6. This was a disputed principle, subject of an important debate in the 1560s. For details, see Marie Axton, *The Queen's Two Bodies: Drama and the English Succession* (London: Royal Historical Society, 1977), 22–23 and 26–28.

7. See *Richard II* 1.2.33–34, 3.2.54–57, and 4.1.122–30.

8. Sigurd Burckhardt, *Shakespearean Meanings* (Princeton: Princeton University Press, 1968), 167. Burckhardt's account of the complementary relation between two modes and models of succession, primogeniture and combat, is indispensable for an understanding of both Tudor ideology and Shakespeare's representation of it: See 163–76 and 180–85.

9. "An exhortation concerning good order and obedience to rulers and Magistrates" (1547, 1559), in *Elizabethan Backgrounds: Historical Documents of the Age of Elizabeth I*, ed. Arthur F. Kinney (Hamden, Conn.: Archon Books, 1975), 64. It was long thought that the reason for the absence of the deposition scene from the original editions of the play was that Queen Elizabeth's government had it suppressed. For a persuasive critique of this view, the evidence on which it is based, and the implications drawn from it, see Leeds Barroll, "A New History for Shakespeare and His Time," *Shakespeare Quarterly* 39, no. 4 (1988): 441–64.

10. *The New Cambridge Shakespeare: King Richard II*, ed. Andrew Gurr (Cambridge: Cambridge University Press, 1984), 19.

11. The classic discussion of this doctrine is in Ernst Kantorowicz, *The King's Two Bodies: A Study in Medieval Political Theology* (Princeton: Princeton University Press, 1957). For an important revisionary account of the use of the doctrine during and after Elizabeth's regime see Axton's *The Queen's Two Bodies.* It is interesting to note that one Elizabethan law case for which the two-bodies doctrine was elaborated concerned the very duchy of Lancaster of which John of Gaunt was the first owner and which the three kings descended from him owned as private property—held "in their Body natural." See Kantorowicz, *King's Two Bodies,* 7–10 and Axton, *Queen's Two Bodies,* 16–17 and 29. For a more recent attempt to explore "the clash of person and office" in the play, see Wolfgang Iser, *Staging Politics: The Lasting Impact of Shakespeare's Histories,* trans. David Henry Wilson (New York: Columbia University Press, 1993), 71–84.

12. Anne Righter, *Shakespeare and the Idea of the Play* (London: Chatto & Windus, 1962), 121. Righter's brilliant book, written a half century ago, remains the best general introduction to Shakespeare's use of the theater metaphor.

13. This is an old problem illustrated in the early Middle Ages by the Donatist Heresy concerning the effect of a priest's personal wickedness on his ritual efficacy. As Elizabethan lawyers put it, "What the King does in his Body politic cannot be invalidated or frustrated by any disability in his natural Body" (Kantorowicz, *King's Two Bodies*, 7).

14. My tendency here and elsewhere is to defend against a flourishing industry of character judgment—worrying whether characters are good or bad, whether they meet our own high moral standards or fall short of them—on the grounds that what characters may think of themselves, how they judge themselves, is more interesting than what I think of them or how I judge them.

15. Holinshed tries to do justice to the pathos of Richard's predicament by balancing his criticism of the king with an emphasis on his victimization: Forsaken by his allies and at the mercy of his enemies, "left desolate, void, and in despaire of all hope and comfort," Richard was "persuaded to renounce his crowne . . . so that in hope of life onelie, he agreed to all things that were of him demanded" (II, 855, 861).

16. When Richard and the Queen visit the dying Gaunt in act 2, scene 1, she greets him in proper form, "How fares our noble uncle Lancaster?" but Richard uses her respectful address as a backboard that gives his bluff greeting a ruder and more derisive bounce: "What comfort, man? How is't with agèd Gaunt?" (2.1.72).

17. John Halverson, "The Lamentable Comedy of Richard II," *English Literary Renaissance* 24, no. 2 (1994): 343–69, esp. 360.

18. *King Lear,* Arden Shakespeare, 3rd series, ed. R. A. Foakes (1997). For a more detailed account of Richard's language in act 3, scene 2 see my *Imaginary Audition: Shakespeare on Stage and Page* (Berkeley: University of California Press, 1989), 79–83, 88–93, and 104–33.

19. That is, "I have been bad, but they have been worse." Lear's statement is complicated because "I am a man" adds a threat: "I am a man, and will have my revenges." The victim/revenger's discourse is developed to a fine art by Bolingbroke's son in *Henry V*, but in *Richard II* the revenger component is muffled deep within the emphasis on victimization—though Richard's sardonic mimicry is itself a form of revenge.

20. Holinshed, for example, puts much emphasis on Richard's attempt to cooperate in making his resignation legal; he praises him for choosing to read aloud the articles of resignation (II, 862), something Shakespeare's Richard refuses to do. Shakespeare's Richard cooperates in a manner that throws a sardonic light on Holinshed's identification of cooperation with passive submission. The play identifies it with passive aggression.

21. Richard reads aloud the articles of resignation and is directly quoted on a few occasions restricted to brief public utterances, but is otherwise represented through and controlled by the narrator's voicing in indirect discourse.

22. Halverson, "Lamentable Comedy," 352, 360. See the interesting and perceptive comments on 362–64, in which Halverson shows how Shakespeare's allusive omissions of episodes in the play's prehistory make his Richard less sympathetic than Holinshed's.

23. *Holinshed's Chronicles*, II, 868. This omission is noted by Halverson ("Lamentable Comedy," 362). Halverson also reminds us that Holinshed partly dissociates himself from this opinion (II, 869), ascribing it to the hostility and ungratefulness of Richard's subjects. In the play, there is one vague reference to the "sinful hours" Richard spent with his evil counselors (3.1.11), but this doesn't come across as information about Richard because it is part of Bolingbroke's gravamen against the counselors, and it contributes to his public justification for putting them to death.

24. In making this suggestion I am applying to *Richard II* an interpretation of Shakespeare's *Richard III* first advanced by Nicholas Brooke in 1968 and recently taken up in some brilliant general comments by Patricia Parker and in an impressively detailed analysis by Linda Charnes: Brooke, *Shakespeare's Early Tragedies* (1968; London: Methuen, 1973), 48–79, especially 55–58 and 77–79; Parker, "Preposterous Events," *Shakespeare Quarterly* 43, no. 2 (1992): 201–4; Charnes, *Notorious Identity: Materializing the Subject in Shakespeare* (Cambridge, Mass.: Harvard University Press, 1993), 20–69. The idea that Richard collaborates in his own downfall is obvious and has often been noted. For a compact statement of the thesis, see Richard Wheeler, *Shakespeare's Development and the Problem Comedies: Turn and Counter-Turn* (Berkeley: University of California Press, 1981), 158–59. My variation on the thesis is to treat it as a project consistently sustained by the language assigned to the name, or speech-prefix, "Richard." I put it this way to emphasize that I am not concerned with what an imaginary person named Richard might actually have been aware of or intended at any moment. Rather, my concern is with a pattern of motivation that can be traced in his language throughout the play. It is entirely conceivable that two actors preparing to per-

form the role of Richard could agree that this project, this pattern, is discernible in the language and yet disagree as to whether at any particular moment Richard should be played as a speaker clearly aware, vaguely aware, or unaware that he is engaged in a scenario and discourse of self-deposition.

25. The suggestion is Andrew Gurr's, in his excellent introduction to the New Cambridge edition of the play (1984), 10–12. Gurr's view is that Richard's stopping the duel is in his own self-interest; I take the opposite view.

26. "When Richard speaks of himself in terms of the conventional sun-king, the image becomes an ironical epithet that emphasizes his failure as God's deputy" (S. K. Heninger, Jr., "The Sun-King Analogy in Richard II," *Shakespeare Quarterly* 11, no. 3 [1960]: 324), to which I add only that the irony seems attributable to the speaker of the words as well as the author of the play.

27. See 1.4.43–64, 2.1.126–27, 155–62, 209–10. Both Gaunt and York accuse him of Gloucester's murder to his face in 2.1.124–31, 163–70.

28. For the more detailed account of these lines from which the present comments are drawn, see my *Imaginary Audition*, 88–93.

29. "If the title is true, God will defend it. . . . If God will not defend it, it isn't true": so Burckhardt paraphrases Richard's logic (*Shakespearean Meanings*, 170). But does Richard think God will defend it even after the king has despoiled his country?

30. Kantorowicz, *King's Two Bodies,* 38, 27.

31. As Meredith Skura notes in *Shakespeare the Actor and the Purposes of Playing* (Chicago: University of Chicago Press, 1993), 299. See her excellent discussion of Richard the "tedious actor," 179–83. The Queen's phrasing suggests more than one sorrow: "I, a gasping new-delivered mother, / Have woe to woe, sorrow to sorrow joined" (2.2.65–66). The sorrow brought forth by Greene's news of what is about to happen to Richard is joined to another sorrow the Queen conceives in response to something that has already happened to Richard.

32. The most interesting attempt to account for the function of the Queen in the play is Graham Holderness's "'A Woman's War': A Feminist Reading of *Richard II*," in *Shakespeare Left and Right*, ed. Ivo Kamps (New York: Routledge, 1991), 167–83.

33. *The Oxford Shakespeare, Henry IV, Part One*, ed. David Bevington (1987; Oxford: Oxford University Press, 2008), 3.2.11.

34. Gurr, *King Richard II*, 32.

35. Preformulated, not premeditated. There is no presumption that speakers who deliver rhymed couplets composed their verse or that they are aware of speaking in rhyme. The shift to rhyme operates at a different rhetorical level; it indicates and characterizes intentions or motives that speak through the speakers whether or not they are aware of them. My views on the various uses to which Shakespeare puts verse are heavily influenced by the wonderful work of George T. Wright: See, for example, "An Almost Oral Art: Shakespeare's Language on Stage and Page," *Shakespeare Quarterly* 43, no. 2 (1992): 159–69.

36. The term is Stephen Booth's: "Syntax as Rhetoric," 91.

37. Against this emphasis on Bolingbroke's ineffectiveness it will be objected that I omit any reference to the two passages in which Richard (1.4.20–36) and York (5.2.7–21) describe him successfully wooing the public. Bolingbroke's popularity is a standard motif in the chronicle sources. Hall mentions it once and Holinshed several times (II, 848, 849, 853). But the joy with which people greet Bolingbroke is described partly as a function of their anticipation of relief from the burden of Richard, and Holinshed dwells on the decline of Bolingbroke's popularity after the questionable circumstances of Richard's death. Shakespeare relegates this motif to the background by keeping it offstage and assigning its description to interested speakers who reveal as much about themselves as they do about Bolingbroke. It is part of the frame within which the play redirects emphasis to the drama of the moral combat going on between the two protagonists.

38. For a compact summary of the Henriad's references to pilgrimage and crusade, see Gurr, *King Richard II,* 4–5.

39. Taken together, the murder of Gloucester and Bolingbroke's accusation set him not only against Mowbray and Richard but also against his father, John of Gaunt, who defends his own inaction in act 1, scene 2 and supports Richard's interruption of the duel. Father and son take different sides in the classic conflict between the claims of loyalty to family or kin group and those of obedience to the monarch. Thus the appeal in which Bolingbroke diplomatically routes an aggressive message to Richard through Mowbray may also be seen to route an equally aggressive and morally more self-endangering message to Gaunt through Mowbray and Richard. During the first three scenes the tension between father and son is frequently hinted at in their language but never directly addressed by either. For a more detailed account of this conflict see my "Psychoanalyzing the Shakespearean Text: The First Three Scenes of the Henriad," in *Shakespeare and the Question of Theory*, ed. Patricia Parker and Geoffrey Hartman (New York: Methuen, 1985), 210–29. See also "Ars Moriendi in Progress, or John of Gaunt and the Practice of Strategic Dying," *Yale Journal of Criticism* 1 (1987): 39–65.

40. John Palmer, *Political Characters of Shakespeare* (London: Macmillan, 1945), 130; Brents Stirling, *Unity in Shakespearian Tragedy: The Interplay of Theme and Character* (New York: Columbia University Press, 1956), 32.

41. Peter Ure, ed., *King Richard II*, 5th ed. (1961; London: Methuen, 1966), 68.

42. We read or hear just enough about the complex legal conventions to suspect that Richard's seizure involved more than brute force; it required manipulations of property law that set up obstructions to Bolingbroke's ability to claim his inheritance. For details see Jack Hexter, "Property, Monopoly, and Shakespeare's *Richard II,*" in *Culture and Politics from Puritanism to the Enlightenment*, ed. Perez Zagorin (Berkeley: University of California Press, 1980), 1–24.

43. Diffuse in the sense that there are several possible answers to why Bolingbroke would return before he knew his property was jeopardized: to mobilize noble and popular hostility to Richard, to continue his effort to purge

the court and crown of corrupt influences, to pursue the project of avenging Gloucester's death, and to do the work his father should have been doing. These aims have been established in the previous scenes. Another concern an exile might be expected to entertain before the situation arose is indicated by the references to the legal procedures necessary to claim an inheritance.

44. Perhaps when Bolingbroke, at the end of the scene, swears to kill Richard's flatterers he speaks from the uneasy experience of finding himself the object of Northumberland's unctuous praise.

45. Hexter, "Property," 9–10, 11.

46. Lois Potter, "The Antic Disposition of Richard II," *Shakespeare Survey* 27 (1974): 35.

47. Rackin, *Stages of History,* 129.

48. Samuel Daniel, *The First Fowre Bookes of the civile wars between the two houses of Lancaster and York,* 3.58, in *The Complete Works in Verse and Prose of Samuel Daniel,* ed. A. B. Grosart, vol. 2 (1885; New York: Russell and Russell, 1963), 121.

49. The phrase is John Palmer's: *Political Characters,* 173.

50. The textual corruption mentioned above makes it impossible to determine whether Bolingbroke's words to Exton were uttered specifically and secretly to him (and on an occasion different from the one in 5.3) or were part of a more general request to the nobles who—according to the existing Q and F stage directions—were present from the beginning of 5.3.

51. Stirling, *Unity in Shakespearian Tragedy,* 38; Palmer, *Political Characters,* 173, 134.

3. *Richard's Soliloquy:* Richard II, *Act 5, Scene 5, Lines 1–166*

1. John Halverson calls these concluding lines "fine-sounding" and "philosophical" but no more than "a gratuitous generalization of Richard's private despair to the rest of mankind"; he rejects the idea that the passage exhibits "much self-knowledge" ("The Lamentable Comedy of Richard II," *English Literary Renaissance* 24, no. 2 [1994]: 346). But I submit that if we listen to these lines with Richard's ears we will recognize a parodic impression of someone else's idea of "fine-sounding, philosophical" sentiments, perhaps those of the Richard who earlier sought out the "sweet way . . . to despair" (3.2.1575), the way he now alludes to and harshly rejects when he speaks of the self-deceiving tendency "to content" by which sinners flatter themselves that they are only victims. What Halverson dismissively terms "Richard's private despair" seems to me to be the motive and motif around which the whole play is organized.

2. Anne Righter, *Shakespeare and the Idea of the Play* (London: Chatto & Windus, 1962), 60.

3. Ibid., 57.

4. Personal communication. My understanding of *Richard II* has benefited enormously from Professor Potter's writings and suggestions about the play, and it gives me pleasure to record my gratitude here.

5. On this, see Wolfgang Iser, *Staging Politics: The Lasting Impact of Shakespeare's Histories,* trans. David Henry Wilson (New York: Columbia University Press, 1993), 94. Richard's words may imply either that he has been trying to make the best of his miserable existence in prison or else that he has been trying to transcend or escape from the prison of himself. If the former, he parades his courage in the face of adversity; if the latter, he parades his desire to reconcile himself to the world and find himself reflected in it. My emphasis is on the word "parades": It is Richard—and not merely "Shakespeare"—who puts his self-pity and desire for self-knowledge or reconciliation on parade for the benefit of the observer in the reviewing stand, that is, himself.

6. Personal communication.

7. Iser, *Staging Politics,* 94.

8. Søren Kierkegaard, *The Sickness unto Death: A Christian Psychological Exposition for Upbuilding and Awakening,* ed. and trans. Howard V. Hong and Edna H. Hong (Princeton: Princeton University Press, 1980), 18, 20. In his analysis of the Queen's forebodings in act 2, scene 2, Iser has recourse to Kierkegaard's *Concept of Anxiety,* but I think the treatise on despair more directly and fully illuminates both passages, since the two are obviously related, Richard's imagery of "still-breeding thoughts" echoing the Queen's presentiment of giving birth to the monster, the "nothing" with which her "inward soul . . . trembles" (2.2.979–89, 1004–6, 1035–39). See Iser, *Staging Politics,* 86–87.

The Queen's rhetoric in act 2, scene 2, is so dense and tortured as to be conspicuously evasive. But what she is evading, what she is trying not to know, or not to think, or to forget, becomes clear as soon as we recall that although she spoke only one line in the preceding scene she—along with Bushy—witnessed Richard's despicable and self-destructive treatment of Gaunt, watched him go out of his way to alienate his uncle York as well as the more hostile peers, and heard Gaunt tell him he is "possessed now to depose" himself. The anxiety she expresses (in 2.2), the "unborn sorrow" she flinches from, is thus more than the bad news Green brings of Richard's imminent political downfall, which, given the excessiveness of her language, is anti-climactic. Her language is haunted by and pregnant with Richard's despair. Critics tend to ignore the effect on her reactions in act 2, scene 2 of the deeply painful spectacle she observed in act 2, scene 1. For an interesting if not very satisfactory exception to this tendency, see Graham Holderness, "'A Woman's War': A Feminist Reading of *Richard II,*" in *Shakespeare Left and Right,* ed. Ivo Kamps (New York: Routledge, 1991), 167–83.1

4. *On the Continuity of the Henriad*

1. See, for example, Herbert Coursen, *The Leasing Out of England: Shakespeare's Second Henriad* (Washington, D.C.: University Presses of America, 1982), 4; Robert Ornstein, *A Kingdom for a Stage: The Achievement of Shakespeare's History*

Plays (Cambridge, Mass.: Harvard University Press, 1972), 221; and E. M. W. Tillyard, *Shakespeare's History Plays* (London: Chatto & Windus, 1959), 236.

2. Thus Ornstein argues that since "the tetralogies, so far as is known, were never performed as such on the Elizabethan stage, Shakespeare had no practical artistic reason or professional obligation to concern himself with their unities. Few members of his audiences would have recognized and objected to inconsistencies of characterization from play to play, just as few would have been able to appreciate the continuities, parallelisms, and symmetries which a critic can discern. Nevertheless, there are in the tetralogies . . . reaches of art that lie beyond the grasp of theatergoers" (*Kingdom for a Stage,* 221).

3. See Harry Berger, Jr., *Imaginary Audition: Shakespeare on Stage and Page* (Berkeley: University of California Press, 1989), 3–42.

4. Tillyard, *Shakespeare's History Plays*, 235–37. See also Norman Rabkin, *Shakespeare and the Problem of Meaning* (Chicago: University of Chicago Press, 1981), 35–36. For a brief survey of the critical debate over the structural unity of the two *Henry IV* plays see David Bevington, Introduction, Oxford Shakespeare edition of *1 Henry IV* (1987; New York: Oxford University Press, 2008), 37–41.

5. Derek A. Traversi, *Shakespeare from Richard II to Henry V* (Stanford: Stanford University Press, 1957), 2.

6. Examples: Sigurd Burckhardt, *Shakespearean Meanings* (Princeton: Princeton University Press, 1968); James L. Calderwood, *Metadrama in Shakespeare's Henriad: Richard II to Henry V* (Berkeley: University of California Press, 1979); John W. Blanpied, *Time and the Artist in Shakespeare's Histories* (Newark: University of Delaware Press, 1983).

7. Examples: Traversi, *Shakespeare from Richard II to Henry V*; Blanpied *Time and the Artist*; Calderwood, *Metadrama in Shakespeare's Henriad*; John Baxter, *Shakespeare's Poetic Styles: Verse into Drama* (London: Routledge, 1980); G. R. Hibbard, *The Making of Shakespeare's Dramatic Poetry* (Toronto: University of Toronto Press, 1981); Richard P. Wheeler, *Shakespeare's Development and Problem Comedies: Turn and Counter-Turn* (Berkeley: University of California Press, 1981), and Wheeler and C. L. Barber, *The Whole Journey: Shakespeare's Power of Development* (Berkeley: University of Calfornia Press, 1986).

8. Examples: Tillyard, *Shakespeare's History Plays,* chap. 4; C. L. Barber, *Shakespeare's Festive Comedy: A Study of Dramatic Form and Its Relation to Social Custom* (Princeton: Princeton University Press, 1957), chap. 8; Eric La Guardia, "Ceremony and History: The Problem of Symbol from *Richard II* to *Henry V*," in *Pacific Coast Studies in Shakespeare*, ed. Waldo F. McNeir and Thelma N. Greenfield (Eugene: University of Oregon Press, 1966), 68–88; Alvin Kernan, "The Henriad: Shakespeare's Major History Plays," in *Modern Shakespearean Criticism: Essays in Style, Dramaturgy, and the Major Plays*, ed. Kernan (New York: Harcourt, 1970), 245–75; Calderwood, *Metadrama in Shakespeare's Henriad*; Joseph A. Porter, *The Drama of Speech Acts: Shakespeare's Lancastrian Tetralogy* (Berkeley: University of California Press, 1979).

9. *Henry V*, 1.2.96.

10. Sigurd Burckhardt, *Shakespearean Meanings* (Princeton: Princeton University Press, 1968), 183–85.

11. Ibid., 183, 172.

12. Jonathan Dollimore and Alan Sinfield, "History and Ideology: The Instance of *Henry V*," in *Alternative Shakespeares*, ed. John Drakakis (London: Methuen, 1985), 206–27, esp. 218.

13. Leonard Tennenhouse, *Power on Display: The Politics of Shakespeare's Genres* (New York: Methuen, 1986), 82–84.

14. Anthony Quayle, introduction to *Shakespeare's Histories at Stratford, 1951*, by John Dover Wilson and T. C. Worsley (London: Max Reinhardt, 1952), vii.

15. Worsley, ibid., 27.

16. Wilson, ibid., 21.

17. Wilson, ibid., 4.

18. Worsley, ibid., 87–88.

19. Ibid., vii.

20. Ibid.

21. *2 Henry IV*, 3.1.81.

22. Sally Beaumann, *The Royal Shakespeare Company* (Oxford: Oxford University Press, 1982), 206–7.

23. Ibid., 207–9.

24. Ibid., 207.

25. Quayle, *Shakespeare's Histories at Stratford, 1951*, vii.

5. *Falstaff and Harry*

1. See M. D. Faber, "Falstaff behind the Arras," *American Imago* 27 (1970): 197–225. See especially 198, 199, 206, 207, 209. Although I resist Faber's psychological emphasis on the struggle between Harry's consciousness and unconscious, I find his observations and interpretations immensely smart and suggestive, and I'm deeply indebted to them.

2. The reading of the soliloquy that follows is identical with that which appears on pages. 306–12 of my *Making Trifles of Terrors: Redistributing Complicities in Shakespeare* (Stanford: Stanford University Press, 1997).

3. Samuel Johnson, *Notes to Shakespeare*, Augustan Reprint Society, vol. 2, part 1, ed. Arthur Sherbo (Los Angeles: William Andrews Clark Memorial Library, 1957), 26. The last part of Johnson's comment is also worth quoting: The speech "exhibits a natural picture of a great mind offering excuses to itself, and palliating those follies which it can neither justify nor forsake."

4. John Dover Wilson, *The Fortunes of Falstaff* (Cambridge: Cambridge University Press, 1961), 41. By "meliorist" I mean a proponent of the idea that Harry gets better and better through the Henriad.

5. William Empson, *Essays on Shakespeare*, ed. David B. Pirie (Cambridge: Cambridge University Press, 1986), 42, 58.

6. The irregular tense relationships are telling: When, in the future, "he please[s] again to be himself," he will break through the vapors "that *did seem* to strangle him." "Did seem" has the force of a future anterior construction, "will have seemed," contingent on his future performance. But the effect of the emphatic preterit form is to accentuate the futility of their assault on the sun, and to anticipate the finality of his triumph. In similar fashion, Harry borrows the symbol of kingship to characterize his pre-kingship plan. Self-attention is displaced to the idealized royal mirror or symbol, the sun, and invested with the idioms of kingly license and condescension: "doth permit" and "when he please."

7. See 4.1.111–12 and *Henry V*, 4.3.100–103 for meteorological analogues. See also *The Tempest* 2.2.1–2: "All the infections that the sun sucks up / From bogs, fens, flats. . . ."

8. On explaining as a discursive strategy see Stephen Greenblatt, *Shakespearean Negotiations: The Circulation of Social Energy in Renaissance England* (Berkeley: University of California Press, 1988), 38–43 and 60–62. The process I'm discussing and the dilemma it involves are described in beautifully precise and compressed terms by Greenblatt, who doesn't dispute the idealizing interpretation of Harry but observes that it "involves as its positive condition the constant production of its own radical subversion and the containment of that subversion." In the soliloquy Harry's "justification of himself threatens to fall away at every moment into its antithesis" (41).

9. Ibid., 30. Johnson inadvertently points this up in the last five words of his comment on the line: "To *falsify hope* is to *exceed hope*, to give much where men hoped for little" (*Notes to Shakespeare* 2:1.26)— to falsify hope is to lower expectations falsely so that they may be exceeded and proved false.

10. Alan Dessen, *Shakespeare and the Late Moral Plays* (Lincoln: University of Nebraska Press, 1986), 81.

11. Leonard Tennenhouse, *Power on Display: The Politics of Shakespeare's Genres* (New York: Methuen, 1986), 83–84.

12. Richard Helgerson, *The Elizabethan Prodigals* (Berkeley: University of California Press, 1976), 3.

13. Joseph A. Porter, *The Drama of Speech Acts: Shakespeare's Lancastrian Tetralogy* (Berkeley: University of Californbia Press, 1979), 76–77. Empson notes two similar possibilities and opts for the more positive one: "not a cynical calculation . . . but a modestly phrased reassurance" ("Falstaff," 58). My point—an Empsonian point—is that the first is present in the language, and in conflict with the second.

14. Porter, *Drama of Speech Acts,* 77.

15. In Q4 and Q5 "foile" is "soile," and in F it is "soyle." "Foile" fits the image better but "soile/soyle" casts a darker shadow over "my fault." My preference is to keep the long "s" lurking within the careful containment of the "f."

16. Ernst Kris, "Prince Hal's Conflict," in *Psychoanalytic Explorations in Art* (New York: International Universities Press, 1952), 273–88.

17. David Bevington, ed., *Henry IV, Part 1*, Oxford Shakespeare (Oxford: Oxford University Press, 1987), 166.

18. For an account of these ethical discourses and their interaction see "What Did the King Know and When Did He Know It?," in *Making Trifles of Terrors*, 211–50.

19. Bevington, *1 Henry IV*, 102.

6. *A Horse Named Cut:* 1 Henry IV, *Act 2, Scene 1*

1. All citations from *1 Henry IV* in this chapter are from the Arden Shakespeare text edited by A. R. Humphreys, 6th ed., rev. (1960; rpt. with minor corrections, London: Methuen, 1974).

2. *The First Part of King Henry the Fourth*, ed. G. L. Kittredge, Kittredge Shakespeare (Boston: Ginn, 1940), 125.

3. References to damp humors, water, and drowning have already been associated with allusions to female power and to violation at 1.2.27–38, 1.3.190–92, and 1.3.199–205.

4. If "Cut" refers to a curtal—a horse with a docked tail—his vulnerability to pests must resemble those of the flea-bitten Carriers.

5. This equation is more accessible to readers than to spectators, since the name "Carrier" is only once uttered on stage.

6. Thomas Rosenmeyer, *The Green Cabinet: Theocritus and the European Pastoral Lyric* (1969; Berkeley: University of California Press, 1973), 63.

7. Bronislaw Malinowski, "The Problem of Meaning in Primitive Languages," Supplement 1 in C. K. Ogden and I. A. Richards, *The Meaning of Meaning: A Study of the Influence of Language upon Thought and of the Science of Symbolism*, 8th ed. (New York: Harcourt, Brace, 1946), 315.

8. Joel Fineman, "Fratricide and Cuckoldry: Shakespeare's Doubles," in *Representing Shakespeare: New Psychoanalytic Essays*, ed. Murray M. Schwartz and Coppélia Kahn (Baltimore: Johns Hopkins University Press, 1980), 83.

9. Stephen Booth, ed., *Shakespeare's Sonnets* (New Haven, Conn.: Yale University Press, 1977), 221–22.

7. *Hydra and Rhizome*

1. A. R. Humphreys, ed., *The First Part of King Henry IV*, 6th ed. (London: Methuen, 1974), 3. All quotations from *1 Henry IV* in this chapter follow this edition; quotations from *2 Henry IV*, *Richard II*, and *Henry V* follow the Arden editions by Humphreys, Peter Ure, and J. H. Walter, respectively.

2. The logic of displacement suggests that this emendation would make the complaint conform to Henry's scenario: "We were enforc'd for your safety to fly / Into your sight."

3. And when Harry does get to perform his glorious deed, he is denied the audience he wanted: No one sees it but Falstaff.

4. Stephen Booth, *"King Lear," "Macbeth," Indefinition, and Tragedy* (New Haven: Yale University Press, 1983), 176.

5. Compare Kenneth Muir, who, after noting that Shakespeare departs from Holinshed in shifting this act from Henry to Harry, thinks the change was made to give the latter "a final touch of magnanimity" (Muir, *The Sources of Shakespeare's Plays* [London: Methuen, 1977], 98). That such a touch is undeniable at the level of manners justifies the act and "covers" its aggressiveness. Readers (including actors) whose interpretation transforms the speaker of Harry's lines into a character may agree to the ambiguity of this speech act but disagree as to its subsequent analysis with respect to Harry's intention, awareness, motivation, and so on.

6. Sigurd Burckhardt, *Shakespearean Meanings* (Princeton: Princeton University Press, 1968), 149.

7. David Bevington, ed., *Henry IV, Part 1* (Oxford: Oxford University Press, 2008), 41.

8. A. R. Humphreys, ed., *The Second Part of King Henry IV*, Arden edition (London: Methuen, 1966), lxii.

9. See my "Sneak's Noise, or, Rumor and Detextualization in *2 Henry IV*," *Kenyon Review*, n.s. 6, no. 4 (1984): 58–78. I choose to refer to Rumor as "she" because Shakespeare's personification reminds me of both Virgil's Fama and Erasmus's Moria. On the latter, see my "Utopian Folly: Erasmus and More on the Perils of Misanthropy," in *Second World and Green World: Studies in Renaissance Fiction-Making*, ed. John P. Lynch (Berkeley: University of California Press, 1988), 229–48.

10. The image is further ambiguated by the fact that in the phrase "the big year," "year" can function as a dialectical variant of "ear" (see 1.2.193–94, along with the textual variants and the Arden note). The ambiguity is consistent with the others that waver between inner and outer, small and large, conditional and circumstantial references.

11. See chapter 12 below for a more sustained account of this passage.

12. Gilles Deleuze and Félix Guattari, *On the Line*, trans. John Johnston (New York: Semiotext[e], 1983), 11–13, an augmented version of the authors' *Rhizome: Introduction* (Paris: Editions de Minuit, 1976). I use this translation here because it is a little closer to the original than Brian Massumi's in Gilles Deleuze and Félix Guattari, *A Thousand Plateaus: Capitalism and Schizophrenia* (Minneapolis: University of Minnesota Press, 1987).

13. Maynard Mack, "The Jacobean Shakespeare," in *Jacobean Theater*, ed. J. R. Brown and Bernard Harris (1960; New York: Capricorn Books, 1967), 26.

14. Ibid., 24.

15. Ibid., 25.

16. Ibid., 26.

17. Ibid.

18. Deleuze and Guattari, *On the Line*, 17–18, 23.

19. *King Lear*, 5.3.295.

20. Barry Weller, "Identity and Representation in Shakespeare," *ELH* 49 (1982): 342. I learned much from this wonderful essay.

21. The idea of relating these mechanisms to Shakespearean dramaturgy was suggested to me by Joel Fineman's brief but characteristically brilliant comments in "Fratricide and Cuckoldry: Shakespeare's Doubles," in *Representing Shakespeare: New Psychoanalytic Essays*, ed. Murray M. Schwartz and Coppélia Kahn (Baltimore: Johns Hopkins University Press, 1980), 72–73.

22. *Henry V*, act 4, Chorus, 20.

23. *2 Henry IV*, 4.3.85–115.

24. Harry Berger, Jr., *Imaginary Audition: Shakespeare on Stage and Page* (Berkeley: University of California Press, 1989).

25. *A Midsummer Night's Dream*, 5.1.14–17.

8. Falstaff, Carnival, and the Perils of Speech-Prefixity

1. A. P. Rossiter, *Angel with Horns and Other Shakespeare Lectures*, ed. Graham Storey (London: Longmans,1961), 53.

2. Valerie Traub, *Desire and Anxiety: Circulations of Sexuality in Shakespearean Drama* (London: Routledge, 1992), 55.

3. Ibid., 56 and 66.

4. Ibid.. 62ff.

5. Jonathan Goldberg, *Sodometries: Renaissance Texts, Modern Sexualities* (Stanford: Stanford University Press, 1992), 153–54, emphasis added.

6. Ibid., 152.

7. Jonathan Goldberg, "The Commodity of Names: 'Falstaff' and 'Oldcastle' in *1 Henry IV*," in *Reconfiguring the Renaissance: Essays in Critical Materialism*, ed. Jonathan Crewe (Lewisburg, Pa.: Bucknell University Press,1992), 81. This is a convincing rebuttal of Gary Taylor's proposal to restore the "Oldcastle" in modern texts of *1 Henry IV*. See Taylor, "The Fortunes of Oldcastle," *Shakespeare Survey* 38 (1985): 85–100. David Bevington's critique of the Taylor thesis in his Oxford edition of the play (106–10) has been questioned by Goldberg on philosophical grounds (87) and defended by John W. Velz on the grounds criticized by Goldberg; see Velz's review of the edition in *Shakespeare Quarterly* 43, no. 1 (1992): 108. For a more inventive and persuasive attempt to work Oldcastle into the field of possible topical allusions around Falstaff, see Charles Whitney, "Festivity and Topicality in the Coventry Scene of *1 Henry IV*," *English Literary Renaissance* 24, no. 2 (1994): 410–48, esp. 412–15, 425–27, and 431–34. I discuss this essay below.

8. Taylor, "Fortunes of Oldcastle," 93–95, 98, 96, and 95.

9. And if he was, why would the Lords Cobham have objected to Shakespeare's portrait? For information on Oldcastle and the debate that swirled around him see *The Oldcastle Controversy*, ed. Peter Corbin and Douglas Sedge (Manchester: Manchester University Press, 1991). For this reference, and also for a wonderfully compact yet complete sketch of the Oldcastle question, I am

grateful to Barbara A. Mowat and Paul Werstine. See their excellent comments in the New Folger Library edition of *Henry IV Part 1* (New York: Washington Square Press, 1994), liv–lvii and 235–41.

10. Whitney, "Festivity and Topicality," 425–27, numerals added.

11. Ibid., 427. Similar topical speculations run into the same rhetorical and referential confusion in the following passage: "Falstaff's parody of Scripture in the Coventry scene *perhaps carries the sense* that Oldcastle was enough of a calculating buffoon to use religion to foment popular revolt—substituting earthly rewards for heavenly. (Of course in this scene revolt is not being fomented; Falstaff is talking to the audience. *The suggestion would only be* that his parables may be alluding to some spiel of Oldcastle's)" (433, my italics). Where is the agency in the italicized phrases? That is, whose sense of Oldcastle does Falstaff's parody carry? Who would be suggesting that the parables might allude to Oldcastle—Whitney, Shakespeare, or Falstaff? The idea that Falstaff directly addresses the theater audience further confuses the issue because it puts him in the actor's place and makes him a surrogate communicating the playwright's messages.

12. Kristen Poole, "Saints Alive! Falstaff, Martin Marprelate, and the Staging of Puritanism," *Shakespeare Quarterly* 46, no.1 (1995): 47–75, esp. 52n.

13. Twice this distinction is marked by the opposition of the plural to the singular: In the phrase, "Shakespeare's audience readily identified Falstaff as a caricature of Oldcastle," "audience" denotes contemporaries familiar with the Oldcastle literature, but in the statement that the Epilogue of *2 Henry IV* "indicates audiences *did* identify Falstaff as Oldcastle," the reference is to people in theaters (Poole, "Saints Alive!," 49). Similarly, an inference about the expectations Shakespeare tapped into, "a register of religious/political language familiar to his Elizabethan audience," reinforces the hypothesis that "Shakespeare's audiences would most likely have recognized Falstaff in the literary tradition of grotesque puritans" (54). In both examples, an allegorical use of "audience" gives way to a statement about empirical audiences in a manner that betrays the virtuality of the latter—virtual not with respect to Shakespeare's plays but with respect to Poole's thesis. In other words, Poole's "audiences" are allegorical personifications of "Shakespeare's Elizabethan audience" (64), which is in turn the personification of "the context of Elizabethan polemical religious discourse."

14. See, for example, Poole's fine closing statement on page 75.

15. William Empson, "Falstaff," in *Essays on Shakespeare*, ed. David B. Pirie (Cambridge: Cambridge University Press, 1986), 52. This is a revised version of "Falstaff and Mr. Dover Wilson," which appeared in 1953 in *The Kenyon Review*. Because there is considerable evidence for the practice Empson mentions—getting soldiers killed to keep their pay—many editors and critics assume that this practice is implied in Falstaff's "I have led my ragamuffins where they are peppered" (*1 Henry IV*, 5.3.35–36). It may be implied, but Empson's attribution of this motive to Falstaff is incorrect. Falstaff makes no such boast.

16. Whitney, "Festivity and Topicality," 424–25. Despite the reservations I express here, this wonderful essay is the best account of both of Falstaff's perfor-

mance in particular and of the differences and tense interactions between festivity and topicality in general.

17. Ibid., 425. There is something wrong with the reference to Bakhtin. Whitney cites a passage from *Problems of Dostoevsky's Poetics* (trans. Caryl Emerson [Minneapolis: University of Minnesota Press, 1984], 108–9), in which "double-voiced" appears just before a discussion of carnivalistic dialogism. The term seems to be applied to the mixing of styles ("multi-toned narration") and to the use of such "inserted genres" as letters, manuscripts, citations, and parodies. This seems less relevant to Falstaff's speech and to the statement Whitney is trying to make about that than does the following passage from *The Dialogic Imagination: Four Essays by M. M. Bakhtin* (ed. Michael Holquist, trans. Caryl Emerson and Michael Holquist [Austin: University of Texas Press, 1981]):

> As a living, socio-ideological concrete thing, as heteroglot opinion, language, for the individual consciousness, lies on the borderline between oneself and the other. The word in language is half someone else's. It becomes "one's own" only when the speaker populates it with his own intention, his own accent, when he appropriates the word. . . . Prior to this moment of appropriation, the word . . . exists in other people's mouths, in other people's contexts, serving other people's intentions: it is from there that one must take the word, and make it one's own. . . . Language is populated—overpopulated—with the intentions of others. (293–94)

Bakhtin's description of the word prior to the moment of appropriation fits Whitney's apparent purpose better than the passage the latter cites because it supports his thesis about the dispersal of interpretive authority among different sectors of the audience.

18. Whitney, "Festivity and Topicality," 422, 439.

9. Interlude: The Clown as Dog

1. Robert Weimann, *Shakespeare and the Popular Tradition in the Theater: Studies in the Social Dimension of Dramatic Form and Function*, ed. Robert Schwartz (Baltimore: Johns Hopkins University Press, 1978), 253–60.

2. Ibid., 256–57.

3. Ibid., 258–60.

4. Ibid., 259.

5. Meredith Anne Skura, *Shakespeare the Actor and the Purposes of Playing* (Chicago: University of Chicago Press, 1993), 162.

6. Ibid., 160.

7. Skura's discussion of this canine conundrum (160–61) follows that of Bert O. States in "The Dog on the Stage," *New Literary History* 14, no. 2 (1983): 373–88, esp. 379–81. See Keir Elam's astute and amusing account of Launce's troubles in this soliloquy: *Shakespeare's Universe of Discourse: Language Games in the Comedies* (Cambridge: Cambridge University Press, 1984), 56.

8. Skura, *Shakespeare the Actor,* 161.

9. Ibid., 163–66.

10. The comedy is increased by the network of puns that bind his language in act 2, scene 3 echoically to that of Julia and Proteus in act 2, scene 2.

11. Once again, Keir Elam throws much light on the relation of conspicuous citation to the dominance of rhetoric over *ethos*: *Shakespeare's Universe of Discourse*, 223–26 and 287–89.

12. Skura, *Shakespeare the Actor*, 162–63.

13. Weimann, *Shakespeare and the Popular Tradition in the Theater*, 257.

10. The King's Names

1. William Babula, "Whatever Happened to Prince Hal? An Essay on 'Henry V,'" *Shakespeare Survey* 30 (1979): 47.

2. Whatever that is. Given the play's emphasis on ethnic group conflict, Captain MacMorris's "What *ish* my nation?" (3.2.125) is a good question.

3. Gary Taylor, *Henry V*, Oxford Shakespeare (Oxford: Oxford University Press, 1982), 69–70.

4. Peter Erickson, *Patriarchal Structures in Shakespeare's Drama* (Berkeley: University of California Press, 1985), 56–57.

5. T. S. Eliot, *Selected Essays, 1917–1932* (New York: Harcourt Brace, 1932), 124.

11. Rabbits, Ducks, Lions, Foxes: A Henrician Bestiary

1. Norman Rabkin, "Rabbits, Ducks, and *Henry V*," *Shakespeare Quarterly* 28, no. 3 (1977): 279–96.

2. Gary Taylor, *Moment by Moment by Shakespeare* (London: Macmillan, 1985), 12.

3. Ibid., 12.

4. A. R. Humphreys, ed., *Henry V*, New Penguin Shakespeare (1968; London: Penguin Books, 1996), 20–21.

5. Taylor, *Moment by Moment*, 150–58.

6. Ibid., 12–13.

7. Humphreys, ed., *Henry V*, 44, 36, 34, 37.

8. Gary Taylor, ed., *King Henry V* (Oxford: Oxford University Press, 2008), 38–39.

9. Ibid., 38–39, 33, 33–34.

10. Stephen Greenblatt, "Invisible Bullets," in Greenblatt, *Shakespearean Negotiations: The Circulation of Social Energy in Renaissance England* (Berkeley: University of California Press, 1988), 21–65.

11. Ibid., 48, 52, 52–53, 55.

12. Ibid., 62–63.

13. Ibid., 62.

14. Ibid., 54.

15. Ibid., 55, 63.
16. Ibid., 63–64.
17. Ibid., 64, 63.
18. Humphreys, ed., *Henry V*, 49.
19. Greenblatt, "Invisible Bullets," 63.
20. Ibid., 55, 63.
21. Ibid., 20.
22. Ibid., 55–56.
23. Ibid., 41, 42, 52, 64.
24. Barry Weller, "Identity and Representation in Shakespeare," *ELH* 49 No.2 (1982): 342.
25. Harry Berger, Jr., "*Troilus and Cressida*: The Observer as Basilisk," *Comparative Drama* 2, no. 2 (1968): 122–36.
26. *Troilus and Cressida,* 2.2.30–31.
27. Peter Erickson, *Patriarchal Structures in Shakespeare's Drama* (Berkeley: University of California Press, 1985), 64–65.

12. Harrying the Stage: Henry V *as Tetralogical Echo Chamber*

1. See J. H. Walter's Arden edition of *King Henry V* (1954; London: Methuen, 1957), xx.
2. Stephen Greenblatt, *Shakespearean Negotiations* (Berkeley: University of California Press, 1988), 62–63.
3. A. R. Humphreys, *William Shakespeare: Four Histories* (London: Penguin, 1994), 737.
4. Samuel Johnson, *Johnson on Shakespeare* (Oxford: Oxford University Press, 1908), 127.
5. See Walter, *King Henry V*, 11, and Humphreys's commentary on these lines in *Four Histories.*
6. *Henry V*, ed. Gary Taylor, in *The Oxford Shakespeare* (1982; Oxford: Oxford University Press, 2008), 97n61.
7. Robert Ornstein, *A Kingdom for a Stage: The Achievement of Shakespeare's History Plays* (Cambridge, Mass.: Harvard University Press, 1972), 180.
8. See Richard Levin, "On Fluellen's Figures, Christ Figures, and James Figures," *PMLA* 89, no. 2 (1974): 302–11, and "The 'Fluellenian' Method," *PMLA* 90, no. 2 (1975): 292–93.

13. Harry's Question

1. Herbert Coursen, *The Leasing Out of England: Shakespeare's Second Henriad* (Washington, D.C.: University Presses of America, 1982), 154.
2. A. R. Humphreys, Introduction to *Henry V* (London: Penguin, 1968), 24.
3. Ibid., 24–25.

4. Geoffrey Bullough, *Narrative and Dramatic Sources of Shakespeare*, Volume 4 (1962; rpt. New York: Columbia University Press, 1975), 378–79.

5. A. R. Humphreys, Introduction to *Henry V*, in *William Shakespeare: Four Histories* (London: Penguin Books, 1994), 686.

6. William Shakespeare, *Henry V*, ed. Gary Taylor, Oxford Shakespeare (Oxford: Oxford University Press, 1984), 37.

7. Ibid., 34.

8. Peter Erickson, *Patriarchal Structures in Shakespeare's Drama* (Berkeley: University of California Press, 1985), 48–49.

9. Coursen, *Leasing Out of England*, 162–64.

10. Ibid., 157–58, 161.

11. Tillyard, *Elizabethan World Picture.*

12. Robert Ornstein, *A Kingdom for a Stage: The Achievement of Shakespeare's History Plays* (Cleveland: Arden Press, 1988), 180.

13. I prefer the Quarto's "lading" to the Folio's "kneading" because honeybees don't knead.

14. C. L. Barber and Richard Wheeler, *The Whole Journey: Shakespeare's Power of Development* (Berkeley: University of California Press, 1986), 220.

15. 5.2.23–67. Compare Harry's words at 1.2.242–43.

16. Alfred Harbage, ed., *The Life of King Henry the Fifth* (Baltimore: Penguin Books, 1966), 22.

17. Taylor, ed., *Henry V*, 43.

18. Ibid., 40.

19. Paul Jorgensen, *Shakespeare's Military World* (Berkeley: University of California Press, 1956), 163–64.

20. Taylor, ed., *Henry V*, 40.

21. Ibid., 71.

22. Jorgensen, *Shakespeare's Military World*, 167.

23. Ibid.

24. *King Richard II*, 5.3.130.

25. Hardin Craig, ed., *The Complete Works of Shakespeare* (Glenview, Ill.: Scott, Foresman, 1961), 756.

26. William Empson, *Essays on Shakespeare* (Cambridge: Cambridge University Press, 1986), 29–78

27. Ibid., 52.

28. Ibid., 52–53.

29. See Richard Levin, "On Fluellen's Figures, Christ Figures, and James Figures," *PMLA* 89, no. 2 (1974): 302–11, and "The 'Fluellenian' Method," *PMLA* 90, no. 2 (1975): 292–93.

30. Jorgensen, *Shakespeare's Military World*, 66.

31. Empson, *Essays on Shakespeare*, 57.

32. *2 Henry IV*, Induction, 39–40.